MARVEL UNIVERSE ULTIMATE SPIDER-MAN VOL. 3. Contains material originally published in magazine form as MARVEL UNIVERSE ULTIMATE SPIDER-MAN #9-12. First printing 2013. ISBN# 978-0-7851-6412-8. Published by MARVEL WORLDWIDE, INC., a subsidiary of MARVEL ENTERTAINMENT, LLC. OFFICE OF PUBLICATION: 135 West 50th Street, New York, NY 10020. Copyright © 2012 and 2013 Marvel Characters, Inc. All rights reserved. All characters featured in this issue and the distinctive names and likenesses thereof, and all related indicia are trademarks of Marvel Characters, Inc. No similarity between any of the names, characters, persons, and/or institutions in this magazine with those of any living or dead person or institution is intended, and any such similarity which may exist is purely coincidental. **Printed in the U.S.A.** ALAN FINE, EVP - Office of the President, Marvel Worldwide, Inc. and EVP & CMO Marvel Characters B.V.; DAN BUCKLEY, Publisher & President - Print, Animation & Digital Divisions; JOE QUESADA, Chief Creative Officer; TOM BREVOORT, SVP of Publishing; DAVID BOGART, SVP of Operations & Procurement, Publishing; C.B. CEBULSKI, SVP of Creator & Content Development; DAVID GABRIEL, SVP of Print & Digital Publishing Sales; JIM O'KEEFE, VP of Operations & Logistics; DAN CARR, Executive Director of Publishing Technology; SUSAN CRESPI, Editorial Operations Manager; ALEX MORALES, Publishing Operations Manager; STAN LEE, Chairman Emeritus. For information regarding advertising in Marvel Comics or on Marvel.com, please contact Niza Disla, Director of Marvel Partnerships, at ndisla@marvel.com. For Marvel subscription inquiries, please call 800-217-9158. **Manufactured between 3/18/2013 and 4/22/2013 by SHERIDAN BOOKS, INC., CHELSEA, MI, USA.**

10 9 8 7 6 5 4 3 2 1

MARVEL
ULTIMATE SPIDER-MAN

WRITERS
CHRIS ELIOPOULOS, KARL KESEL, BRIAN CLEVINGER, TY TEMPLETON & JOE CARAMAGNA

ARTISTS
NUNO PLATI, TY TEMPLETON AND RAMON BACHS & RAUL FONTS

COLOR ARTISTS
NUNO PLATI, TY TEMPLETON, PETE PANTAZIS & ANDREW DALHOUSE

LETTERERS
VC'S JOE SABINO, JOE CARAMAGNA & CLAYTON COWLES

EDITORS
TOM BRENNAN & ELLIE PYLE

SENIOR EDITOR
STEPHEN WACKER

Collection Editor: **Cory Levine**
Assistant Editors: **Alex Starbuck & Nelson Ribeiro**
Editors, Special Projects: **Jennifer Grünwald & Mark D. Beazley**
Senior Editor, Special Projects: **Jeff Youngquist**
SVP of Print & Digital Publishing Sales: **David Gabriel**
Head of Marvel Television: **Jeph Loeb**

Editor In Chief: **Axel Alonso**
Chief Creative Officer: **Joe Quesada**
Publisher: **Dan Buckley**
Executive Producer: **Alan Fine**

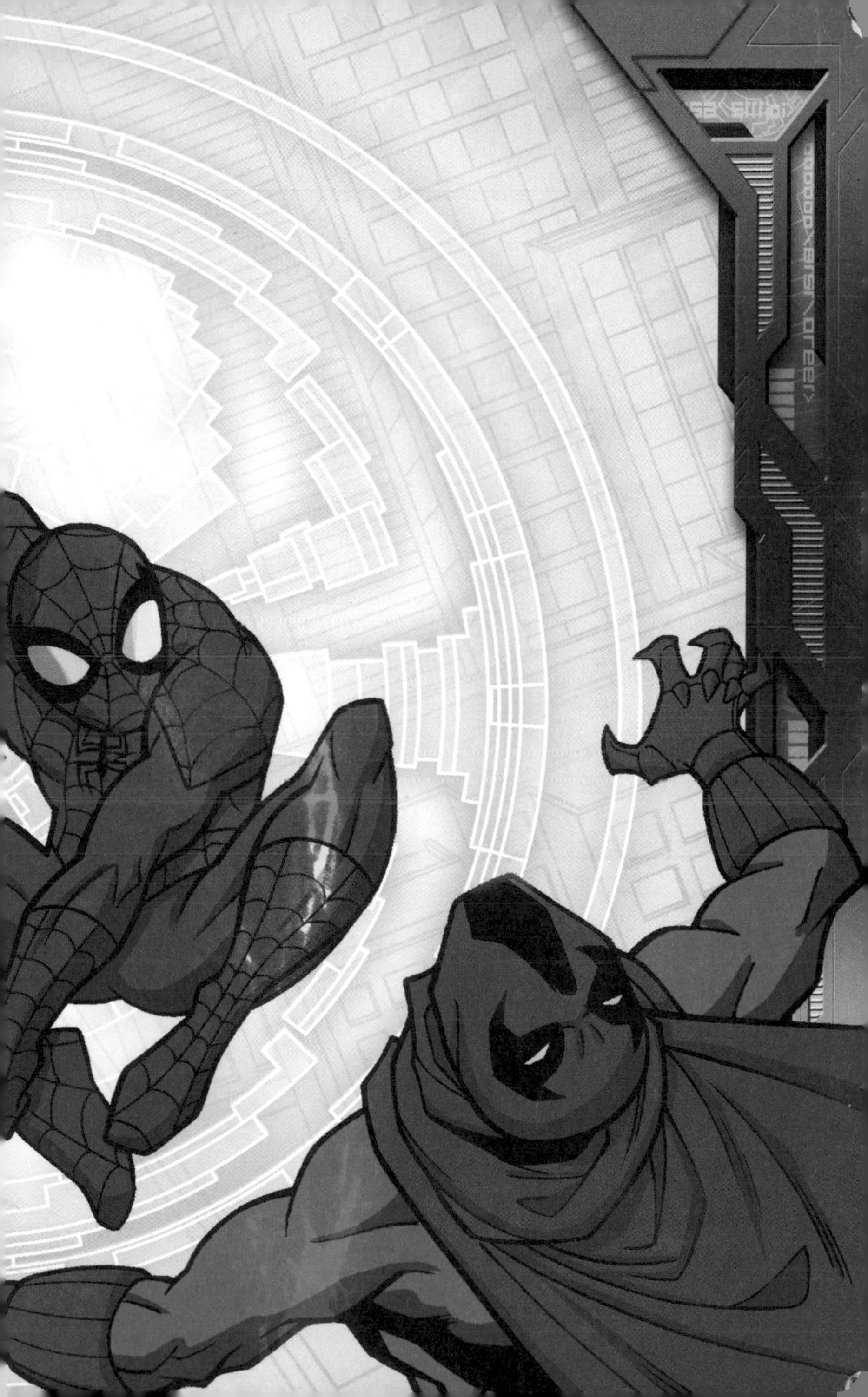

WHILE ATTENDING A DEMONSTRATION IN RADIOLOGY, HIGH SCHOOL STUDENT PETER PARKER WAS BITTEN BY A SPIDER THAT HAD ACCIDENTALLY BEEN EXPOSED TO RADIOACTIVE RAYS. THROUGH A MIRACLE OF SCIENCE, PETER SOON FOUND THAT HE HAD GAINED THE SPIDER'S POWERS...AND HAD, IN EFFECT, BECOME A HUMAN SPIDER! FROM THAT DAY ON, HE HAS ENDEAVORED TO BECOME THE...

MARVEL ULTIMATE SPIDER-MAN™

This one's Spider-Man (duh!)

NICK FURY

PRINCIPAL COULSON

MARY JANE WATSON

HARRY OSBORN

FLASH THOMPSON

AUNT MAY

A DONUT (YUM!)

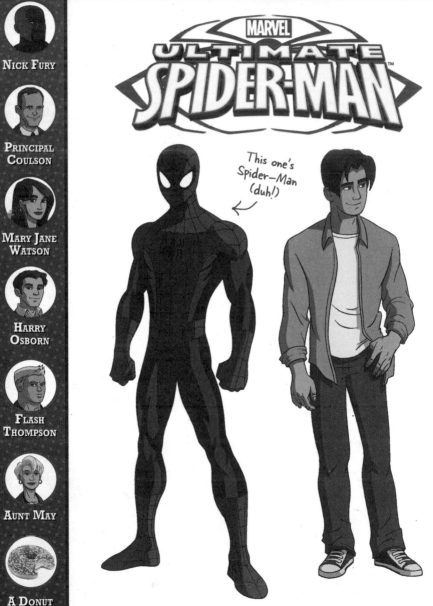

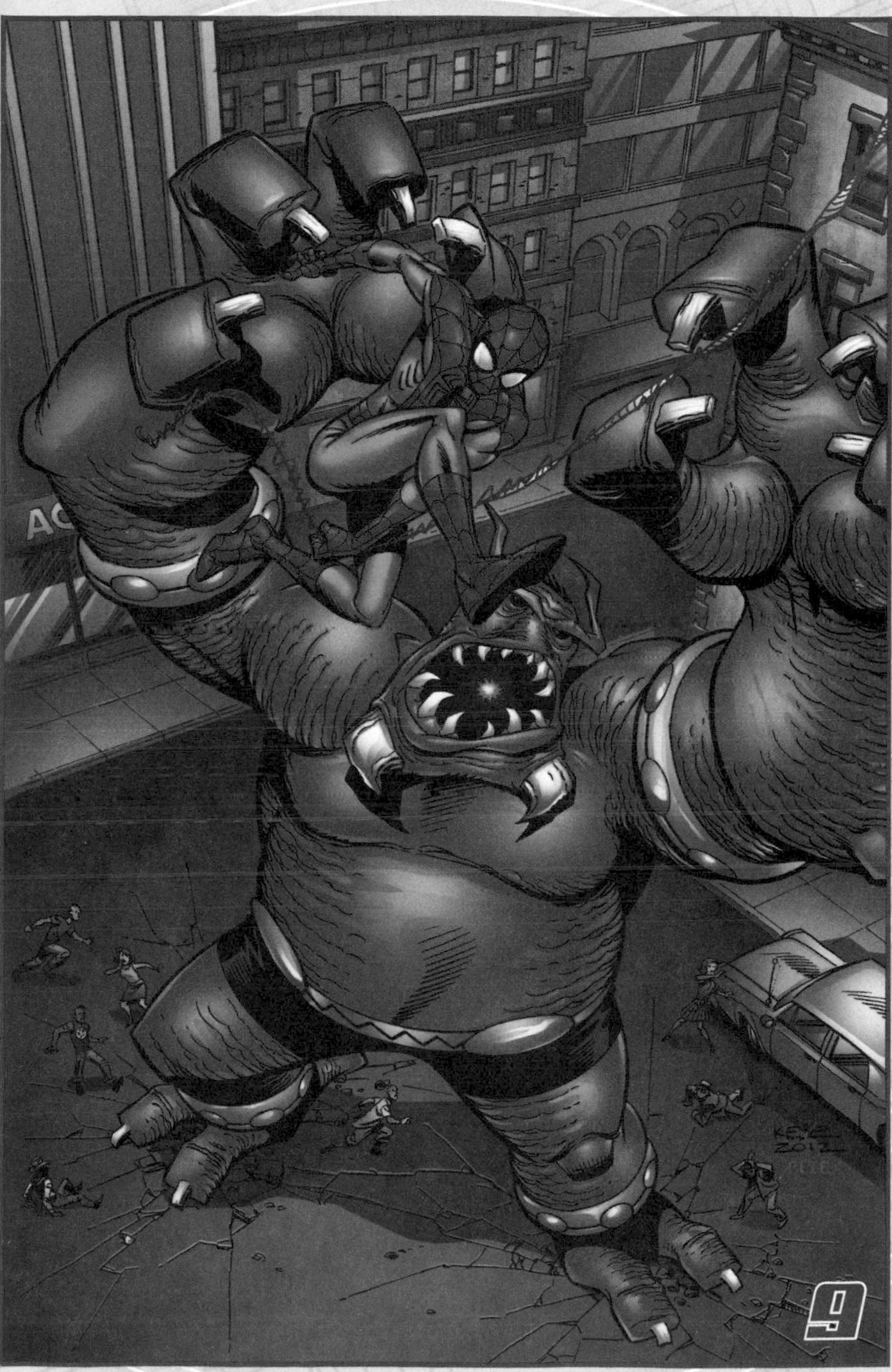
9

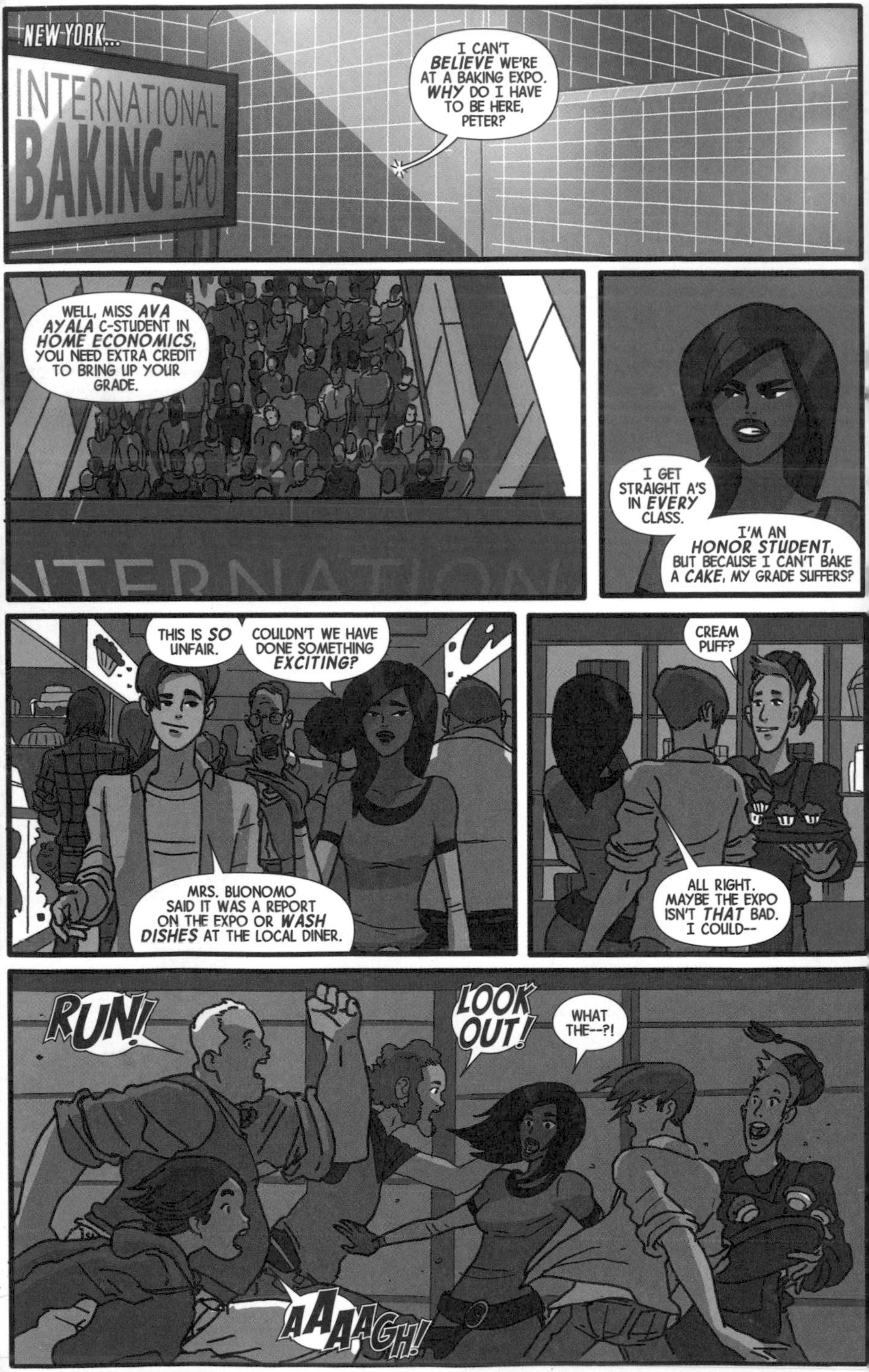
NEW YORK...
INTERNATIONAL BAKING EXPO
I CAN'T BELIEVE WE'RE AT A BAKING EXPO. WHY DO I HAVE TO BE HERE, PETER?
WELL, MISS AVA AYALA C-STUDENT IN HOME ECONOMICS, YOU NEED EXTRA CREDIT TO BRING UP YOUR GRADE.
I GET STRAIGHT A'S IN EVERY CLASS.
I'M AN HONOR STUDENT, BUT BECAUSE I CAN'T BAKE A CAKE, MY GRADE SUFFERS?
THIS IS SO UNFAIR.
COULDN'T WE HAVE DONE SOMETHING EXCITING?
MRS. BUONOMO SAID IT WAS A REPORT ON THE EXPO OR WASH DISHES AT THE LOCAL DINER.
CREAM PUFF?
ALL RIGHT. MAYBE THE EXPO ISN'T THAT BAD. I COULD--
RUN!
LOOK OUT!
WHAT THE--?!
AAAAGH!

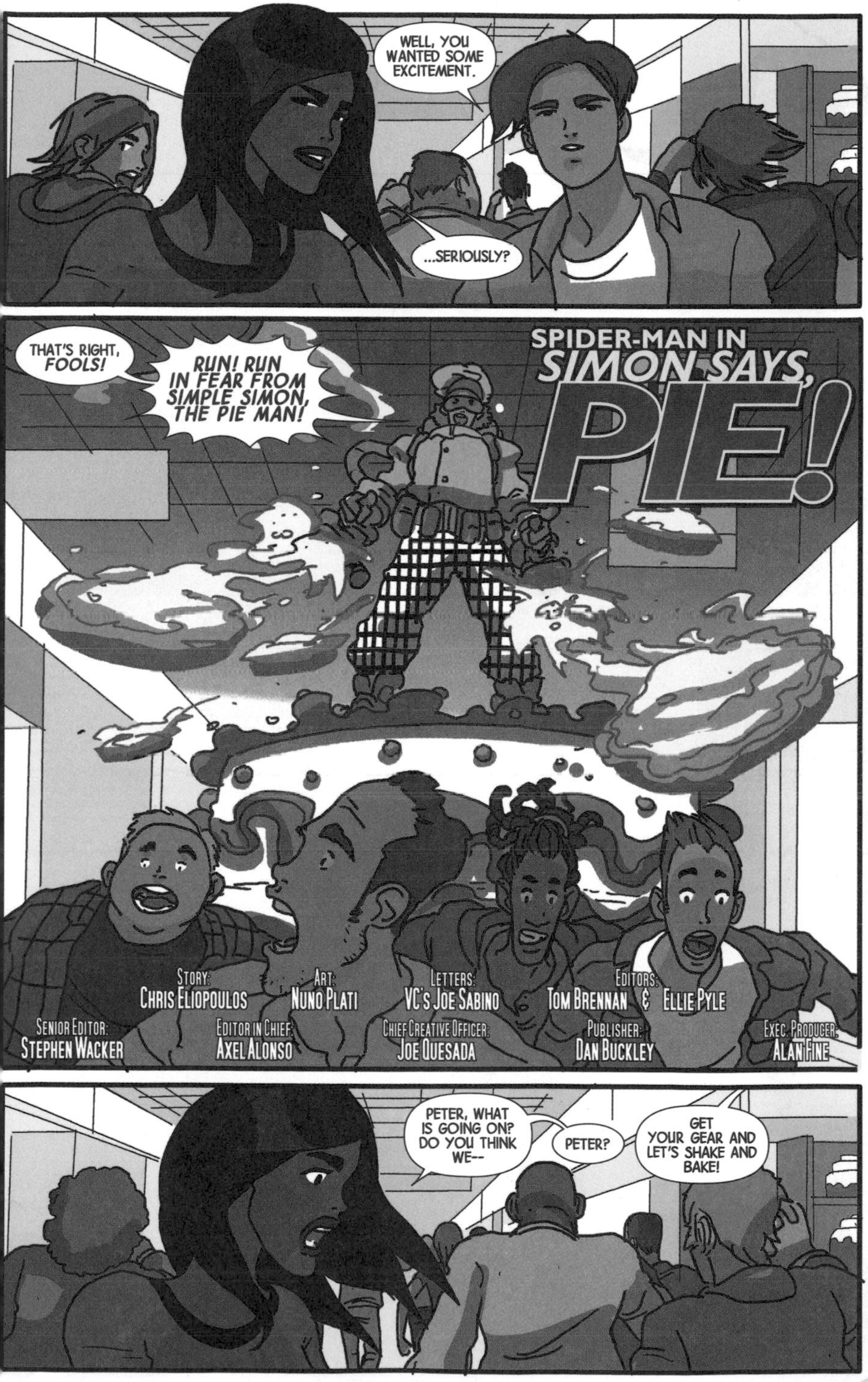
WELL, YOU WANTED SOME EXCITEMENT.
...SERIOUSLY?
THAT'S RIGHT, FOOLS!
RUN! RUN IN FEAR FROM SIMPLE SIMON, THE PIE MAN!
SPIDER-MAN IN SIMON SAYS, PIE!
STORY: CHRIS ELIOPOULOS
ART: NUNO PLATI
LETTERS: VC's JOE SABINO
EDITORS: TOM BRENNAN & ELLIE PYLE
SENIOR EDITOR: STEPHEN WACKER
EDITOR IN CHIEF: AXEL ALONSO
CHIEF CREATIVE OFFICER: JOE QUESADA
PUBLISHER: DAN BUCKLEY
EXEC. PRODUCER: ALAN FINE
PETER, WHAT IS GOING ON? DO YOU THINK WE--
PETER?
GET YOUR GEAR AND LET'S SHAKE AND BAKE!

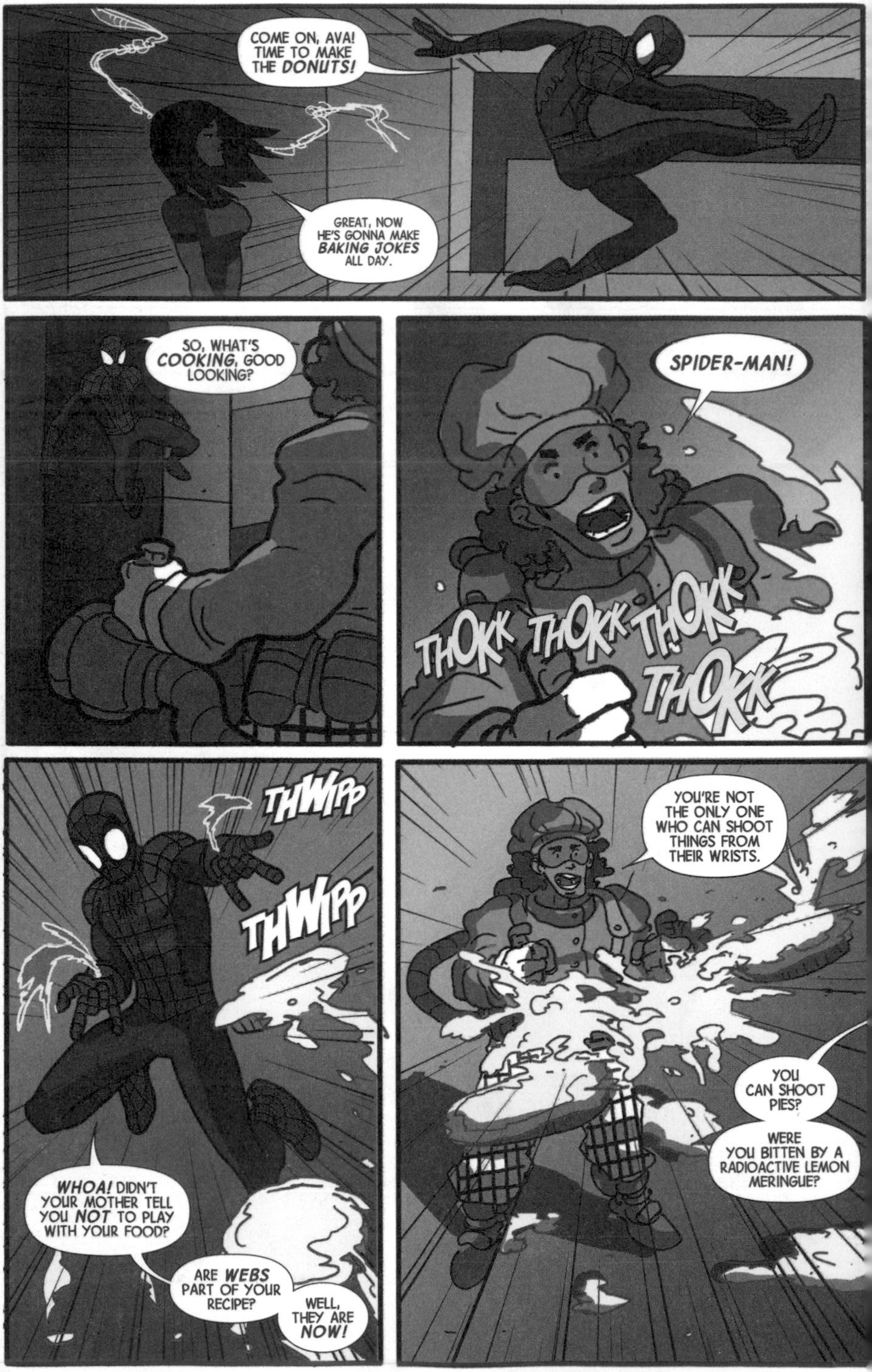
COME ON, AVA! TIME TO MAKE THE DONUTS!
GREAT, NOW HE'S GONNA MAKE BAKING JOKES ALL DAY.
SO, WHAT'S COOKING, GOOD LOOKING?
SPIDER-MAN!
THOKK THOKK THOKK THOKK
THWIPP
THWIPP
WHOA! DIDN'T YOUR MOTHER TELL YOU NOT TO PLAY WITH YOUR FOOD?
ARE WEBS PART OF YOUR RECIPE?
WELL, THEY ARE NOW!
YOU'RE NOT THE ONLY ONE WHO CAN SHOOT THINGS FROM THEIR WRISTS.
YOU CAN SHOOT PIES?
WERE YOU BITTEN BY A RADIOACTIVE LEMON MERINGUE?

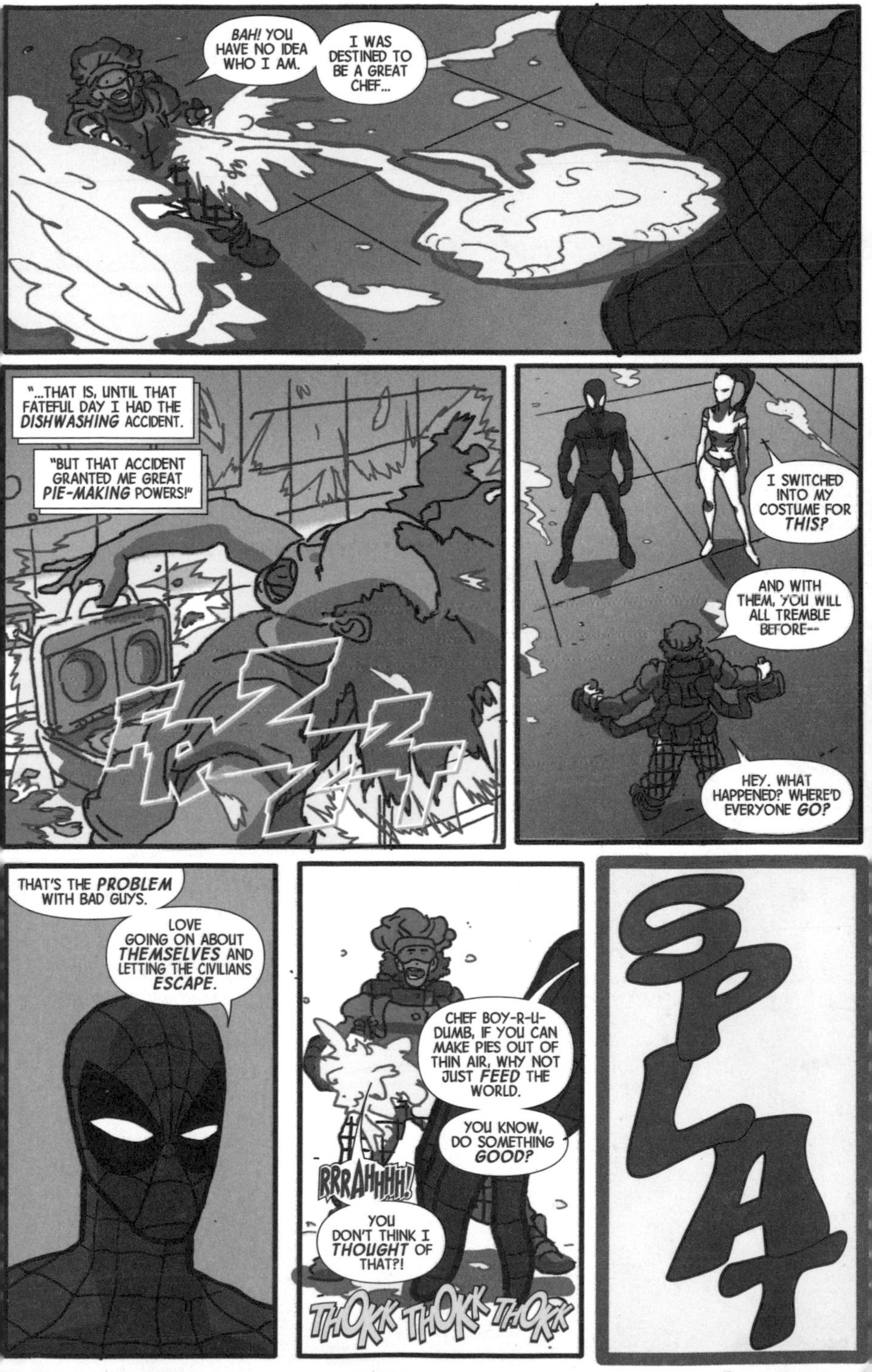
BAH! YOU HAVE NO IDEA WHO I AM.
I WAS DESTINED TO BE A GREAT CHEF...
"...THAT IS, UNTIL THAT FATEFUL DAY I HAD THE DISHWASHING ACCIDENT.
"BUT THAT ACCIDENT GRANTED ME GREAT PIE-MAKING POWERS!"
I SWITCHED INTO MY COSTUME FOR THIS?
AND WITH THEM, YOU WILL ALL TREMBLE BEFORE--
HEY. WHAT HAPPENED? WHERE'D EVERYONE GO?
THAT'S THE PROBLEM WITH BAD GUYS.
LOVE GOING ON ABOUT THEMSELVES AND LETTING THE CIVILIANS ESCAPE.
CHEF BOY-R-U-DUMB, IF YOU CAN MAKE PIES OUT OF THIN AIR, WHY NOT JUST FEED THE WORLD.
YOU KNOW, DO SOMETHING GOOD?
RRRAHHHH!
YOU DON'T THINK I THOUGHT OF THAT?!
THOKK THOKK THOKK
SPLAT

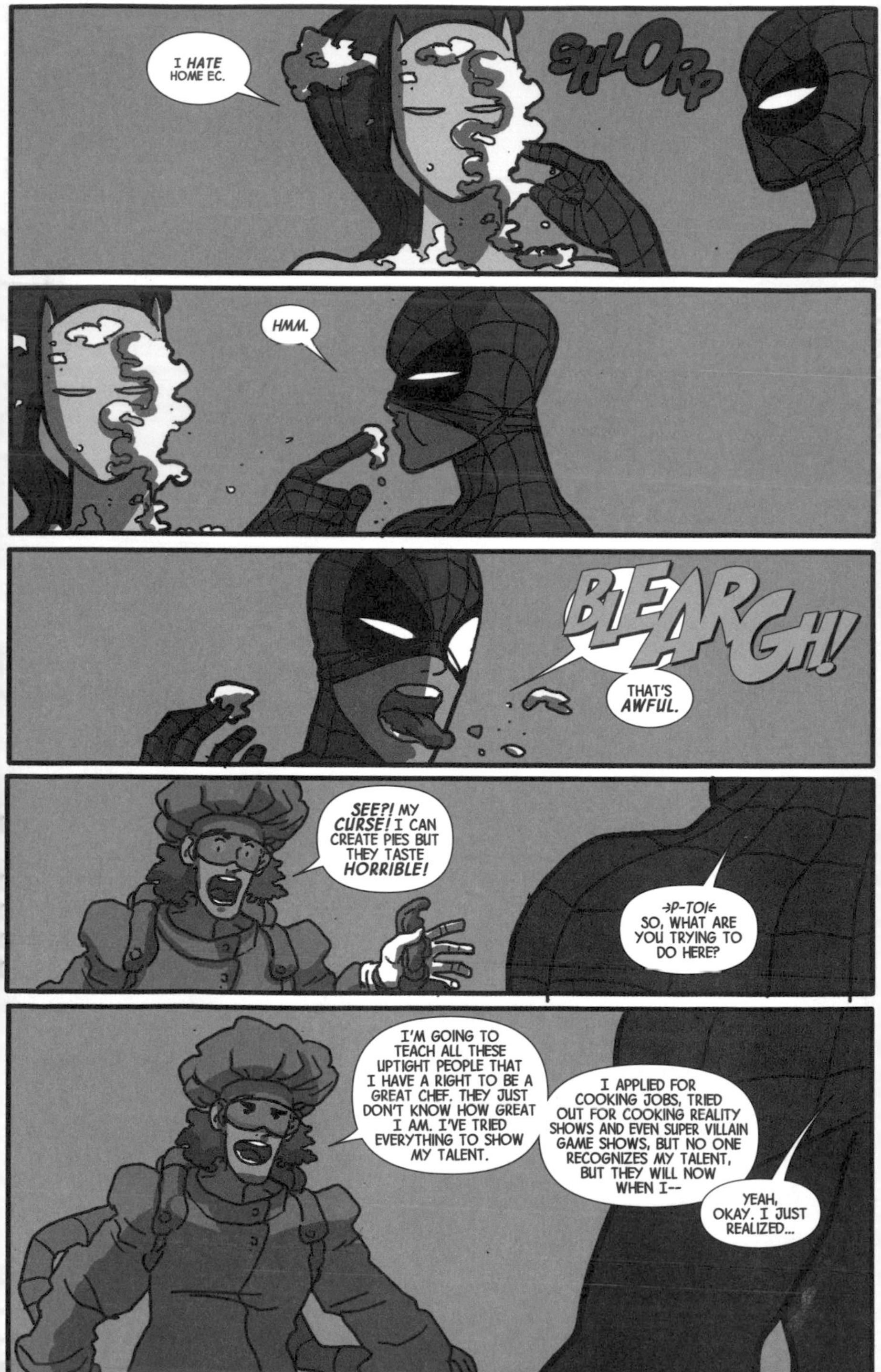

I HATE HOME EC.
SHLORP
HMM.
BLEARGH!
THAT'S AWFUL.
SEE?! MY CURSE! I CAN CREATE PIES BUT THEY TASTE HORRIBLE!
P-TOI
SO, WHAT ARE YOU TRYING TO DO HERE?
I'M GOING TO TEACH ALL THESE UPTIGHT PEOPLE THAT I HAVE A RIGHT TO BE A GREAT CHEF. THEY JUST DON'T KNOW HOW GREAT I AM. I'VE TRIED EVERYTHING TO SHOW MY TALENT.
I APPLIED FOR COOKING JOBS, TRIED OUT FOR COOKING REALITY SHOWS AND EVEN SUPER VILLAIN GAME SHOWS, BUT NO ONE RECOGNIZES MY TALENT, BUT THEY WILL NOW WHEN I--
YEAH, OKAY. I JUST REALIZED...

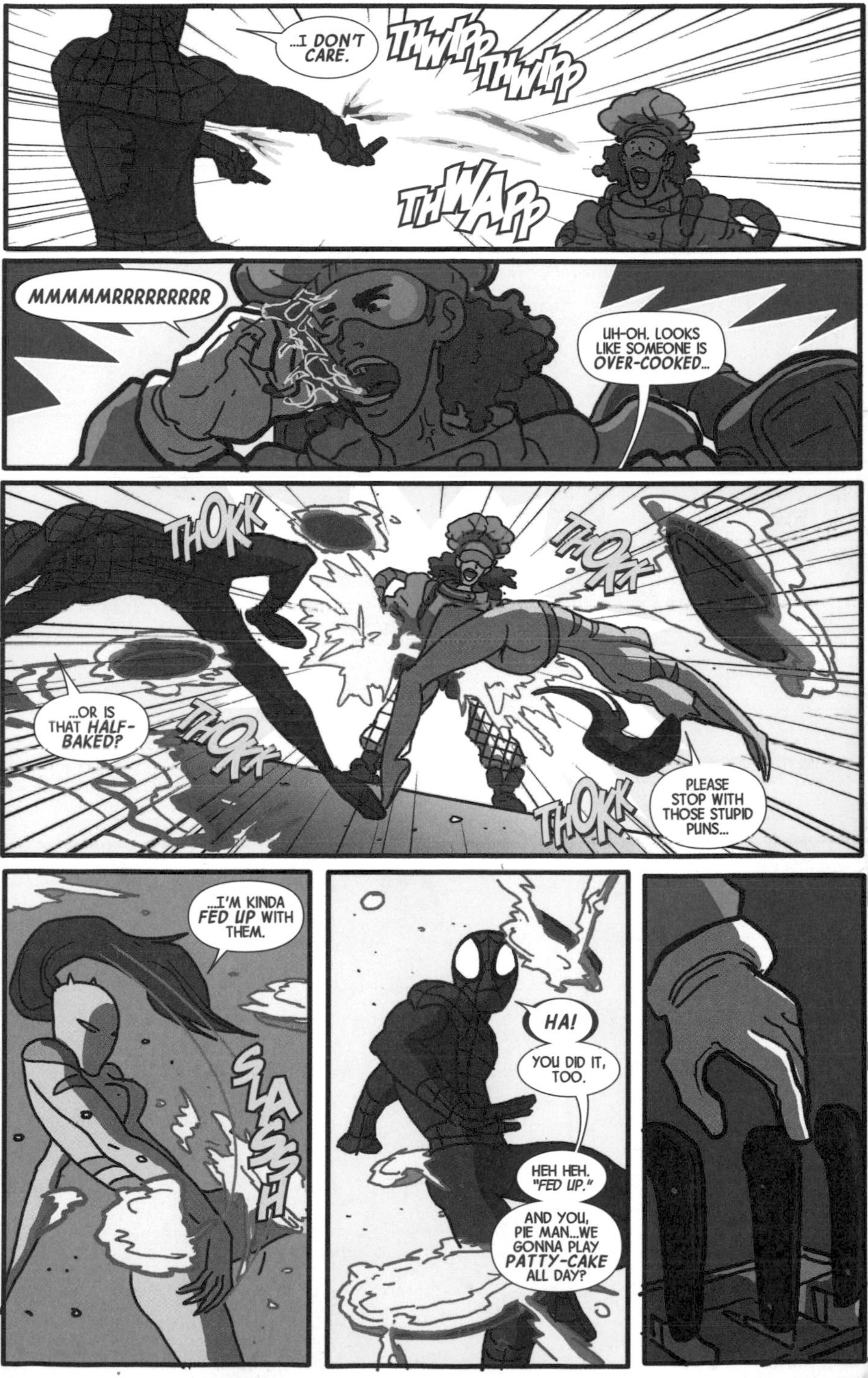
...I DON'T CARE.
THWIPP THWIPP
THWAPP
MMMMMRRRRRRRRR
UH-OH. LOOKS LIKE SOMEONE IS OVER-COOKED...
THOKK
THOKK
...OR IS THAT HALF-BAKED?
THOKK
THOKK
PLEASE STOP WITH THOSE STUPID PUNS...
...I'M KINDA FED UP WITH THEM.
SLASSSH
HA!
YOU DID IT, TOO.
HEH HEH. "FED UP."
AND YOU, PIE MAN...WE GONNA PLAY PATTY-CAKE ALL DAY?

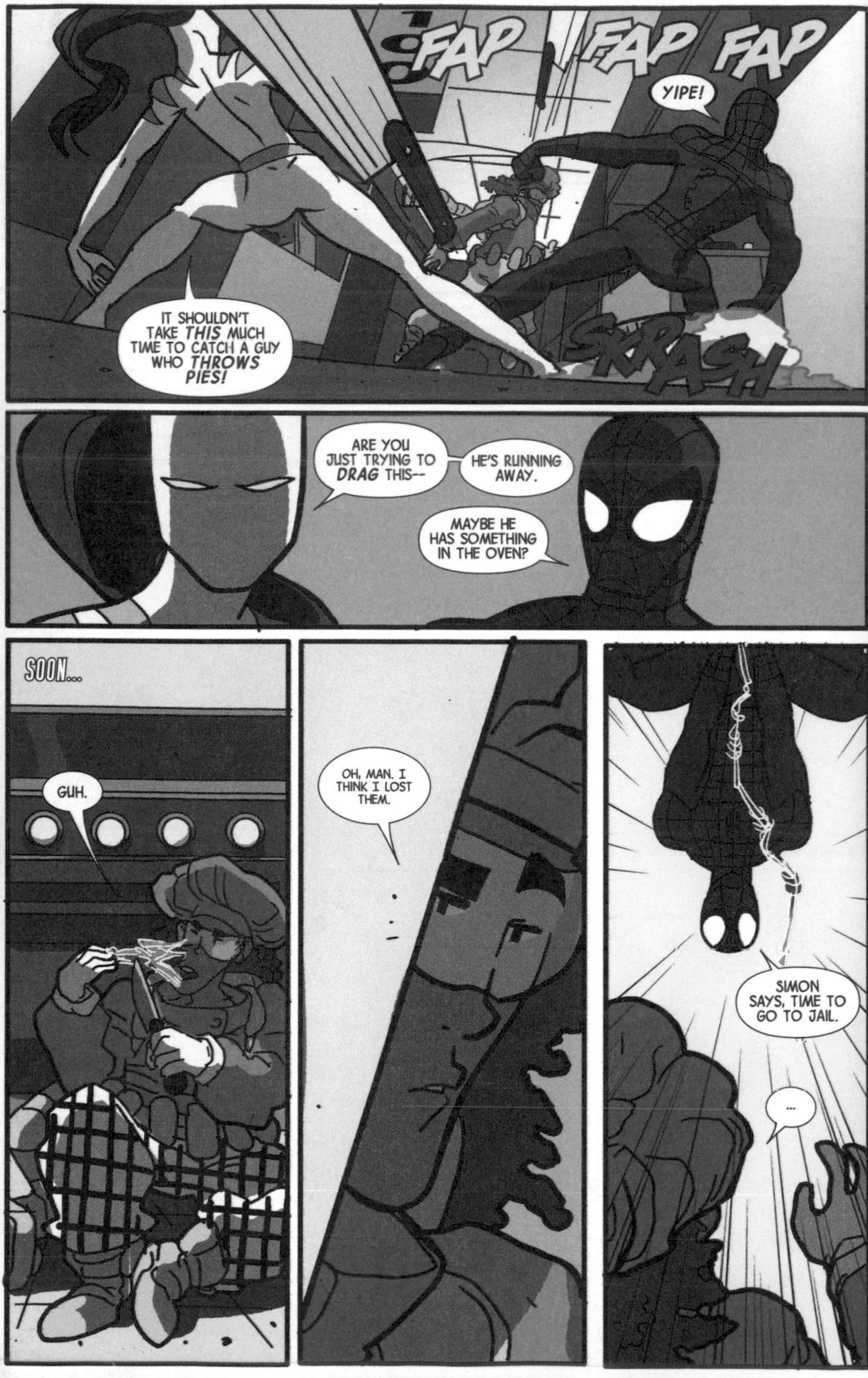
FAP FAP FAP
YIPE!
IT SHOULDN'T TAKE THIS MUCH TIME TO CATCH A GUY WHO THROWS PIES!
SKRASH
ARE YOU JUST TRYING TO DRAG THIS--
HE'S RUNNING AWAY.
MAYBE HE HAS SOMETHING IN THE OVEN?
SOON...
GUH.
OH, MAN. I THINK I LOST THEM.
SIMON SAYS, TIME TO GO TO JAIL.
...

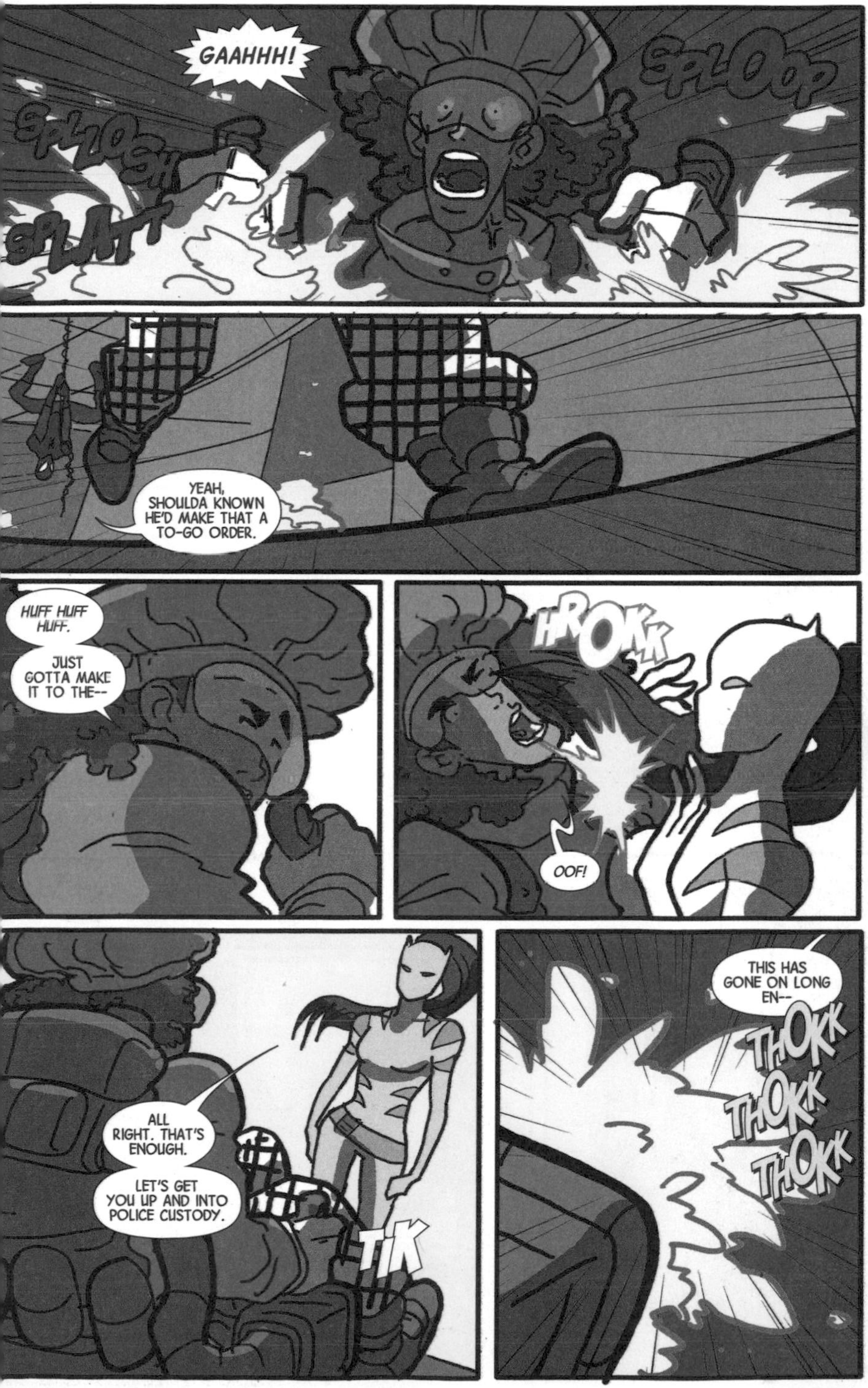
GAAHHH!
SPLOOP
SPLOOSH
SPLATT
YEAH, SHOULDA KNOWN HE'D MAKE THAT A TO-GO ORDER.
HUFF HUFF HUFF.
JUST GOTTA MAKE IT TO THE--
HROKK
OOF!
ALL RIGHT. THAT'S ENOUGH.
LET'S GET YOU UP AND INTO POLICE CUSTODY.
TIK
THIS HAS GONE ON LONG EN--
THOKK
THOKK
THOKK

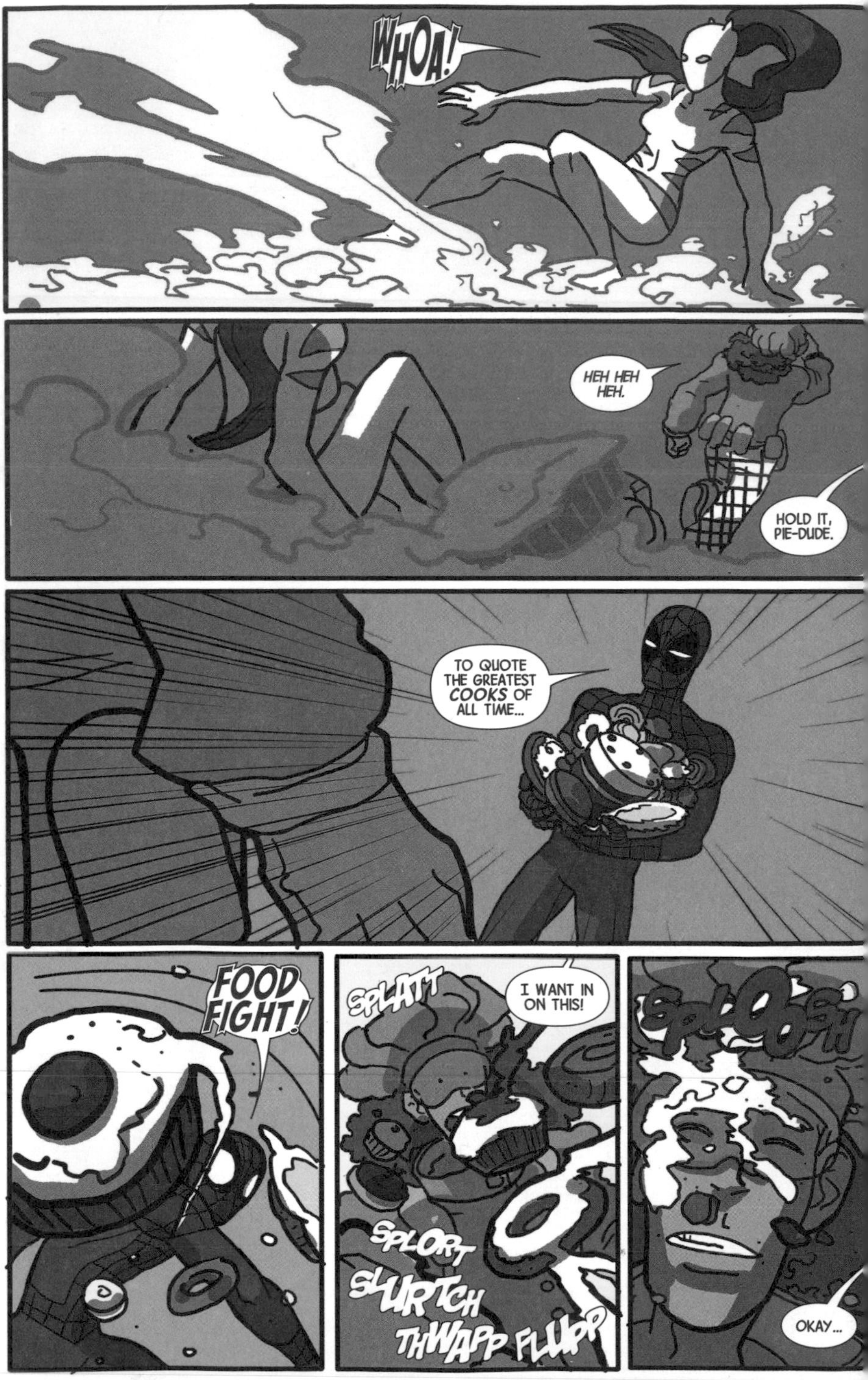
WHOA!
HEH HEH HEH.
HOLD IT, PIE-DUDE.
TO QUOTE THE GREATEST COOKS OF ALL TIME...
FOOD FIGHT!
SPLATT
I WANT IN ON THIS!
SPLORT
SLURTCH
THWAPP FLUPP
SPLOOOSH
OKAY...

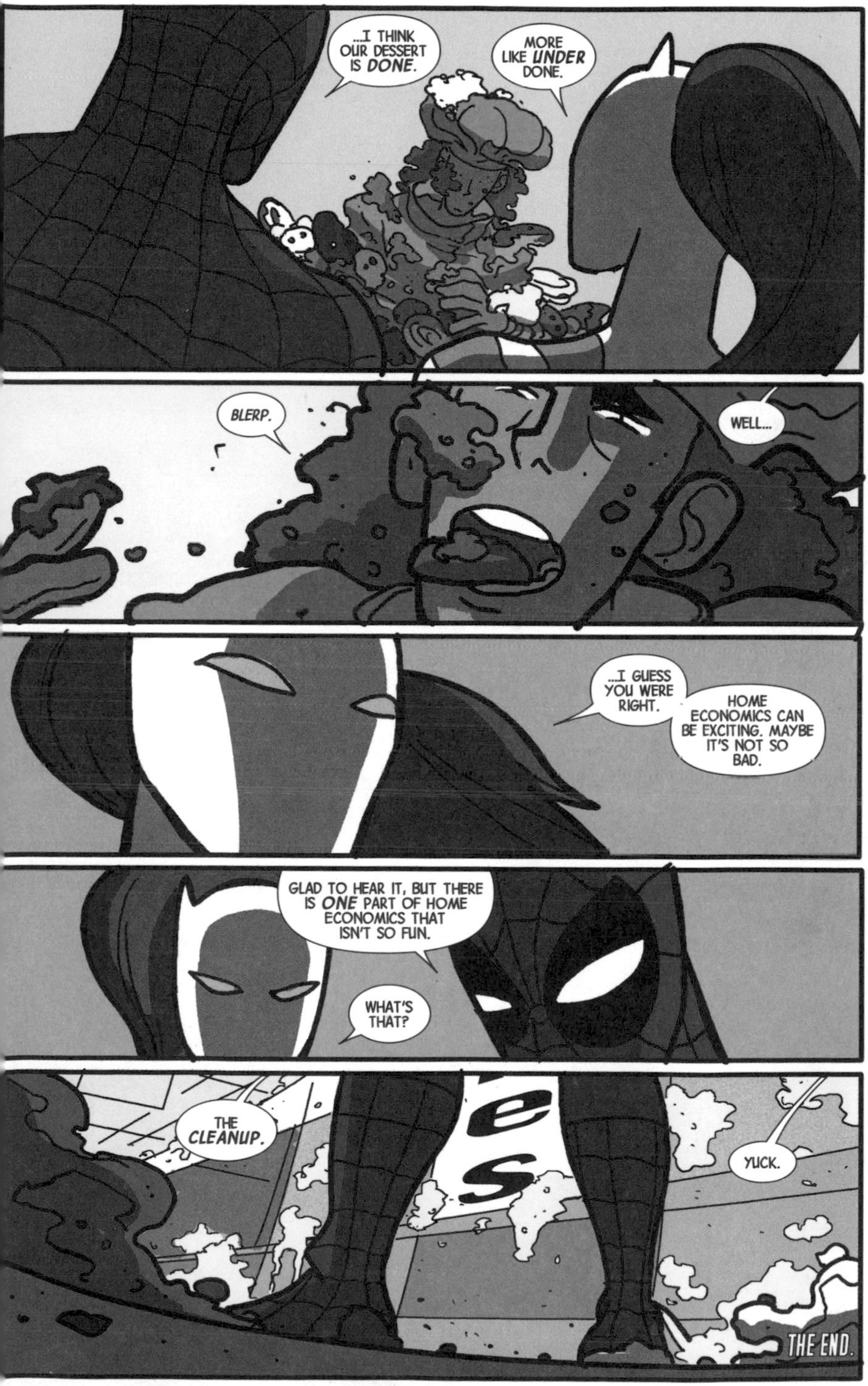
...I THINK OUR DESSERT IS DONE.
MORE LIKE UNDER DONE.
BLERP.
WELL...
...I GUESS YOU WERE RIGHT.
HOME ECONOMICS CAN BE EXCITING. MAYBE IT'S NOT SO BAD.
GLAD TO HEAR IT, BUT THERE IS ONE PART OF HOME ECONOMICS THAT ISN'T SO FUN.
WHAT'S THAT?
THE CLEANUP.
YUCK.
THE END.

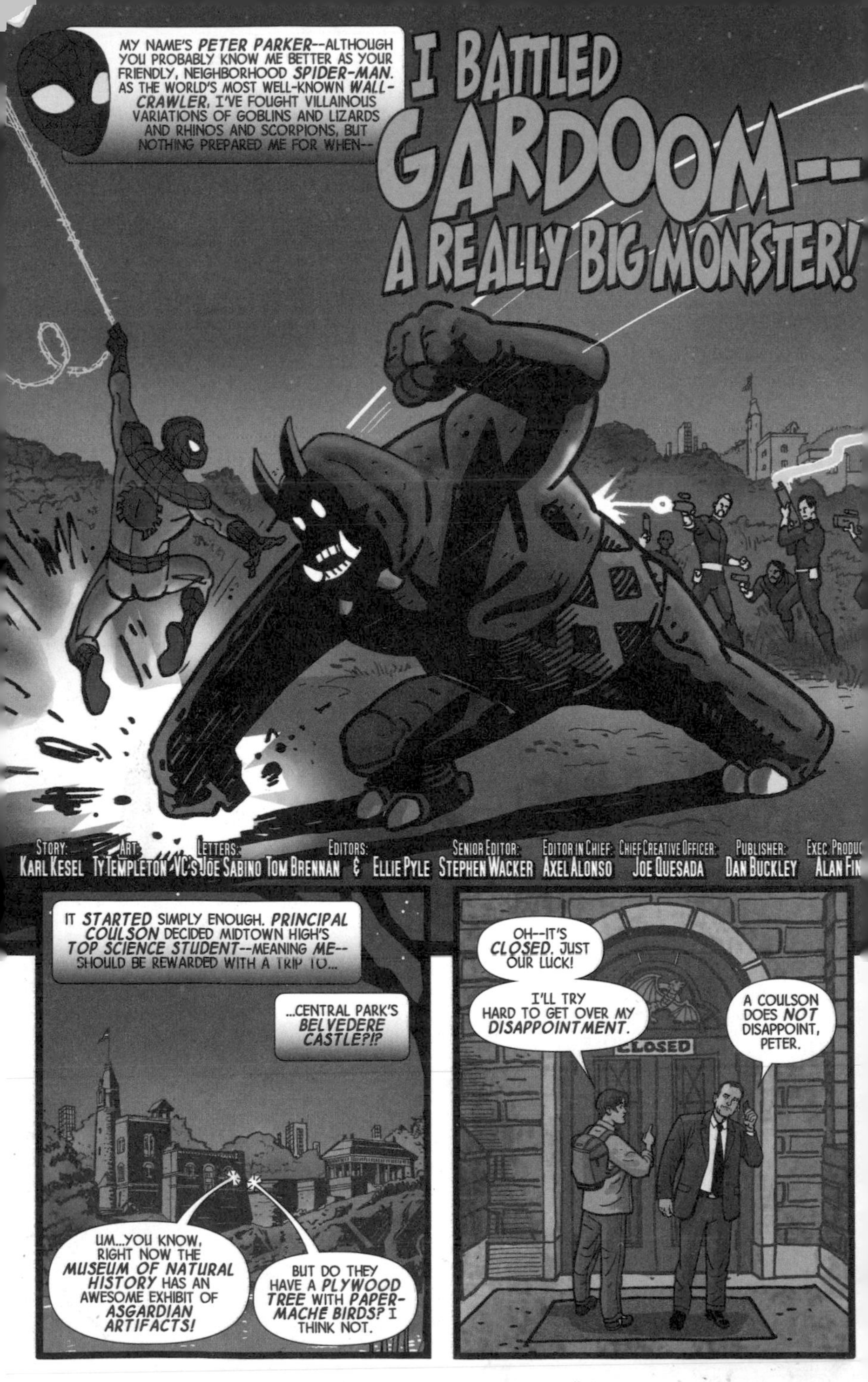
MY NAME'S PETER PARKER--ALTHOUGH YOU PROBABLY KNOW ME BETTER AS YOUR FRIENDLY, NEIGHBORHOOD SPIDER-MAN. AS THE WORLD'S MOST WELL-KNOWN WALL-CRAWLER, I'VE FOUGHT VILLAINOUS VARIATIONS OF GOBLINS AND LIZARDS AND RHINOS AND SCORPIONS, BUT NOTHING PREPARED ME FOR WHEN--
I BATTLED GARDOOM--A REALLY BIG MONSTER!
STORY: KARL KESEL ART: TY TEMPLETON LETTERS: VC's JOE SABINO EDITORS: TOM BRENNAN & ELLIE PYLE SENIOR EDITOR: STEPHEN WACKER EDITOR IN CHIEF: AXEL ALONSO CHIEF CREATIVE OFFICER: JOE QUESADA PUBLISHER: DAN BUCKLEY EXEC. PRODUC ALAN FIN
IT STARTED SIMPLY ENOUGH. PRINCIPAL COULSON DECIDED MIDTOWN HIGH'S TOP SCIENCE STUDENT--MEANING ME--SHOULD BE REWARDED WITH A TRIP TO...
...CENTRAL PARK'S BELVEDERE CASTLE?!?
UM...YOU KNOW, RIGHT NOW THE MUSEUM OF NATURAL HISTORY HAS AN AWESOME EXHIBIT OF ASGARDIAN ARTIFACTS!
BUT DO THEY HAVE A PLYWOOD TREE WITH PAPER-MACHE BIRDS? I THINK NOT.
OH--IT'S CLOSED. JUST OUR LUCK!
I'LL TRY HARD TO GET OVER MY DISAPPOINTMENT.
CLOSED
A COULSON DOES NOT DISAPPOINT, PETER.

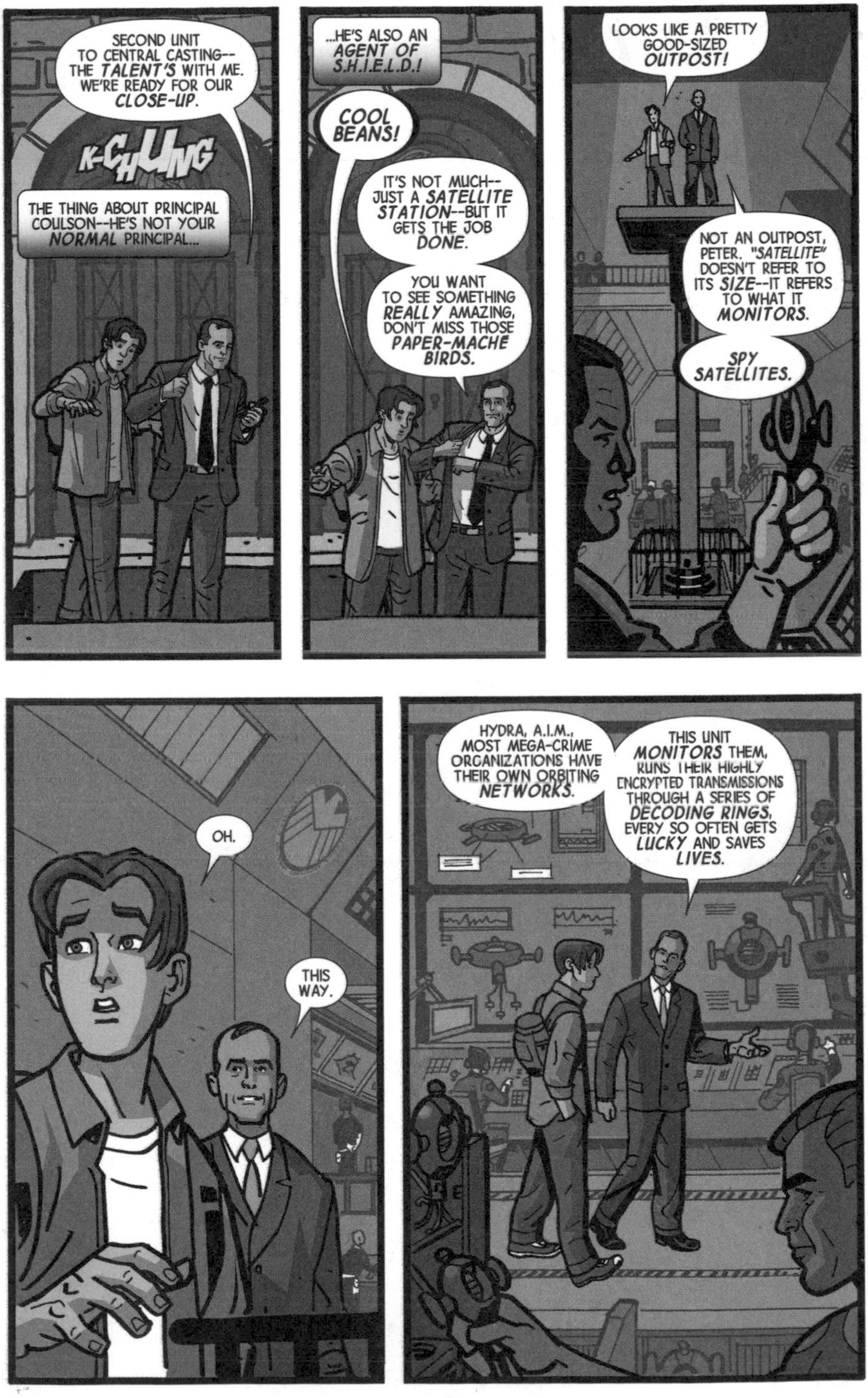

SECOND UNIT TO CENTRAL CASTING-- THE TALENT'S WITH ME. WE'RE READY FOR OUR CLOSE-UP.
K-CHUNG
THE THING ABOUT PRINCIPAL COULSON--HE'S NOT YOUR NORMAL PRINCIPAL...
...HE'S ALSO AN AGENT OF S.H.I.E.L.D.!
COOL BEANS!
IT'S NOT MUCH-- JUST A SATELLITE STATION--BUT IT GETS THE JOB DONE.
YOU WANT TO SEE SOMETHING REALLY AMAZING, DON'T MISS THOSE PAPER-MACHE BIRDS.
LOOKS LIKE A PRETTY GOOD-SIZED OUTPOST!
NOT AN OUTPOST, PETER. "SATELLITE" DOESN'T REFER TO ITS SIZE--IT REFERS TO WHAT IT MONITORS.
SPY SATELLITES.
OH.
THIS WAY.
HYDRA, A.I.M., MOST MEGA-CRIME ORGANIZATIONS HAVE THEIR OWN ORBITING NETWORKS.
THIS UNIT MONITORS THEM, RUNS THEIR HIGHLY ENCRYPTED TRANSMISSIONS THROUGH A SERIES OF DECODING RINGS, EVERY SO OFTEN GETS LUCKY AND SAVES LIVES.

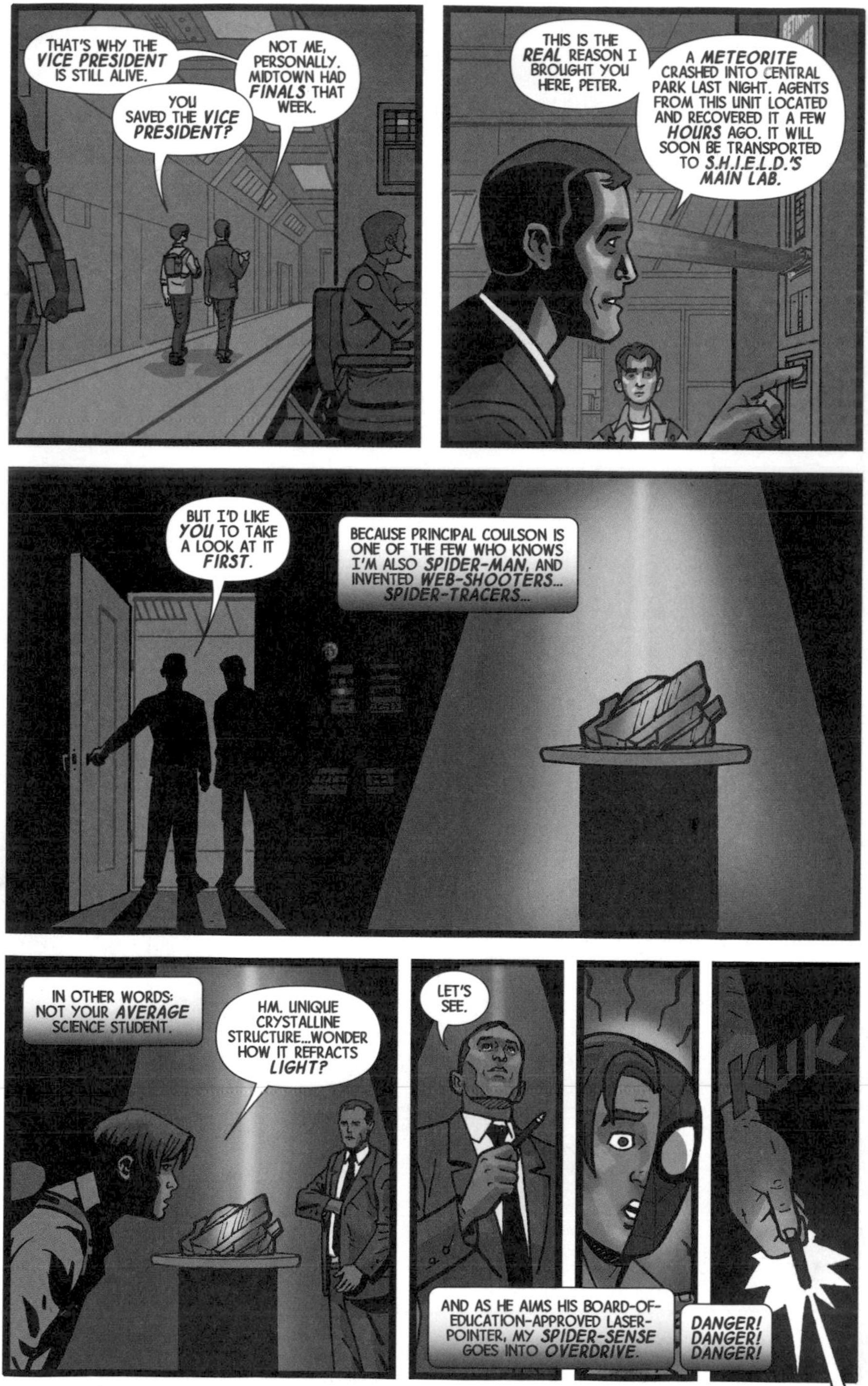
THAT'S WHY THE VICE PRESIDENT IS STILL ALIVE.
YOU SAVED THE VICE PRESIDENT?
NOT ME, PERSONALLY. MIDTOWN HAD FINALS THAT WEEK.
THIS IS THE REAL REASON I BROUGHT YOU HERE, PETER.
A METEORITE CRASHED INTO CENTRAL PARK LAST NIGHT. AGENTS FROM THIS UNIT LOCATED AND RECOVERED IT A FEW HOURS AGO. IT WILL SOON BE TRANSPORTED TO S.H.I.E.L.D.'S MAIN LAB.
BUT I'D LIKE YOU TO TAKE A LOOK AT IT FIRST.
BECAUSE PRINCIPAL COULSON IS ONE OF THE FEW WHO KNOWS I'M ALSO SPIDER-MAN, AND INVENTED WEB-SHOOTERS... SPIDER-TRACERS...
IN OTHER WORDS: NOT YOUR AVERAGE SCIENCE STUDENT.
HM. UNIQUE CRYSTALLINE STRUCTURE...WONDER HOW IT REFRACTS LIGHT?
LET'S SEE.
KLIK
AND AS HE AIMS HIS BOARD-OF-EDUCATION-APPROVED LASER-POINTER, MY SPIDER-SENSE GOES INTO OVERDRIVE.
DANGER! DANGER! DANGER!

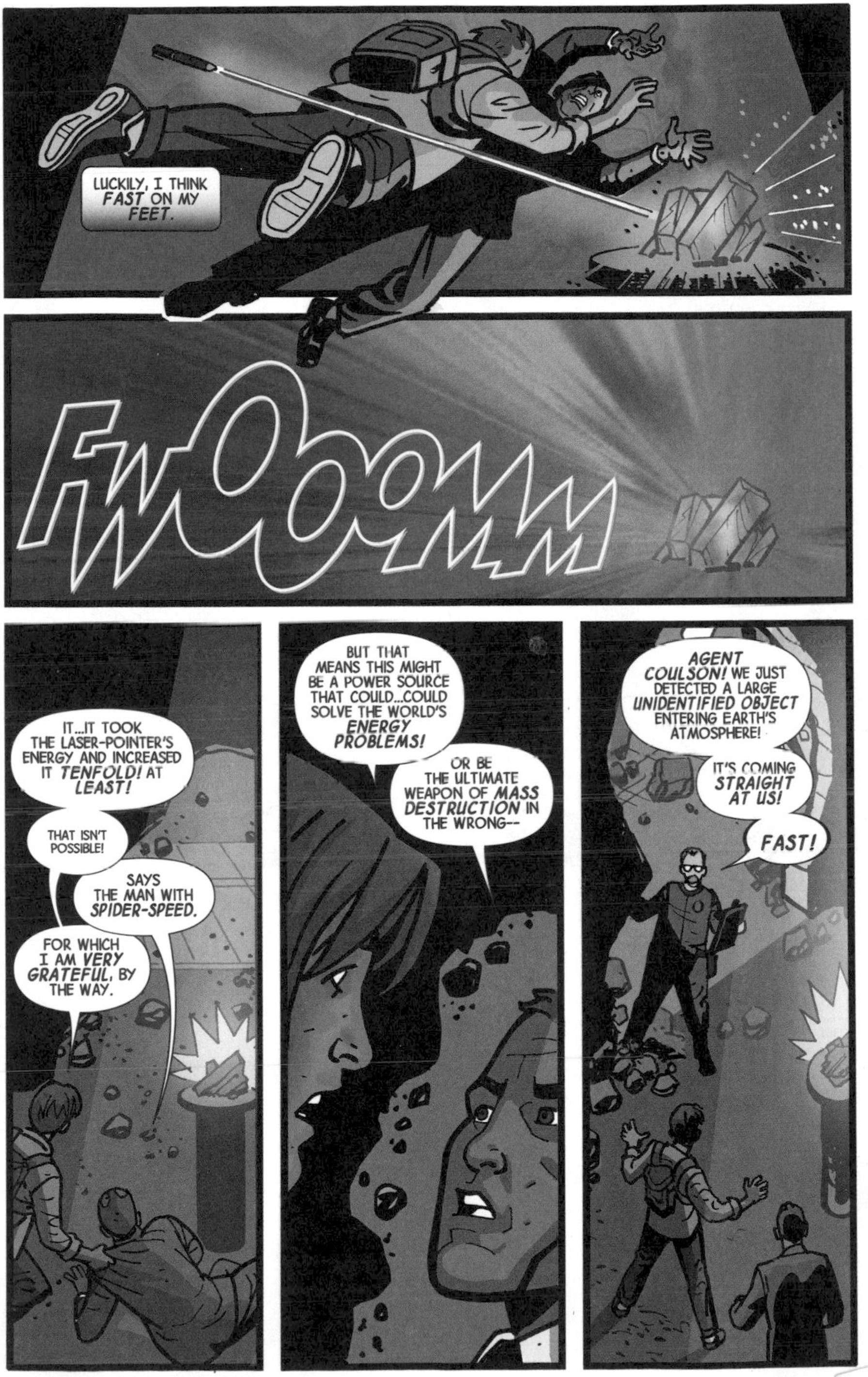
LUCKILY, I THINK FAST ON MY FEET.
FWOOOMM
IT...IT TOOK THE LASER-POINTER'S ENERGY AND INCREASED IT TENFOLD! AT LEAST!
THAT ISN'T POSSIBLE!
SAYS THE MAN WITH SPIDER-SPEED.
FOR WHICH I AM VERY GRATEFUL, BY THE WAY.
BUT THAT MEANS THIS MIGHT BE A POWER SOURCE THAT COULD...COULD SOLVE THE WORLD'S ENERGY PROBLEMS!
OR BE THE ULTIMATE WEAPON OF MASS DESTRUCTION IN THE WRONG--
AGENT COULSON! WE JUST DETECTED A LARGE UNIDENTIFIED OBJECT ENTERING EARTH'S ATMOSPHERE!
IT'S COMING STRAIGHT AT US!
FAST!

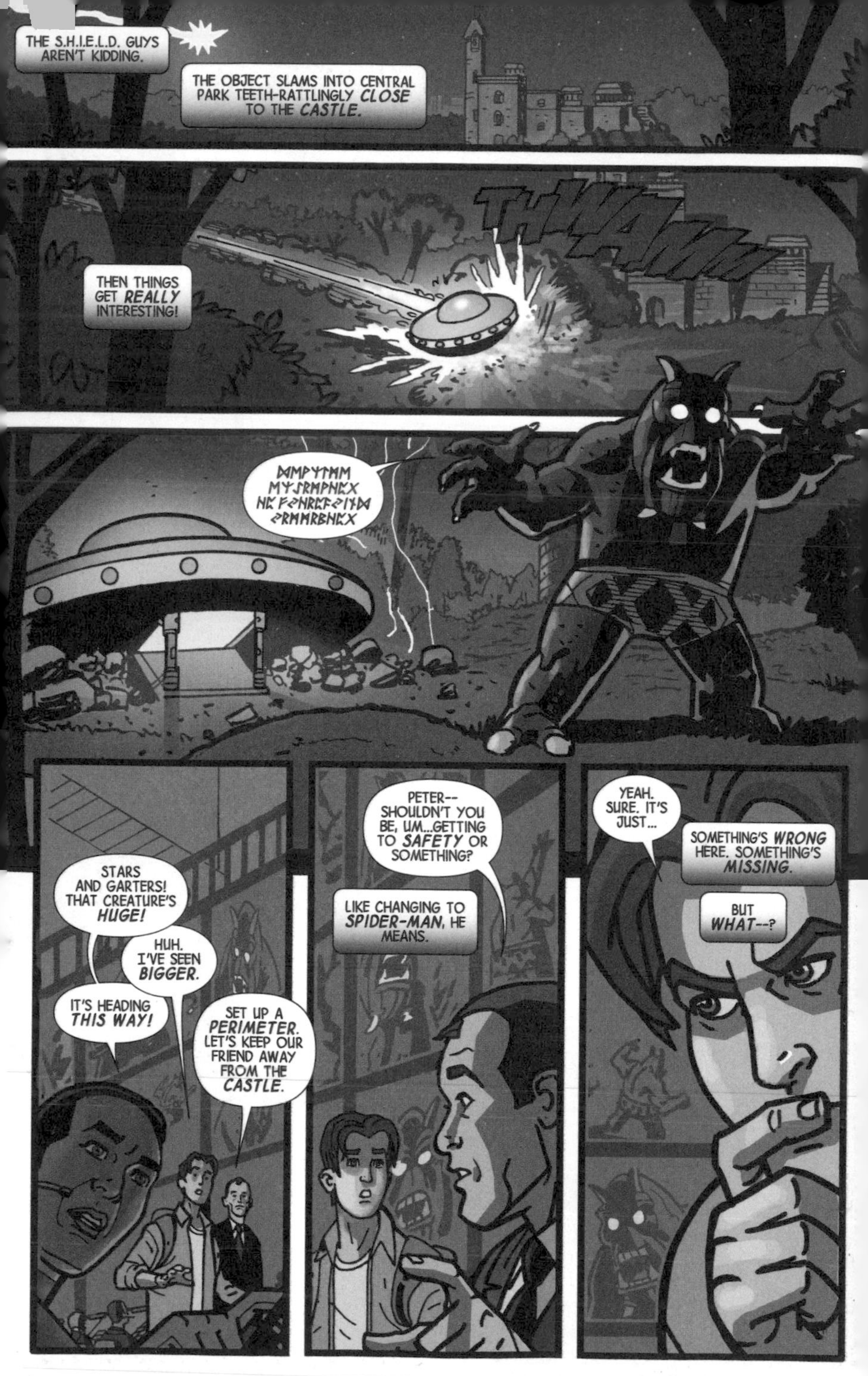
THE S.H.I.E.L.D. GUYS AREN'T KIDDING.
THE OBJECT SLAMS INTO CENTRAL PARK TEETH-RATTLINGLY CLOSE TO THE CASTLE.
THWAMM
THEN THINGS GET REALLY INTERESTING!
STARS AND GARTERS! THAT CREATURE'S HUGE!
HUH. I'VE SEEN BIGGER.
IT'S HEADING THIS WAY!
SET UP A PERIMETER. LET'S KEEP OUR FRIEND AWAY FROM THE CASTLE.
PETER-- SHOULDN'T YOU BE, UM...GETTING TO SAFETY OR SOMETHING?
LIKE CHANGING TO SPIDER-MAN, HE MEANS.
YEAH. SURE. IT'S JUST...
SOMETHING'S WRONG HERE. SOMETHING'S MISSING.
BUT WHAT--?

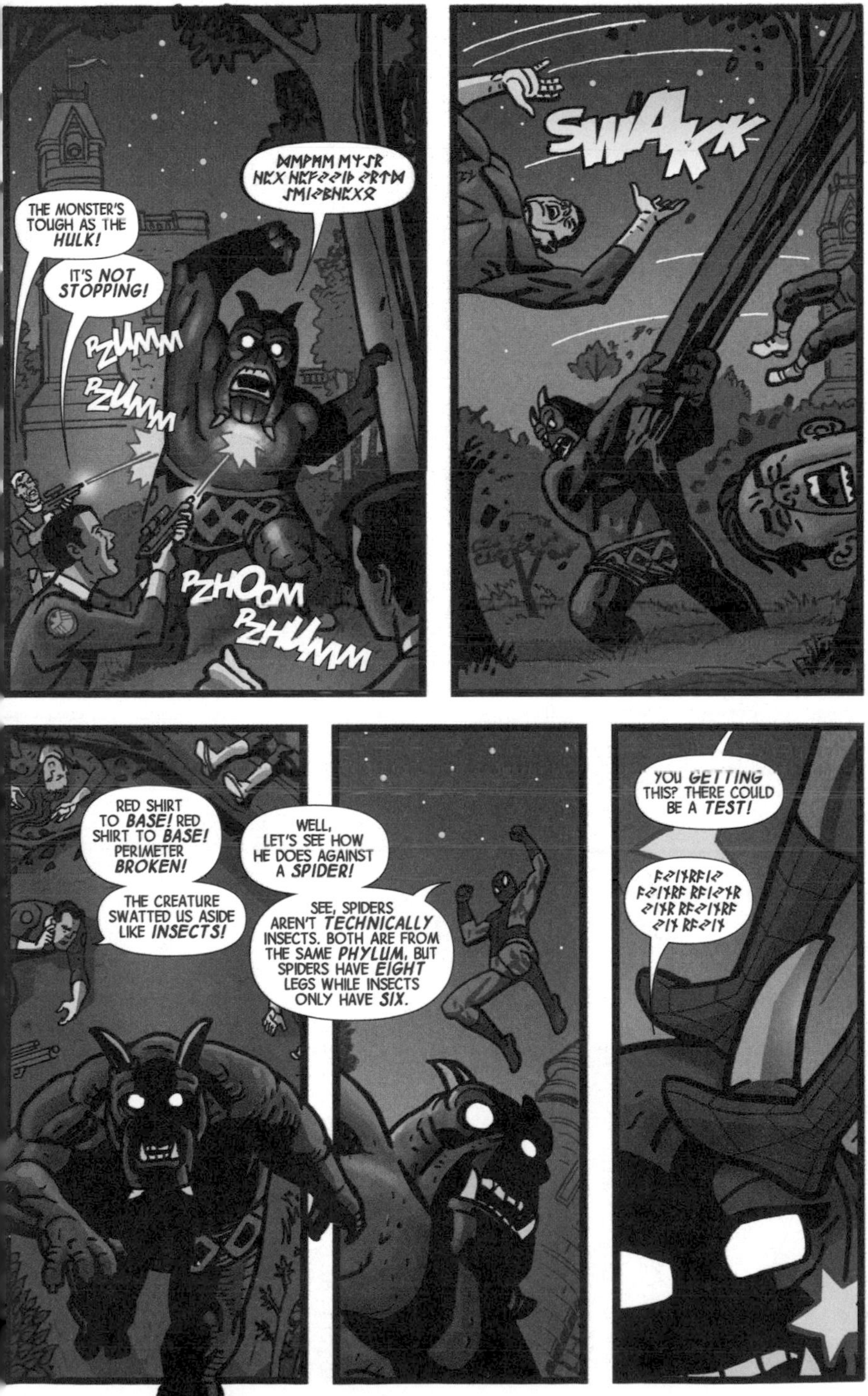

THE MONSTER'S TOUGH AS THE HULK!
IT'S NOT STOPPING!
PZUMM
PZUMM
PZHOOM
PZHUMM
SWAKK
RED SHIRT TO BASE! RED SHIRT TO BASE! PERIMETER BROKEN!
THE CREATURE SWATTED US ASIDE LIKE INSECTS!
WELL, LET'S SEE HOW HE DOES AGAINST A SPIDER!
SEE, SPIDERS AREN'T TECHNICALLY INSECTS. BOTH ARE FROM THE SAME PHYLUM, BUT SPIDERS HAVE EIGHT LEGS WHILE INSECTS ONLY HAVE SIX.
YOU GETTING THIS? THERE COULD BE A TEST!

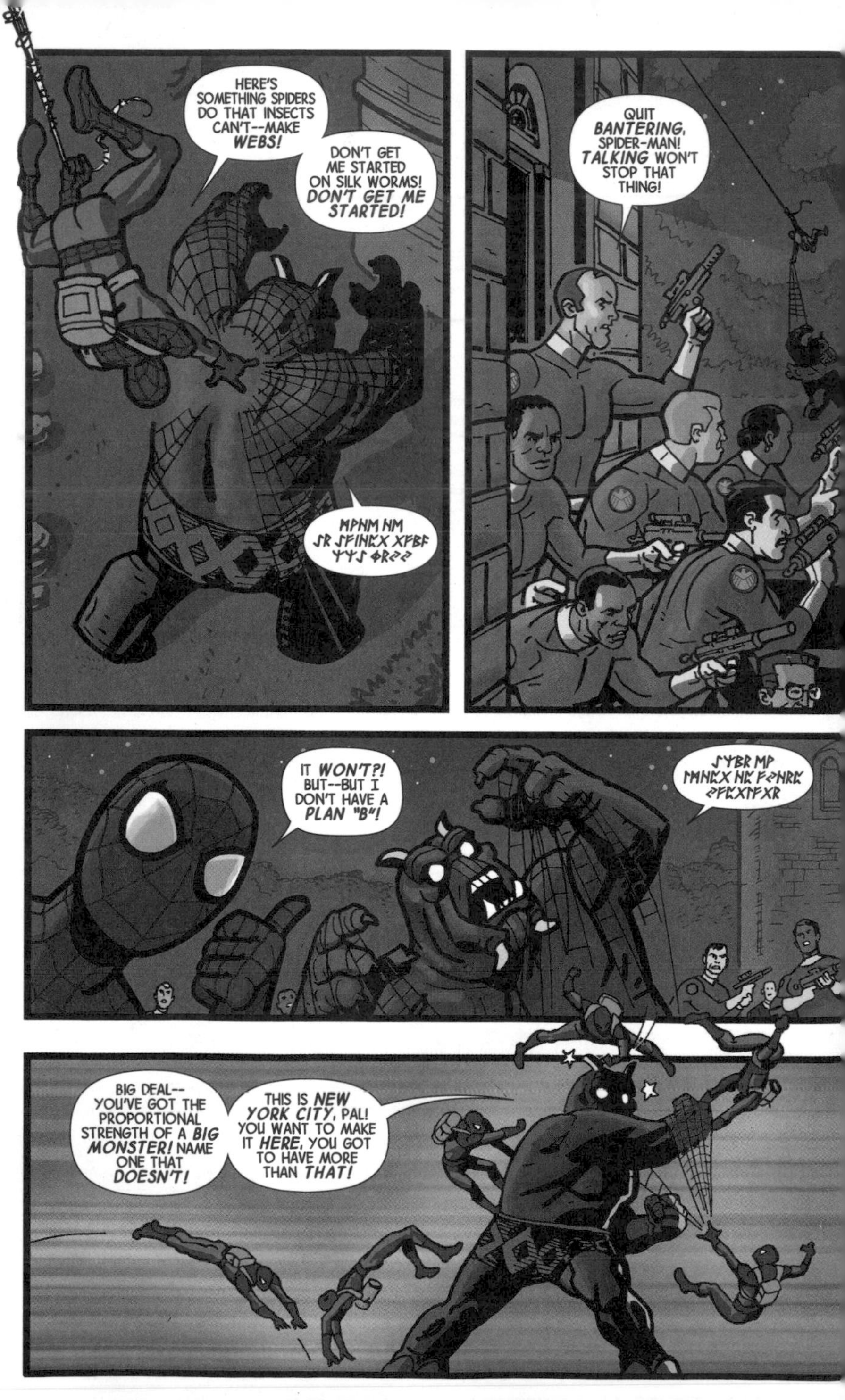
HERE'S SOMETHING SPIDERS DO THAT INSECTS CAN'T--MAKE WEBS!
DON'T GET ME STARTED ON SILK WORMS! DON'T GET ME STARTED!
QUIT BANTERING, SPIDER-MAN! TALKING WON'T STOP THAT THING!
IT WON'T?! BUT--BUT I DON'T HAVE A PLAN "B"!
BIG DEAL-- YOU'VE GOT THE PROPORTIONAL STRENGTH OF A BIG MONSTER! NAME ONE THAT DOESN'T!
THIS IS NEW YORK CITY, PAL! YOU WANT TO MAKE IT HERE, YOU GOT TO HAVE MORE THAN THAT!

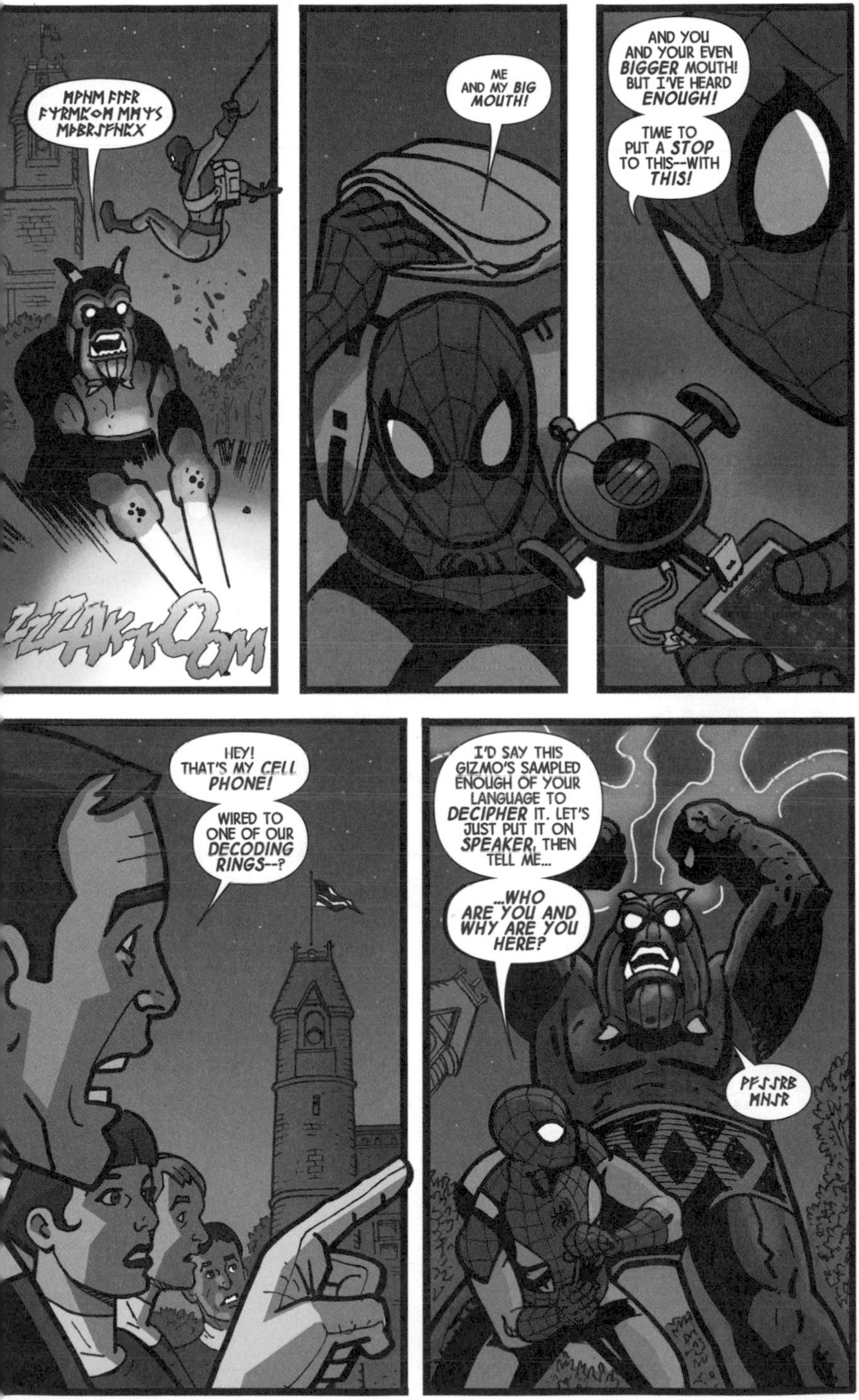
ZZZAKKOOM
ME AND MY BIG MOUTH!
AND YOU AND YOUR EVEN BIGGER MOUTH! BUT I'VE HEARD ENOUGH!
TIME TO PUT A STOP TO THIS--WITH THIS!
HEY! THAT'S MY CELL PHONE!
WIRED TO ONE OF OUR DECODING RINGS--?
I'D SAY THIS GIZMO'S SAMPLED ENOUGH OF YOUR LANGUAGE TO DECIPHER IT. LET'S JUST PUT IT ON SPEAKER, THEN TELL ME...
...WHO ARE YOU AND WHY ARE YOU HERE?

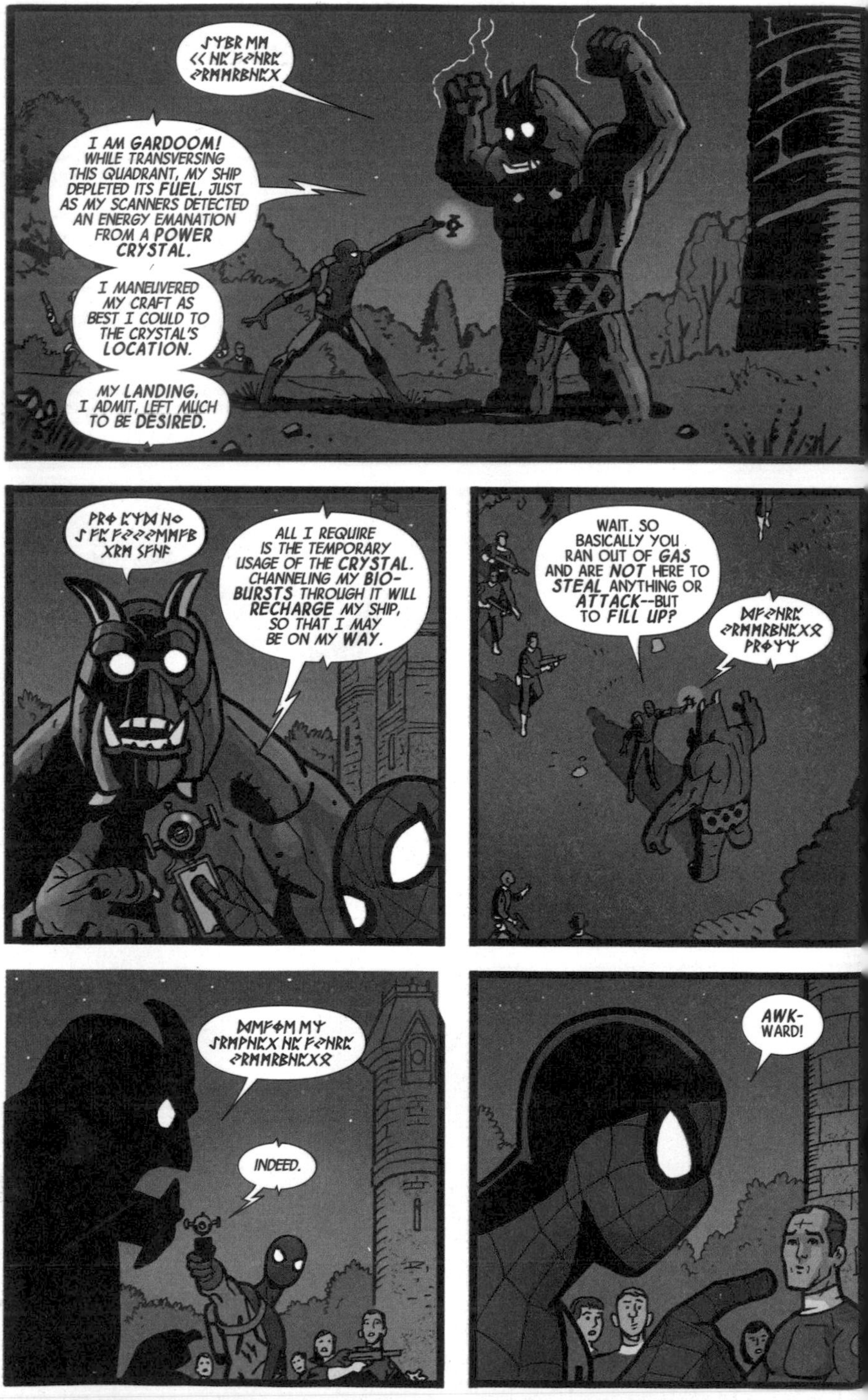
I AM GARDOOM! WHILE TRANSVERSING THIS QUADRANT, MY SHIP DEPLETED ITS FUEL, JUST AS MY SCANNERS DETECTED AN ENERGY EMANATION FROM A POWER CRYSTAL.
I MANEUVERED MY CRAFT AS BEST I COULD TO THE CRYSTAL'S LOCATION.
MY LANDING, I ADMIT, LEFT MUCH TO BE DESIRED.
ALL I REQUIRE IS THE TEMPORARY USAGE OF THE CRYSTAL. CHANNELING MY BIO-BURSTS THROUGH IT WILL RECHARGE MY SHIP, SO THAT I MAY BE ON MY WAY.
WAIT. SO BASICALLY YOU RAN OUT OF GAS AND ARE NOT HERE TO STEAL ANYTHING OR ATTACK--BUT TO FILL UP?
INDEED.
AWK-WARD!

A QUICK REFUELING LATER...

AGAIN, MR. GARDOOM, I OFFER MY DEEPEST *APOLOGIES* AS A REPRESENTATIVE OF S.H.I.E.L.D. AND MIDTOWN HIGH SCHOOL.

ᚠᚷᚠᚾᚲᛁ ᛋᛒ. ᚷᚠᛒᚠᛁᛁᛋᛁ ᚾ ᚣᚢ ᚲᚱᛒ ᛋᚢ ᚠᚱᚱᛋᚱᛗᛗ ᚠᛋᚣᚢᚣᚲᚾᚱᛗ.

ᚾᛗ ᚾᛗ ᛏᚾᚾᚺᚱ ᛒᚾᚷᛕᛗ. ᚱᚠᛒᛗᛕ ᚠᛗ ᚠ ᚷᚠᚢᛕᛗᚾᛒ ᛒᚱᛋᛁᛗᚠᛗᚾᚣᚲ ᚠᛗ ᚠ ᛋᚢᚠᛒᚱ ᛒᚢᛕᚱᛕᚣᛒᚢ ᚠᚣ ᚢᚣᛏ ᛗᚠᚢ ᚾᛗ

IT IS QUITE ALL RIGHT. EARTH HAS A GALACTIC REPUTATION AS A PLACE WHERE--HOW DO YOU SAY IT?--FIRST YOU *FIGHT*, THEN *TEAM-UP*.

ALL RIGHT, SPIDER-MAN--YOU'RE A *SCIENCE WHIZ*, SO IT'S NO SURPRISE YOU COBBLED TOGETHER AN *INTERGALACTIC TRANSLATOR* WHILE CHANGING CLOTHES...

...MY QUESTION IS: HOW'D YOU KNOW TO DO THAT? ALL INDICATIONS WERE MR. GARDOOM WAS A *THREAT*.

ALL EXCEPT ONE--MY *SPIDER-SENSE*.

IT *DIDN'T* GO OFF. THAT MEANT THERE WAS *NO DANGER!*

GOTTA SAY-- I'M GLAD IT WORKED OUT LIKE IT DID.

'CAUSE GARDOOM WAS *BIG*--*REALLY* BIG.

YOU SAID YOU'D SEEN *BIGGER*--BUT YOU'RE NOT TALKING ABOUT HIS *SIZE*, ARE YOU?

NO.

NO, I'M TALKING ABOUT HIS *SPIRIT*.

AND WE'D BETTER HOPE THERE'S A LOT MORE LIKE *HIM* OUT THERE!

END.

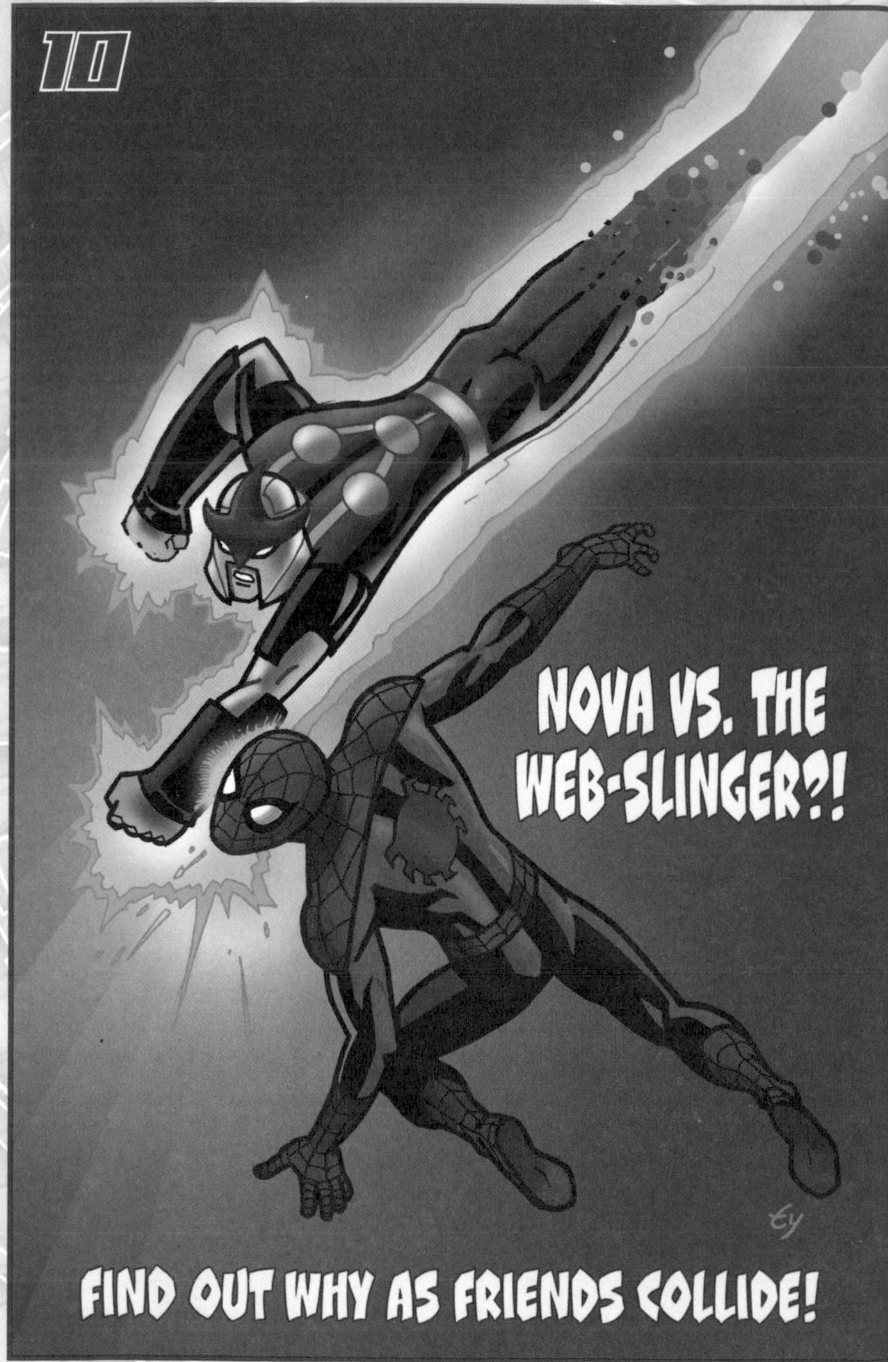
10
NOVA VS. THE WEB-SLINGER?!
FIND OUT WHY AS FRIENDS COLLIDE!

WOOO!

YOU SAID IT, BRO!

REC

HD

THESE SKATEBOARDING SUPER-JERKS ARE KNOWN AS THE *"XTREME KRHYME CREW"* AND THEY'VE BEEN RIPPING OFF NEW YORK FOR A FEW WEEKS.

THEN THEY POST THEIR CRIMES ON THE INTERNET. WISH I COULD SAY IT WAS AS STUPID AN IDEA AS IT SOUNDS, BUT THEY'VE BECOME THE BIGGEST INTERNET SENSATIONS SINCE THAT CAT WHO JUMPS IN THE BOX.

Toob — **Xtreme Krhyme Crew**

BRIAN CLEVINGER
writer
RAMON BACHS
pencils
RAUL FONTS
inks
PETER PANTAZIS
colorist
VC's JOE CARAMAGNA
letterer
ELLIE PYLE &
TOM BRENNAN
editors
STEPHEN WACKER
senior editor
AXEL ALONSO
editor in chief
JOE QUESADA
chief creative officer
DAN BUCKLEY
publisher
ALAN FINE
executive producer

Views: 3.467.512

I'VE GOTTA PUT THESE GUYS OUT OF COMMISSION. THEY'RE CRIMINALS AND I CAN'T LET THEM-- *3 MILLION VIEWERS?!*

lcome to the newe ... video! This time we ...pelled into the se ... e Bank just off Times ...uare. We rolled (a ... n of cash. Cops chased ...but watch the who ... ot away! Like and share ...r videos and follow us on Tweetster for clues on our next heist!

SPIDEY DOESN'T GET THREE MILLION VIEWS...

Comments: 7.824

come to the newest Xtreme Krhyme Crew video
time we rappelled into the second floor of
pire State Bank just off Times Square. We rolled
d LOL!!!-ed) out with a ton of cash. Cops chase
but watch the whole video to see how we got
ay! Like and share our videos and follow us on
eetster for clues on our next heist!

ANNOUNCING YOUR NEXT CRIME, HUH?

WELL THE AMAZING, SENSATIONAL AND, YES, ULTIMATE SPIDER-MAN WILL BE THERE TO STOP 'EM.

I JUST *HAVE* TO.

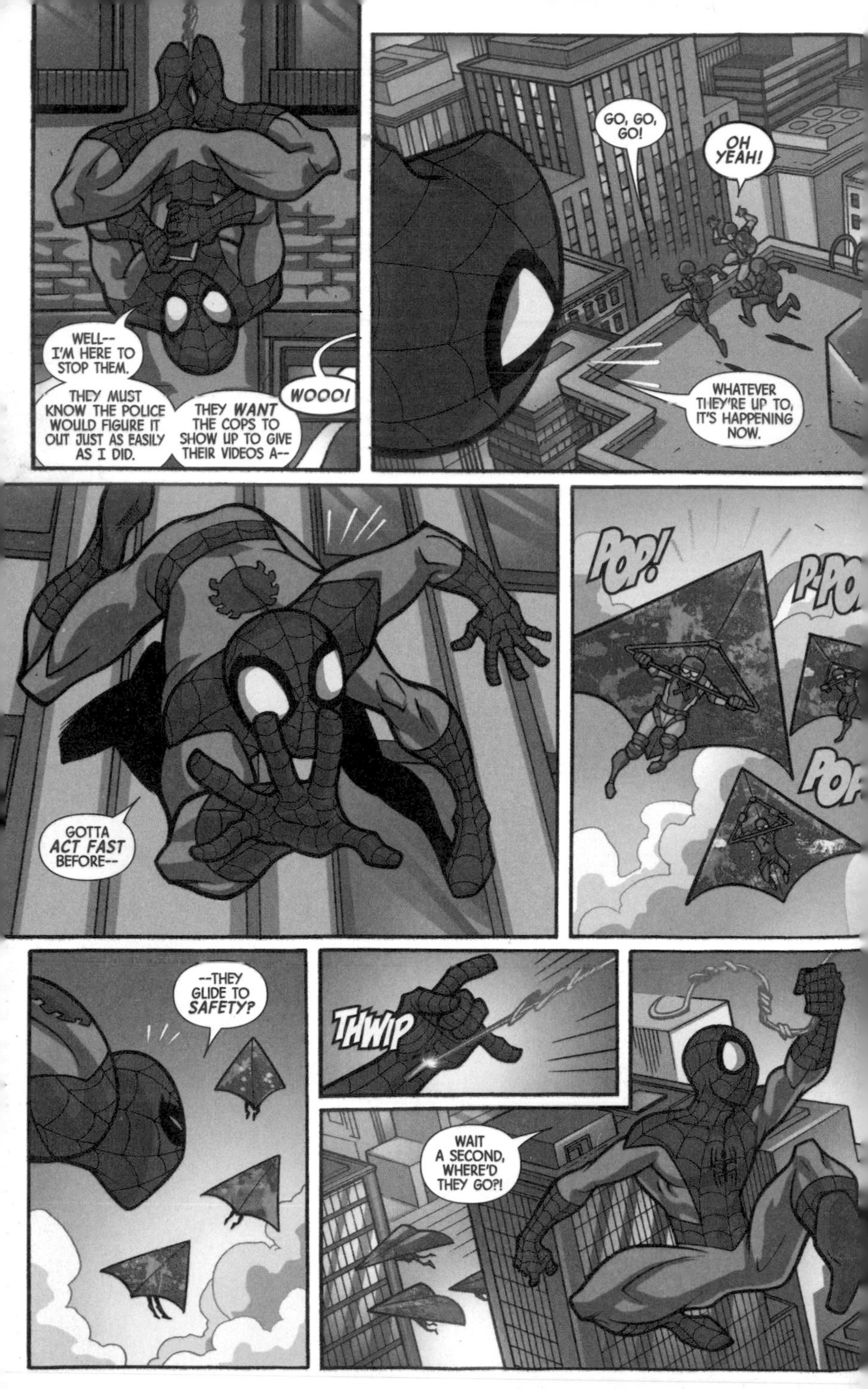
WELL-- I'M HERE TO STOP THEM.
THEY MUST KNOW THE POLICE WOULD FIGURE IT OUT JUST AS EASILY AS I DID.
THEY WANT THE COPS TO SHOW UP TO GIVE THEIR VIDEOS A--
WOOO!
GO, GO, GO!
OH YEAH!
WHATEVER THEY'RE UP TO, IT'S HAPPENING NOW.
GOTTA ACT FAST BEFORE--
POP!
--THEY GLIDE TO SAFETY?
THWIP
WAIT A SECOND, WHERE'D THEY GO?!

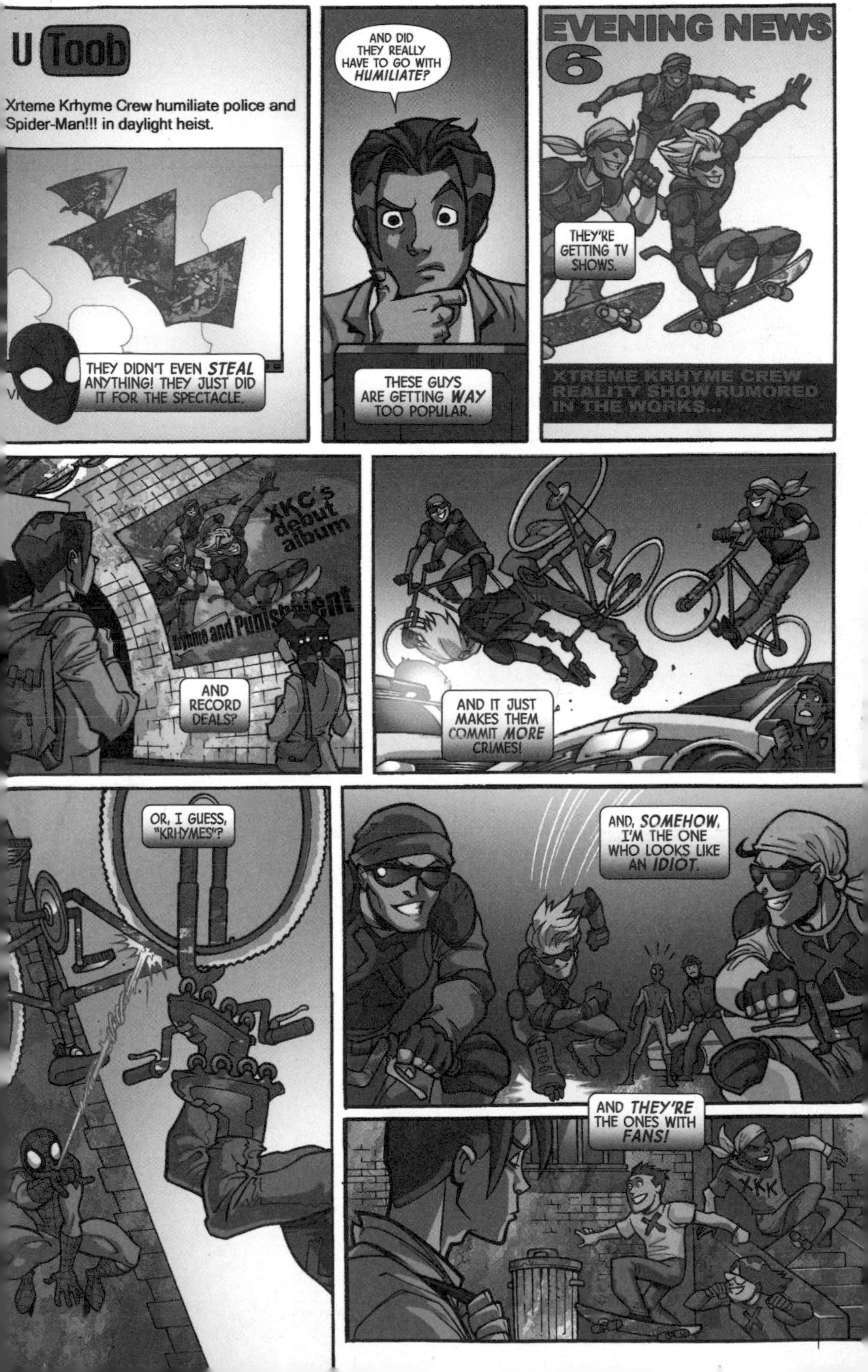
U Toob
Xrteme Krhyme Crew humiliate police and Spider-Man!!! in daylight heist.
THEY DIDN'T EVEN STEAL ANYTHING! THEY JUST DID IT FOR THE SPECTACLE.
AND DID THEY REALLY HAVE TO GO WITH HUMILIATE?
THESE GUYS ARE GETTING WAY TOO POPULAR.
EVENING NEWS 6
THEY'RE GETTING TV SHOWS.
XTREME KRHYME CREW REALITY SHOW RUMORED IN THE WORKS...
XKC's debut album
Krhyme and Punishment
AND RECORD DEALS?
AND IT JUST MAKES THEM COMMIT MORE CRIMES!
OR, I GUESS, "KRHYMES"?
AND, SOMEHOW, I'M THE ONE WHO LOOKS LIKE AN IDIOT.
AND THEY'RE THE ONES WITH FANS!

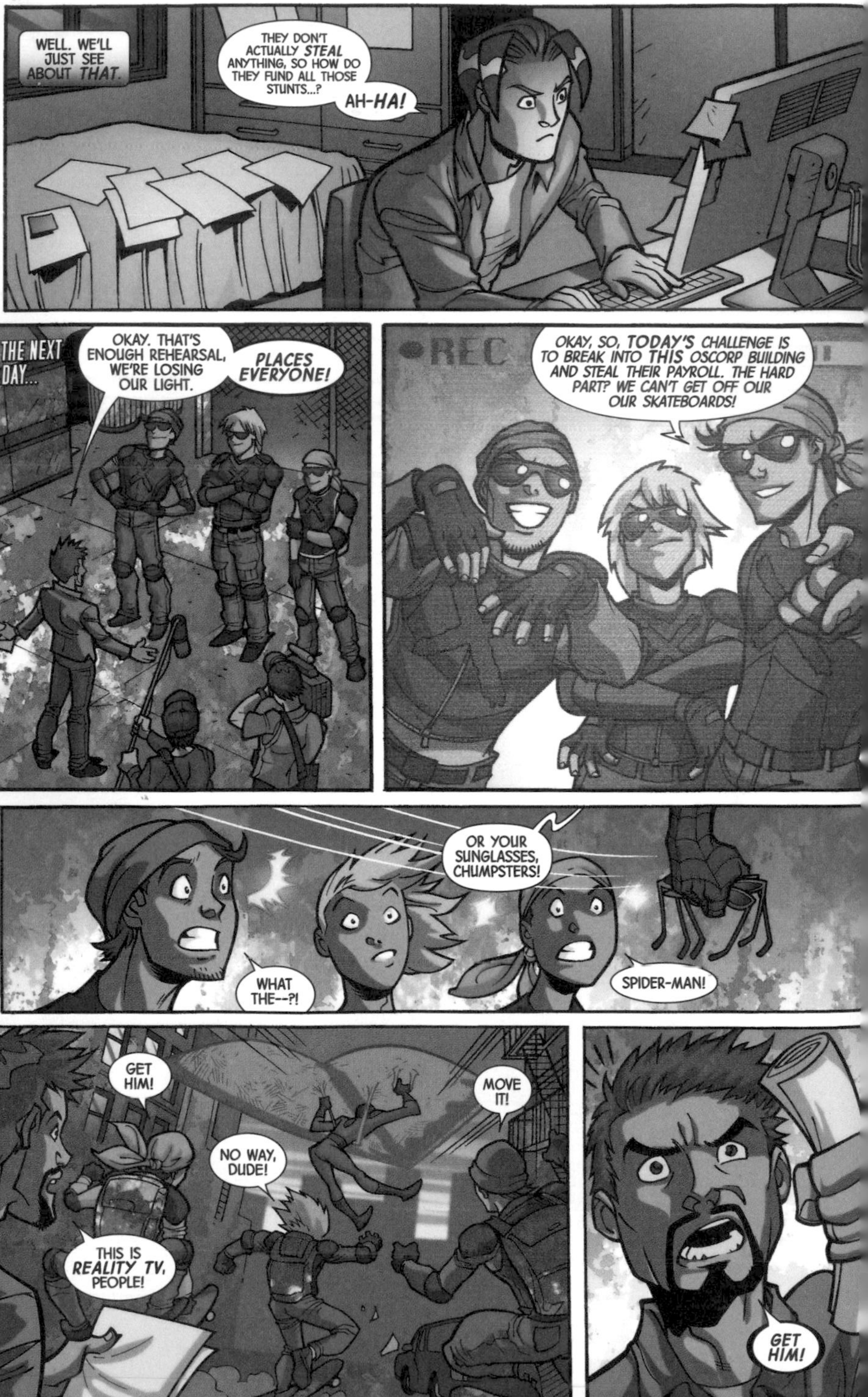
WELL. WE'LL JUST SEE ABOUT THAT.
THEY DON'T ACTUALLY STEAL ANYTHING, SO HOW DO THEY FUND ALL THOSE STUNTS...?
AH-HA!
THE NEXT DAY...
OKAY. THAT'S ENOUGH REHEARSAL, WE'RE LOSING OUR LIGHT.
PLACES EVERYONE!
REC
OKAY, SO, TODAY'S CHALLENGE IS TO BREAK INTO THIS OSCORP BUILDING AND STEAL THEIR PAYROLL. THE HARD PART? WE CAN'T GET OFF OUR OUR SKATEBOARDS!
OR YOUR SUNGLASSES, CHUMPSTERS!
WHAT THE--?!
SPIDER-MAN!
GET HIM!
MOVE IT!
NO WAY, DUDE!
THIS IS REALITY TV, PEOPLE!
GET HIM!

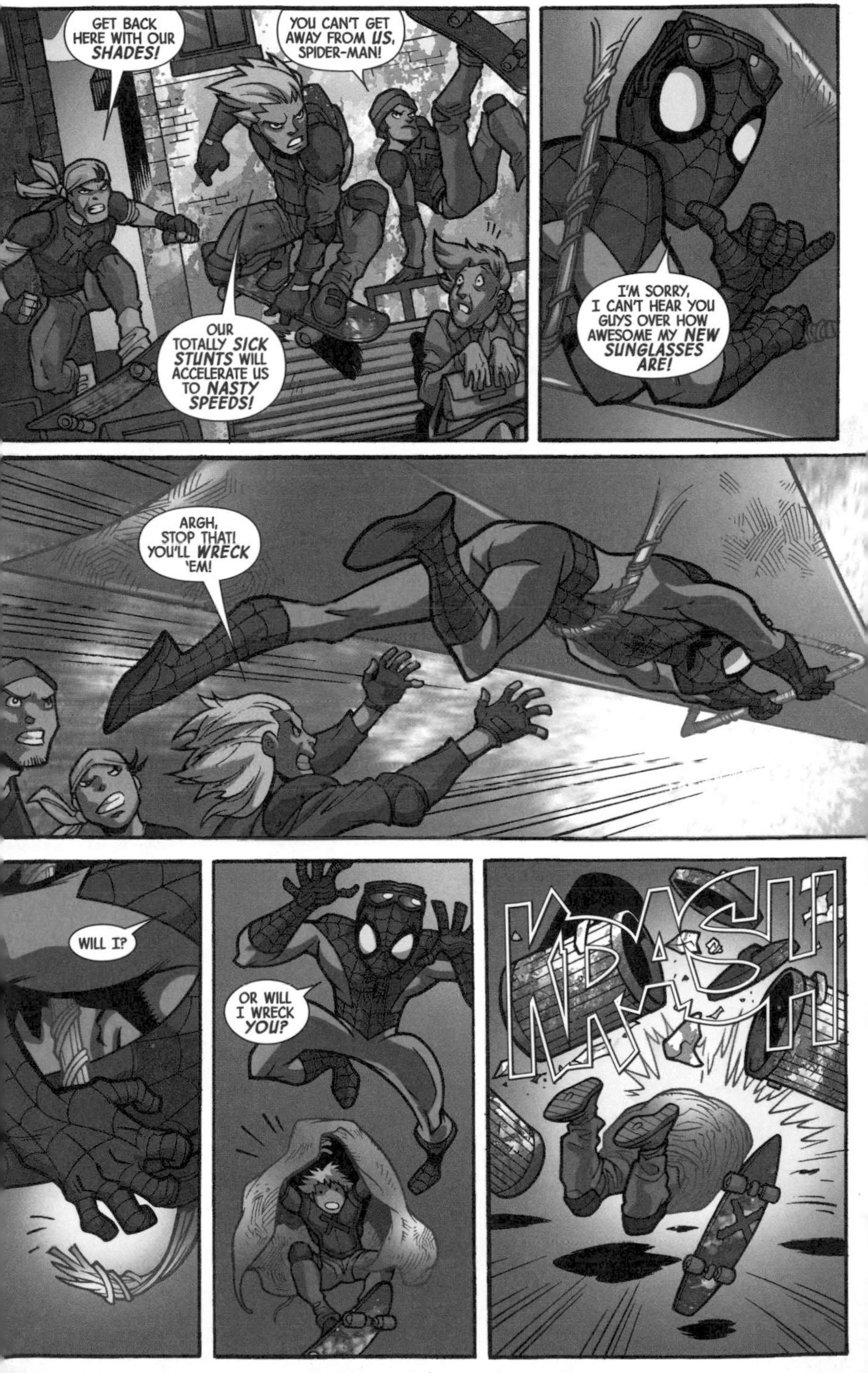
GET BACK HERE WITH OUR SHADES!
YOU CAN'T GET AWAY FROM US, SPIDER-MAN!
OUR TOTALLY SICK STUNTS WILL ACCELERATE US TO NASTY SPEEDS!
I'M SORRY, I CAN'T HEAR YOU GUYS OVER HOW AWESOME MY NEW SUNGLASSES ARE!
ARGH, STOP THAT! YOU'LL WRECK 'EM!
WILL I?
OR WILL I WRECK YOU?
KRASH

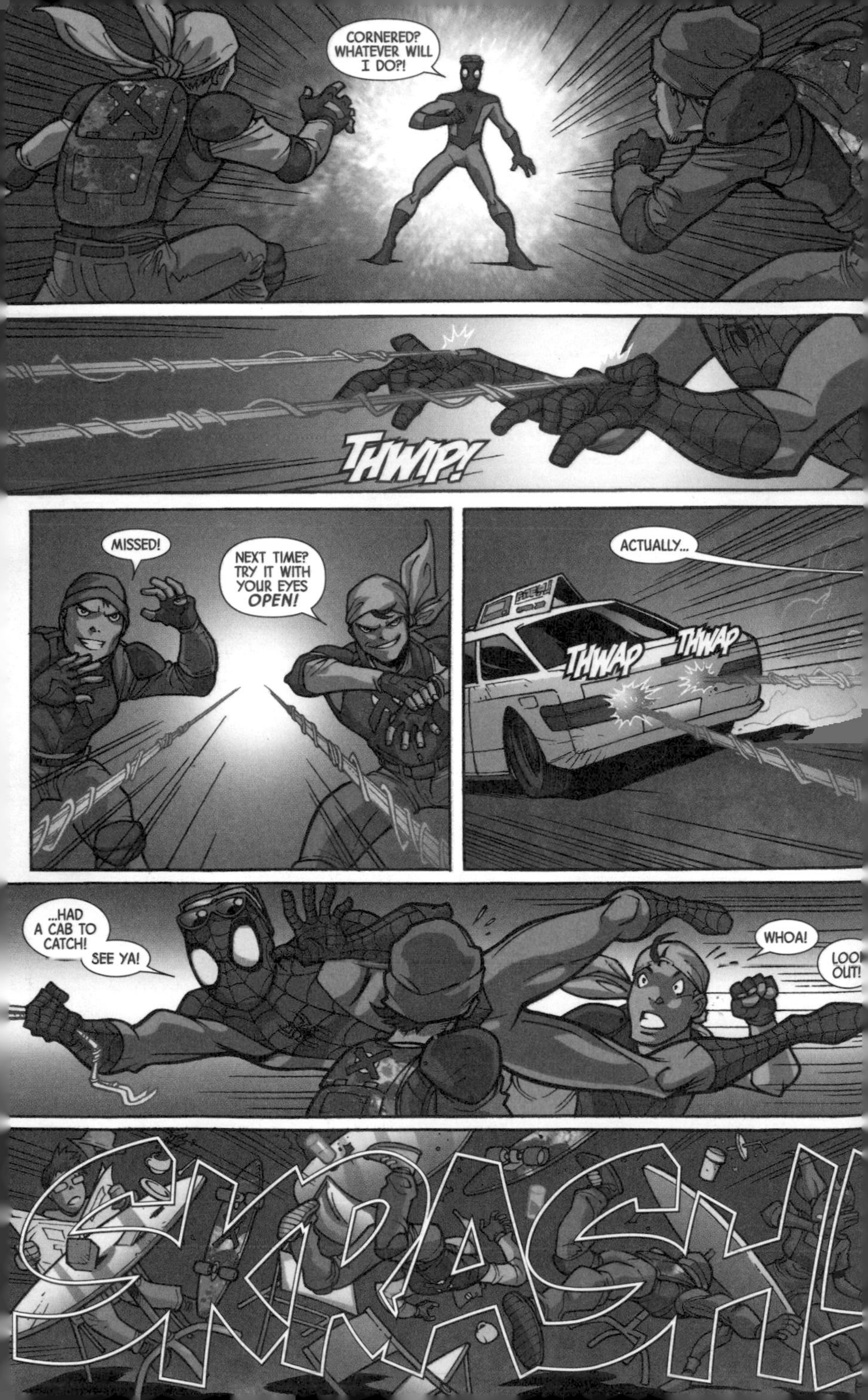
CORNERED? WHATEVER WILL I DO?!
THWIP!
MISSED!
NEXT TIME? TRY IT WITH YOUR EYES OPEN!
ACTUALLY...
THWAP THWAP
...HAD A CAB TO CATCH!
SEE YA!
WHOA!
LOO OUT!

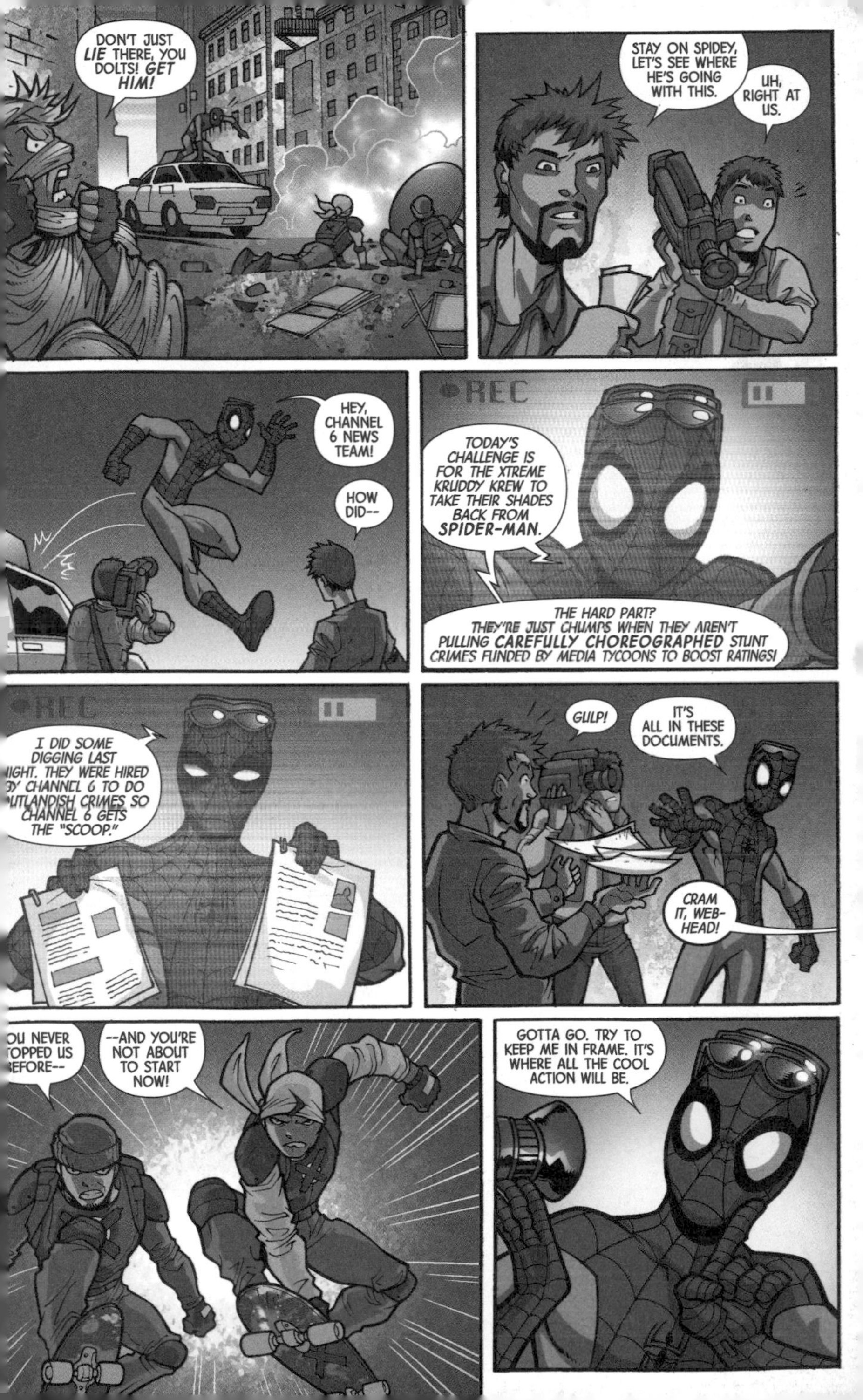

DON'T JUST LIE THERE, YOU DOLTS! GET HIM!
STAY ON SPIDEY, LET'S SEE WHERE HE'S GOING WITH THIS.
UH, RIGHT AT US.
HEY, CHANNEL 6 NEWS TEAM!
HOW DID--
REC
TODAY'S CHALLENGE IS FOR THE XTREME KRUDDY KREW TO TAKE THEIR SHADES BACK FROM SPIDER-MAN.
THE HARD PART? THEY'RE JUST CHUMPS WHEN THEY AREN'T PULLING CAREFULLY CHOREOGRAPHED STUNT CRIMES FUNDED BY MEDIA TYCOONS TO BOOST RATINGS!
REC
I DID SOME DIGGING LAST NIGHT. THEY WERE HIRED BY CHANNEL 6 TO DO OUTLANDISH CRIMES SO CHANNEL 6 GETS THE "SCOOP."
GULP!
IT'S ALL IN THESE DOCUMENTS.
CRAM IT, WEB-HEAD!
YOU NEVER STOPPED US BEFORE--
--AND YOU'RE NOT ABOUT TO START NOW!
GOTTA GO. TRY TO KEEP ME IN FRAME. IT'S WHERE ALL THE COOL ACTION WILL BE.

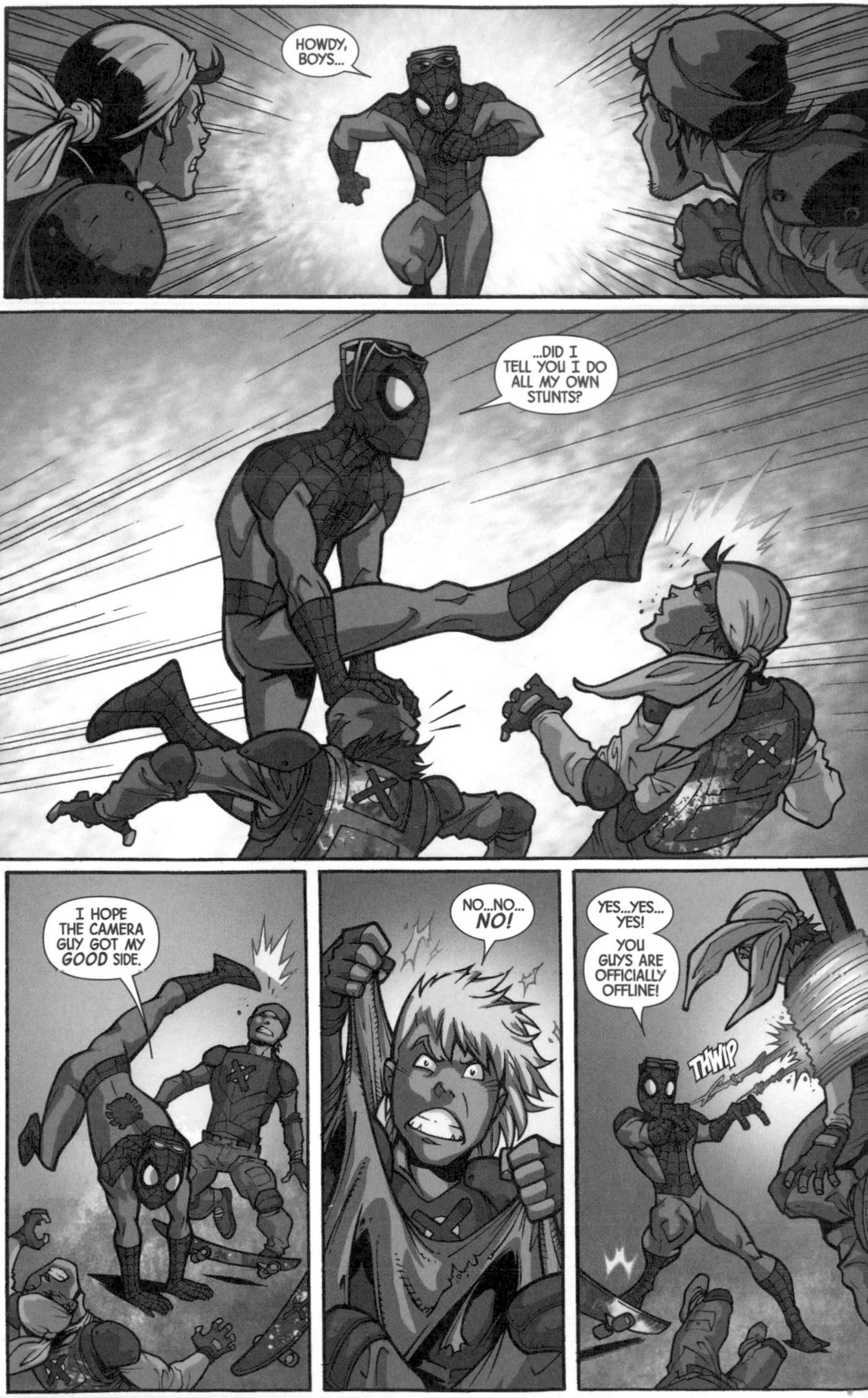
HOWDY, BOYS...
...DID I TELL YOU I DO ALL MY OWN STUNTS?
I HOPE THE CAMERA GUY GOT MY *GOOD* SIDE.
NO...NO... *NO!*
YES...YES... YES!
YOU GUYS ARE OFFICIALLY OFFLINE!
THWIP

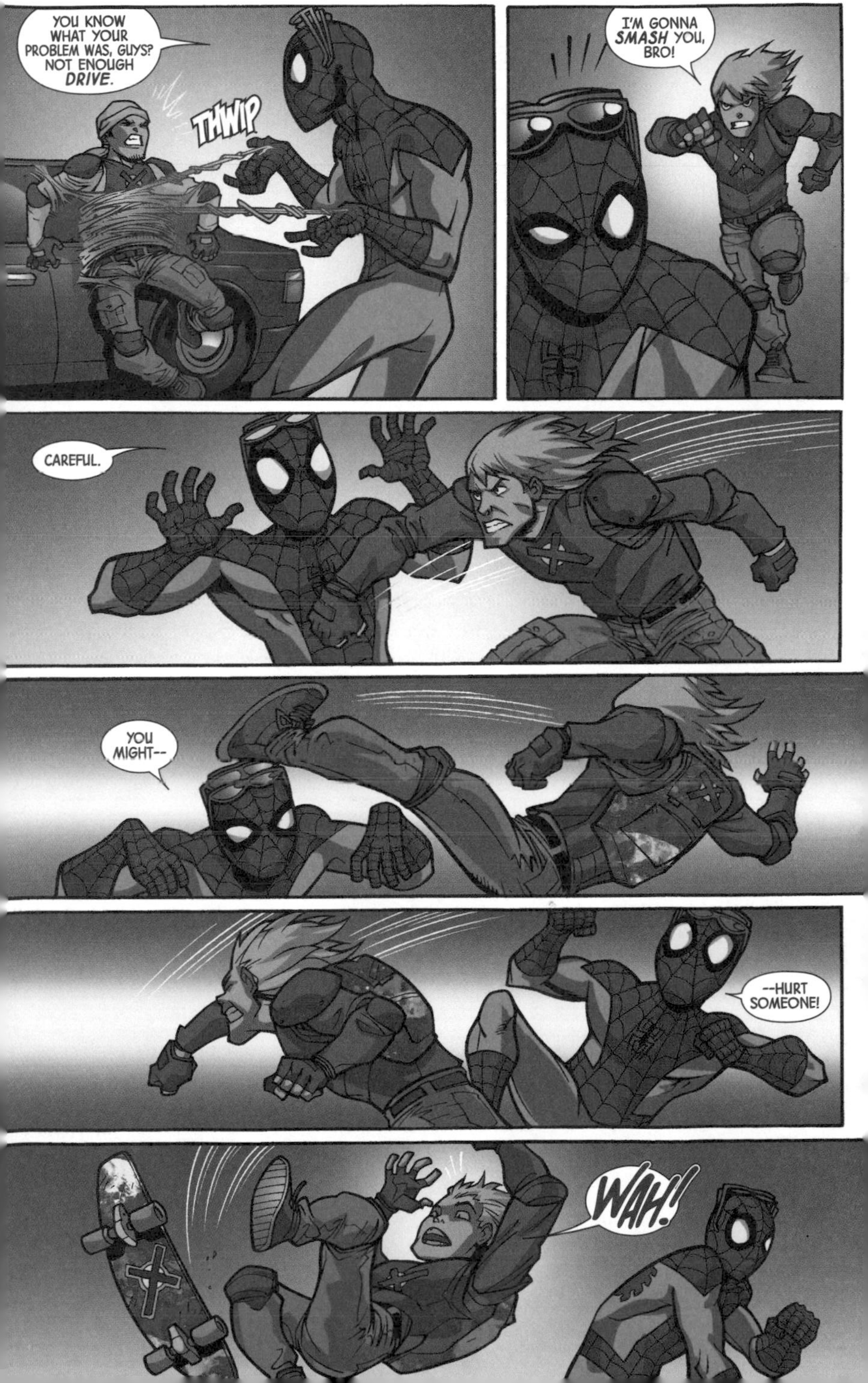

YOU KNOW WHAT YOUR PROBLEM WAS, GUYS? NOT ENOUGH DRIVE.
THWIP
I'M GONNA SMASH YOU, BRO!
CAREFUL.
YOU MIGHT--
--HURT SOMEONE!
WAH!

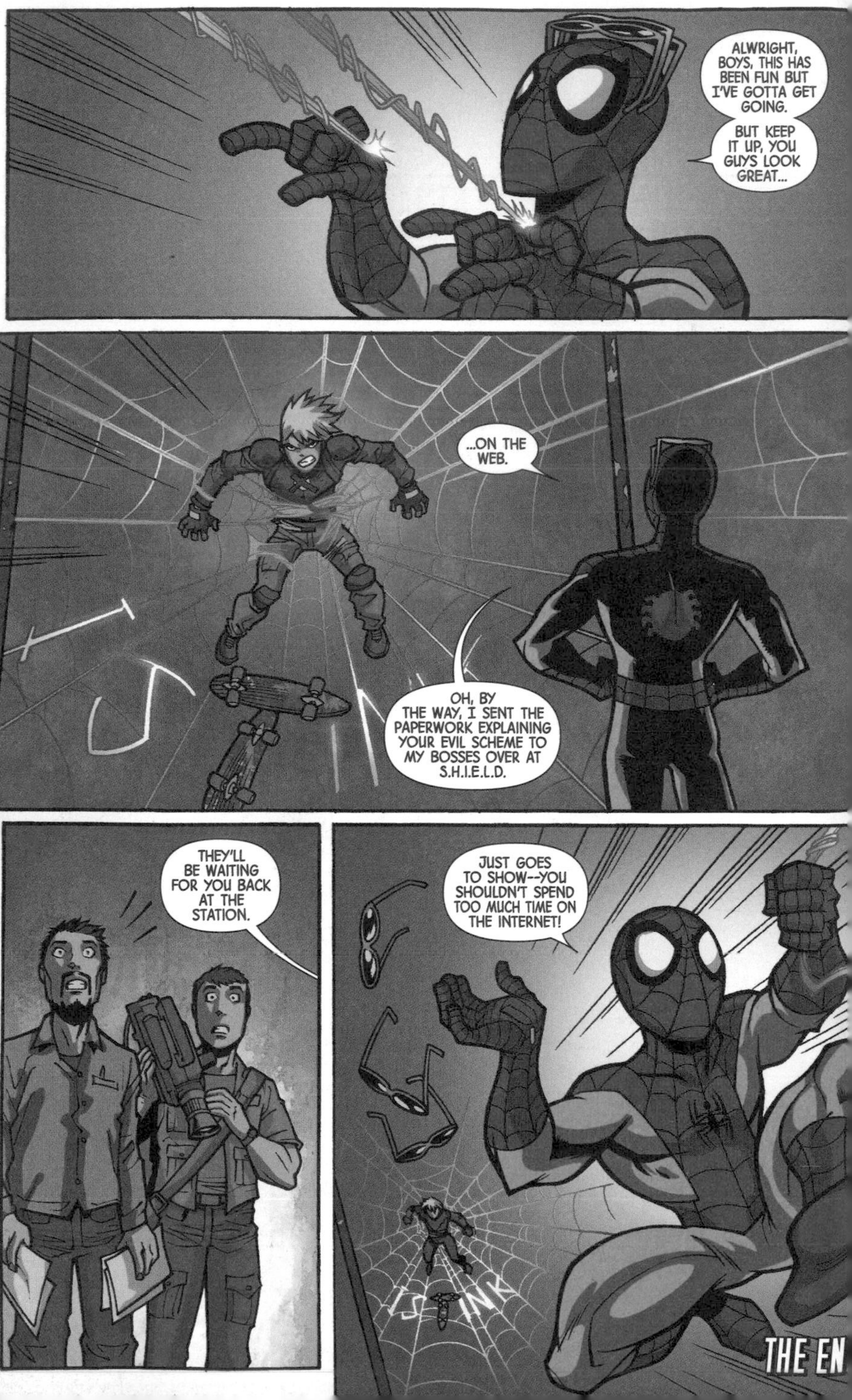
ALWRIGHT, BOYS, THIS HAS BEEN FUN BUT I'VE GOTTA GET GOING.
BUT KEEP IT UP, YOU GUYS LOOK GREAT...
...ON THE WEB.
OH, BY THE WAY, I SENT THE PAPERWORK EXPLAINING YOUR EVIL SCHEME TO MY BOSSES OVER AT S.H.I.E.L.D.
THEY'LL BE WAITING FOR YOU BACK AT THE STATION.
JUST GOES TO SHOW--YOU SHOULDN'T SPEND TOO MUCH TIME ON THE INTERNET!
STINK
THE EN

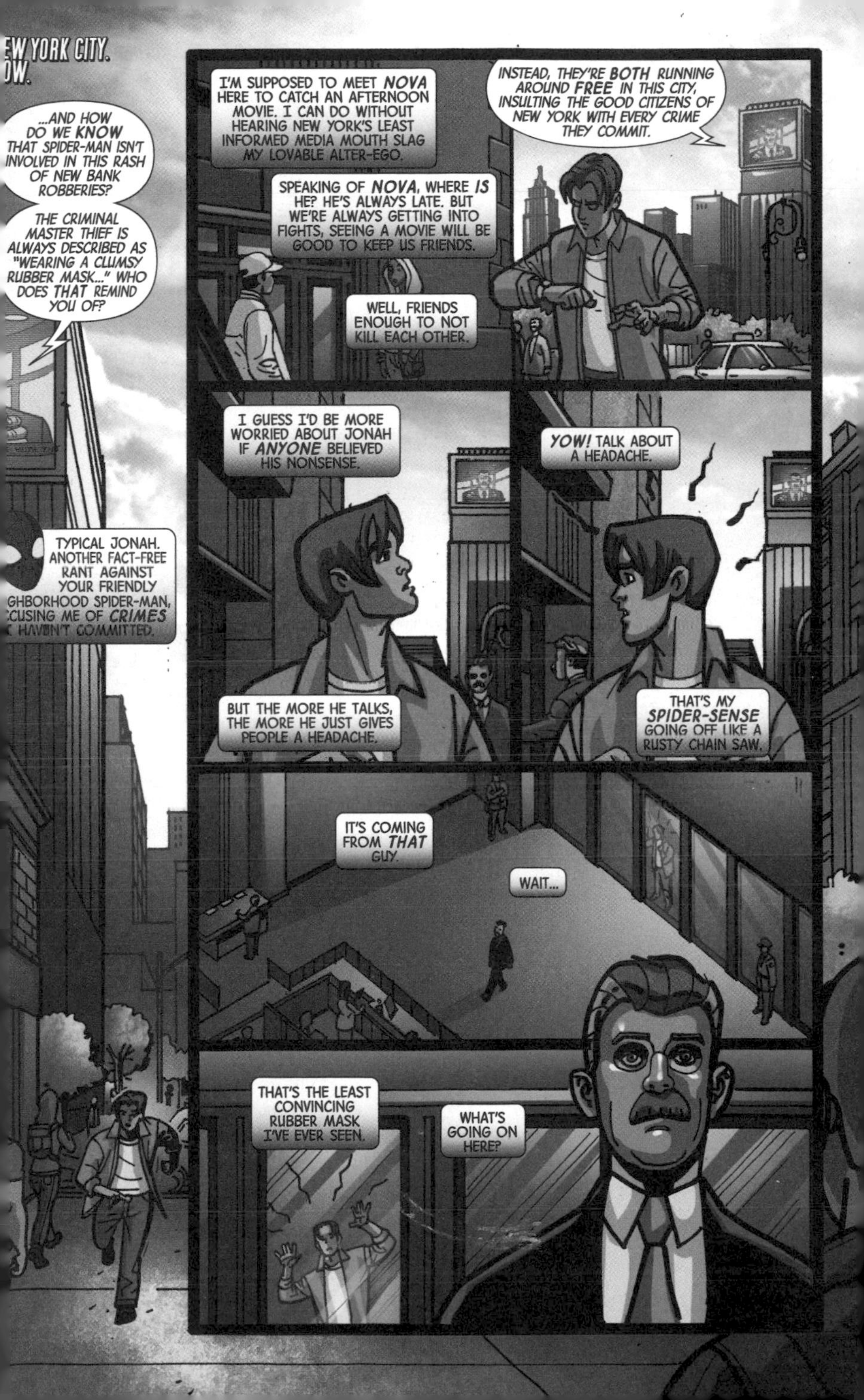

EW YORK CITY.
OW.
...AND HOW DO WE KNOW THAT SPIDER-MAN ISN'T INVOLVED IN THIS RASH OF NEW BANK ROBBERIES?
THE CRIMINAL MASTER THIEF IS ALWAYS DESCRIBED AS "WEARING A CLUMSY RUBBER MASK..." WHO DOES THAT REMIND YOU OF?
TYPICAL JONAH. ANOTHER FACT-FREE RANT AGAINST YOUR FRIENDLY GHBORHOOD SPIDER-MAN, CUSING ME OF CRIMES HAVEN'T COMMITTED.
I'M SUPPOSED TO MEET NOVA HERE TO CATCH AN AFTERNOON MOVIE. I CAN DO WITHOUT HEARING NEW YORK'S LEAST INFORMED MEDIA MOUTH SLAG MY LOVABLE ALTER-EGO.
INSTEAD, THEY'RE BOTH RUNNING AROUND FREE IN THIS CITY, INSULTING THE GOOD CITIZENS OF NEW YORK WITH EVERY CRIME THEY COMMIT.
SPEAKING OF NOVA, WHERE IS HE? HE'S ALWAYS LATE. BUT WE'RE ALWAYS GETTING INTO FIGHTS, SEEING A MOVIE WILL BE GOOD TO KEEP US FRIENDS.
WELL, FRIENDS ENOUGH TO NOT KILL EACH OTHER.
I GUESS I'D BE MORE WORRIED ABOUT JONAH IF ANYONE BELIEVED HIS NONSENSE.
BUT THE MORE HE TALKS, THE MORE HE JUST GIVES PEOPLE A HEADACHE.
YOW! TALK ABOUT A HEADACHE.
THAT'S MY SPIDER-SENSE GOING OFF LIKE A RUSTY CHAIN SAW.
IT'S COMING FROM THAT GUY.
WAIT...
THAT'S THE LEAST CONVINCING RUBBER MASK I'VE EVER SEEN.
WHAT'S GOING ON HERE?

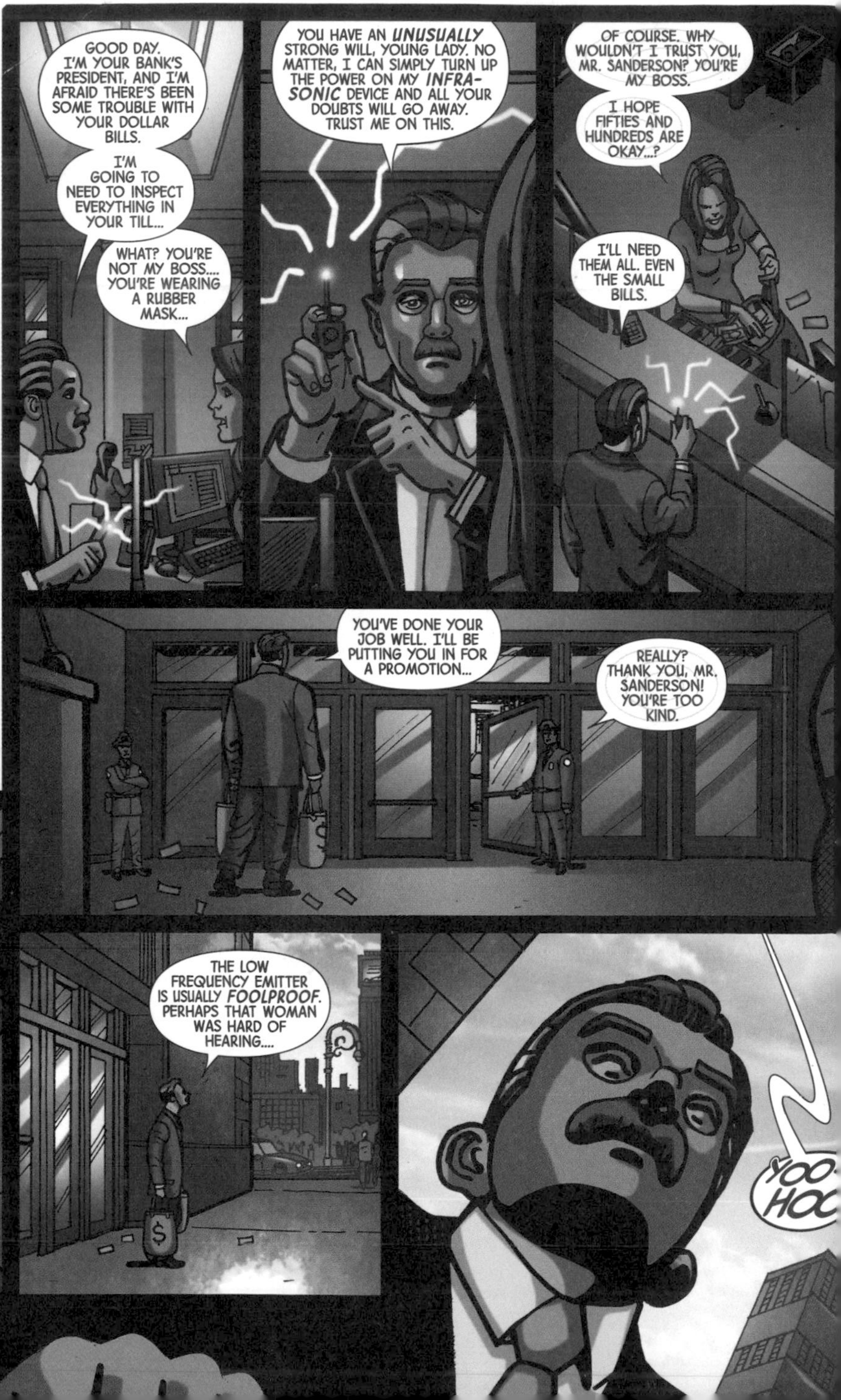
GOOD DAY. I'M YOUR BANK'S PRESIDENT, AND I'M AFRAID THERE'S BEEN SOME TROUBLE WITH YOUR DOLLAR BILLS.
I'M GOING TO NEED TO INSPECT EVERYTHING IN YOUR TILL...
WHAT? YOU'RE NOT MY BOSS.... YOU'RE WEARING A RUBBER MASK...
YOU HAVE AN UNUSUALLY STRONG WILL, YOUNG LADY. NO MATTER, I CAN SIMPLY TURN UP THE POWER ON MY INFRA-SONIC DEVICE AND ALL YOUR DOUBTS WILL GO AWAY. TRUST ME ON THIS.
OF COURSE. WHY WOULDN'T I TRUST YOU, MR. SANDERSON? YOU'RE MY BOSS.
I HOPE FIFTIES AND HUNDREDS ARE OKAY...?
I'LL NEED THEM ALL. EVEN THE SMALL BILLS.
YOU'VE DONE YOUR JOB WELL. I'LL BE PUTTING YOU IN FOR A PROMOTION...
REALLY? THANK YOU, MR. SANDERSON! YOU'RE TOO KIND.
THE LOW FREQUENCY EMITTER IS USUALLY FOOLPROOF. PERHAPS THAT WOMAN WAS HARD OF HEARING....

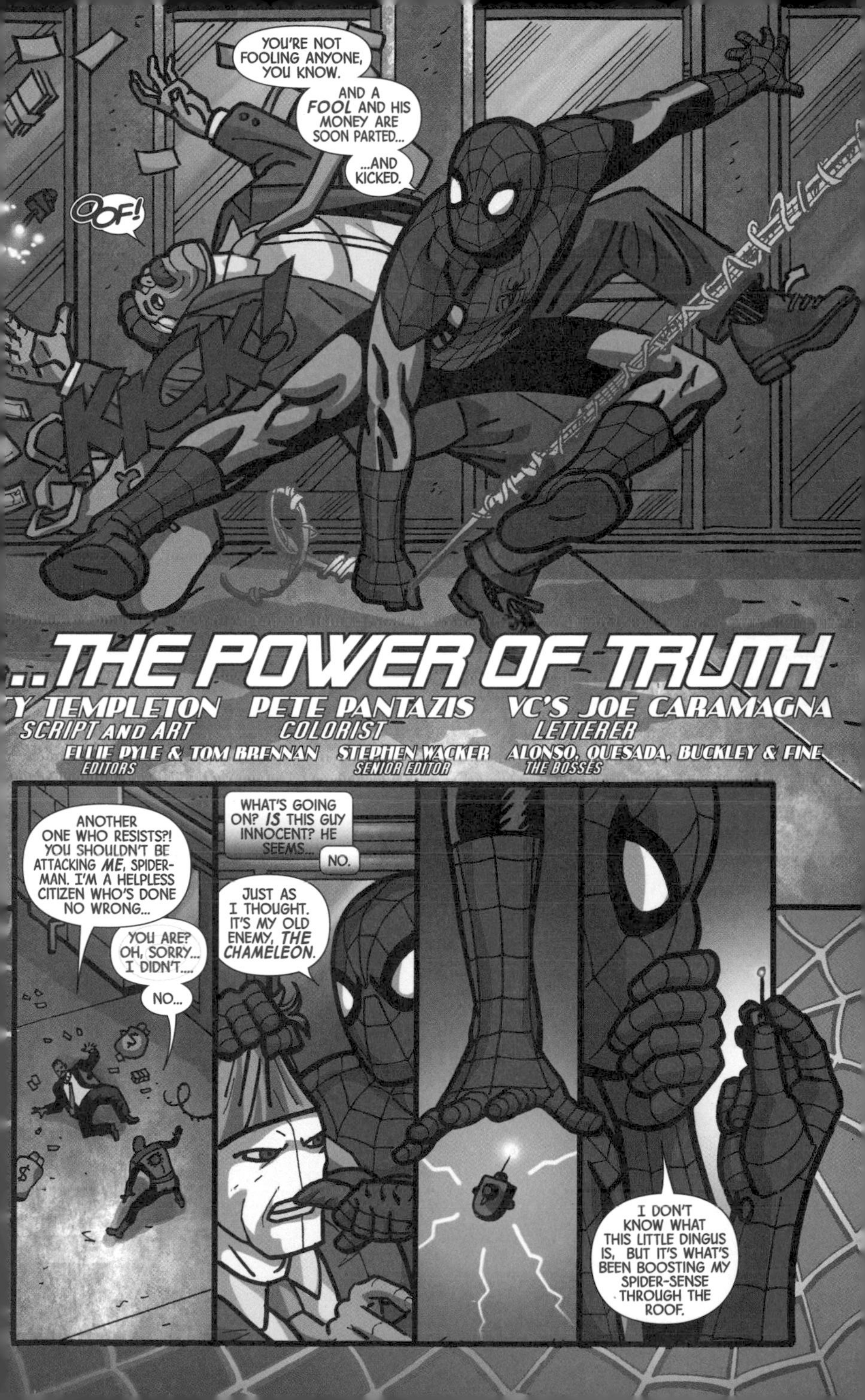

YOU'RE NOT FOOLING ANYONE, YOU KNOW.
AND A FOOL AND HIS MONEY ARE SOON PARTED...
...AND KICKED.
OOF!
..THE POWER OF TRUTH
Y TEMPLETON SCRIPT AND ART
PETE PANTAZIS COLORIST
VC'S JOE CARAMAGNA LETTERER
ELLIE PYLE & TOM BRENNAN EDITORS
STEPHEN WACKER SENIOR EDITOR
ALONSO, QUESADA, BUCKLEY & FINE THE BOSSES
ANOTHER ONE WHO RESISTS?! YOU SHOULDN'T BE ATTACKING ME, SPIDER-MAN. I'M A HELPLESS CITIZEN WHO'S DONE NO WRONG...
YOU ARE? OH, SORRY... I DIDN'T....
NO...
WHAT'S GOING ON? IS THIS GUY INNOCENT? HE SEEMS...
NO.
JUST AS I THOUGHT. IT'S MY OLD ENEMY, THE CHAMELEON.
I DON'T KNOW WHAT THIS LITTLE DINGUS IS, BUT IT'S WHAT'S BEEN BOOSTING MY SPIDER-SENSE THROUGH THE ROOF.

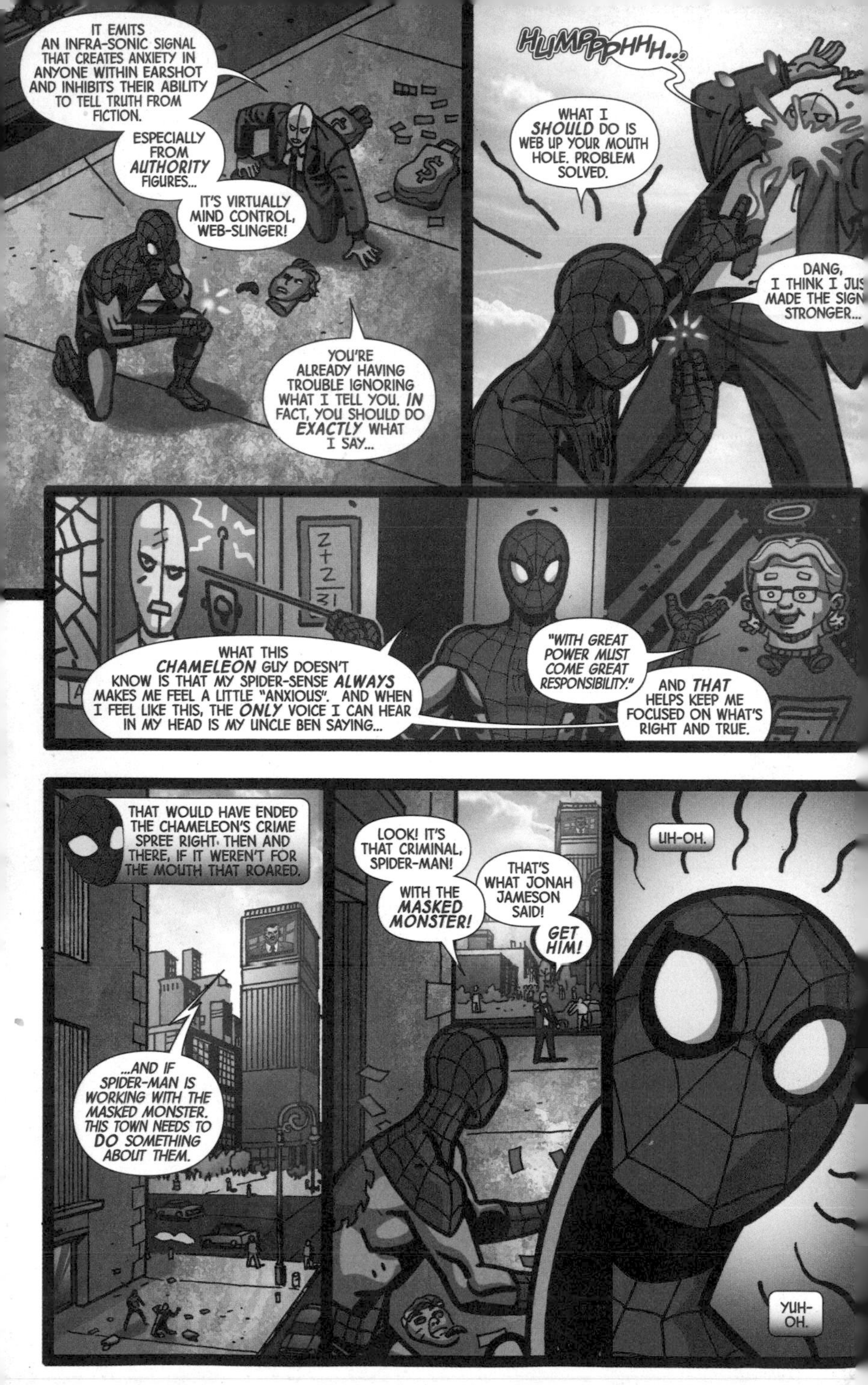
IT EMITS AN INFRA-SONIC SIGNAL THAT CREATES ANXIETY IN ANYONE WITHIN EARSHOT AND INHIBITS THEIR ABILITY TO TELL TRUTH FROM FICTION.
ESPECIALLY FROM AUTHORITY FIGURES...
IT'S VIRTUALLY MIND CONTROL, WEB-SLINGER!
YOU'RE ALREADY HAVING TROUBLE IGNORING WHAT I TELL YOU. IN FACT, YOU SHOULD DO EXACTLY WHAT I SAY...
HUMPPPHHH...
WHAT I SHOULD DO IS WEB UP YOUR MOUTH HOLE. PROBLEM SOLVED.
DANG, I THINK I JUS MADE THE SIGN STRONGER...
WHAT THIS CHAMELEON GUY DOESN'T KNOW IS THAT MY SPIDER-SENSE ALWAYS MAKES ME FEEL A LITTLE "ANXIOUS". AND WHEN I FEEL LIKE THIS, THE ONLY VOICE I CAN HEAR IN MY HEAD IS MY UNCLE BEN SAYING...
"WITH GREAT POWER MUST COME GREAT RESPONSIBILITY."
AND THAT HELPS KEEP ME FOCUSED ON WHAT'S RIGHT AND TRUE.
THAT WOULD HAVE ENDED THE CHAMELEON'S CRIME SPREE RIGHT THEN AND THERE, IF IT WEREN'T FOR THE MOUTH THAT ROARED.
...AND IF SPIDER-MAN IS WORKING WITH THE MASKED MONSTER. THIS TOWN NEEDS TO DO SOMETHING ABOUT THEM.
LOOK! IT'S THAT CRIMINAL, SPIDER-MAN!
WITH THE MASKED MONSTER!
THAT'S WHAT JONAH JAMESON SAID!
GET HIM!
UH-OH.
YUH-OH.

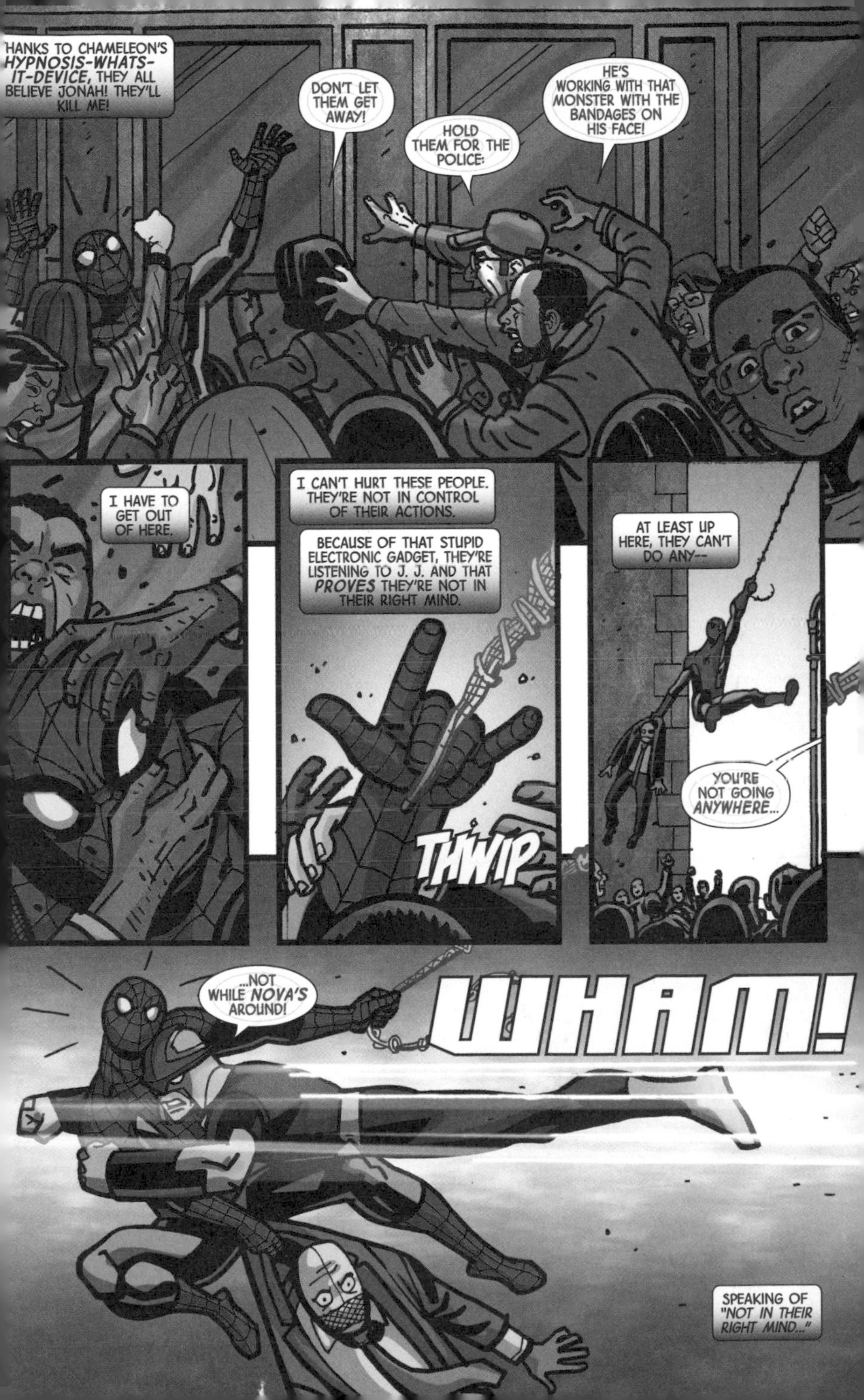
HANKS TO CHAMELEON'S HYPNOSIS-WHATS-IT-DEVICE, THEY ALL BELIEVE JONAH! THEY'LL KILL ME!
DON'T LET THEM GET AWAY!
HOLD THEM FOR THE POLICE!
HE'S WORKING WITH THAT MONSTER WITH THE BANDAGES ON HIS FACE!
I HAVE TO GET OUT OF HERE.
I CAN'T HURT THESE PEOPLE. THEY'RE NOT IN CONTROL OF THEIR ACTIONS.
BECAUSE OF THAT STUPID ELECTRONIC GADGET, THEY'RE LISTENING TO J. J. AND THAT PROVES THEY'RE NOT IN THEIR RIGHT MIND.
THWIP
AT LEAST UP HERE, THEY CAN'T DO ANY--
YOU'RE NOT GOING ANYWHERE...
...NOT WHILE NOVA'S AROUND!
WHAM!
SPEAKING OF "NOT IN THEIR RIGHT MIND..."

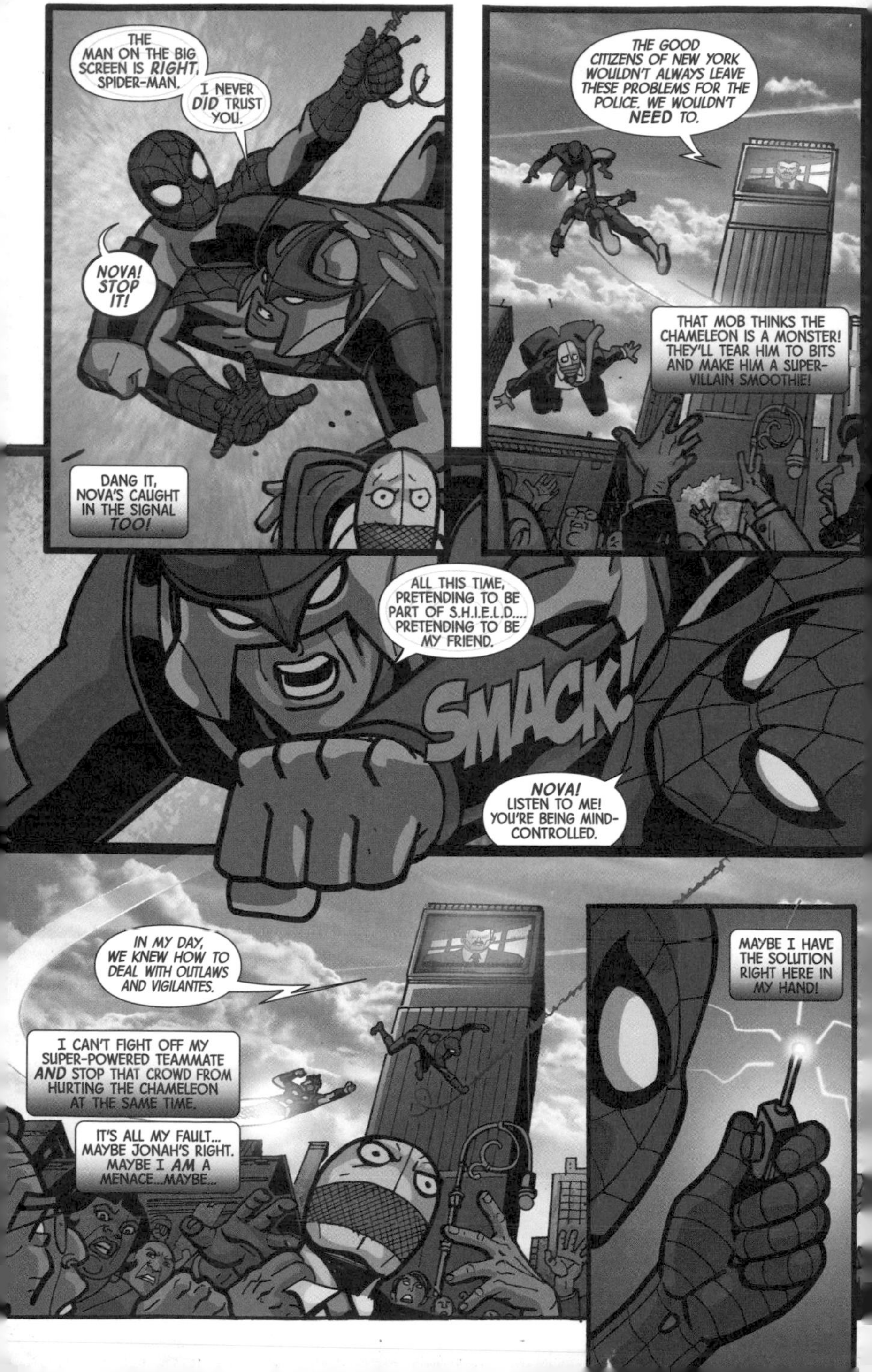
THE MAN ON THE BIG SCREEN IS RIGHT, SPIDER-MAN.
I NEVER DID TRUST YOU.
NOVA! STOP IT!
DANG IT, NOVA'S CAUGHT IN THE SIGNAL TOO!
THE GOOD CITIZENS OF NEW YORK WOULDN'T ALWAYS LEAVE THESE PROBLEMS FOR THE POLICE. WE WOULDN'T NEED TO.
THAT MOB THINKS THE CHAMELEON IS A MONSTER! THEY'LL TEAR HIM TO BITS AND MAKE HIM A SUPER-VILLAIN SMOOTHIE!
ALL THIS TIME, PRETENDING TO BE PART OF S.H.I.E.L.D.... PRETENDING TO BE MY FRIEND.
SMACK!
NOVA! LISTEN TO ME! YOU'RE BEING MIND-CONTROLLED.
IN MY DAY, WE KNEW HOW TO DEAL WITH OUTLAWS AND VIGILANTES.
I CAN'T FIGHT OFF MY SUPER-POWERED TEAMMATE AND STOP THAT CROWD FROM HURTING THE CHAMELEON AT THE SAME TIME.
IT'S ALL MY FAULT... MAYBE JONAH'S RIGHT. MAYBE I AM A MENACE...MAYBE...
MAYBE I HAVE THE SOLUTION RIGHT HERE IN MY HAND!

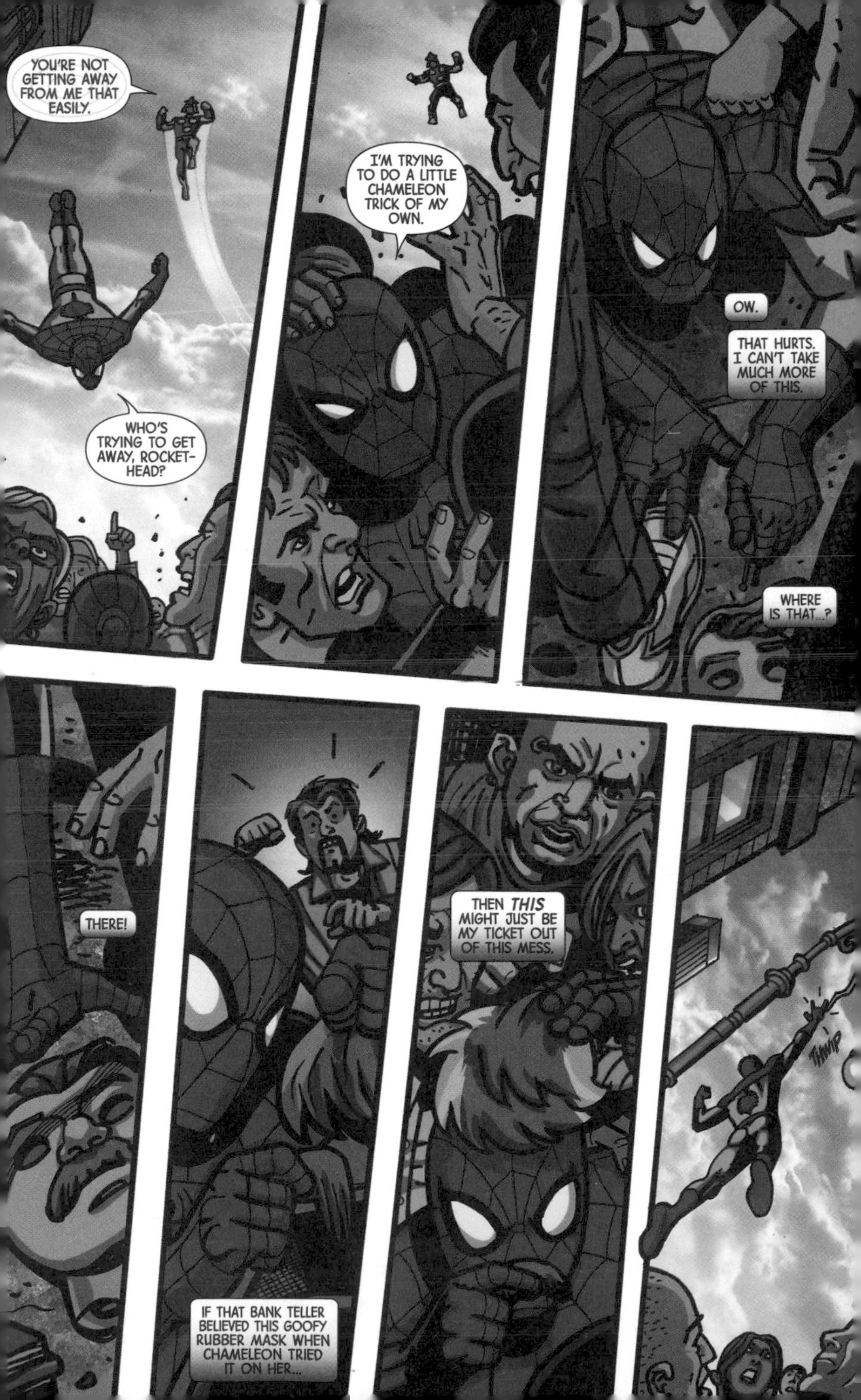

YOU'RE NOT GETTING AWAY FROM ME THAT EASILY.
WHO'S TRYING TO GET AWAY, ROCKET-HEAD?
I'M TRYING TO DO A LITTLE CHAMELEON TRICK OF MY OWN.
OW.
THAT HURTS. I CAN'T TAKE MUCH MORE OF THIS.
WHERE IS THAT...?
THERE!
IF THAT BANK TELLER BELIEVED THIS GOOFY RUBBER MASK WHEN CHAMELEON TRIED IT ON HER...
THEN *THIS* MIGHT JUST BE MY TICKET OUT OF THIS MESS.
THWIP

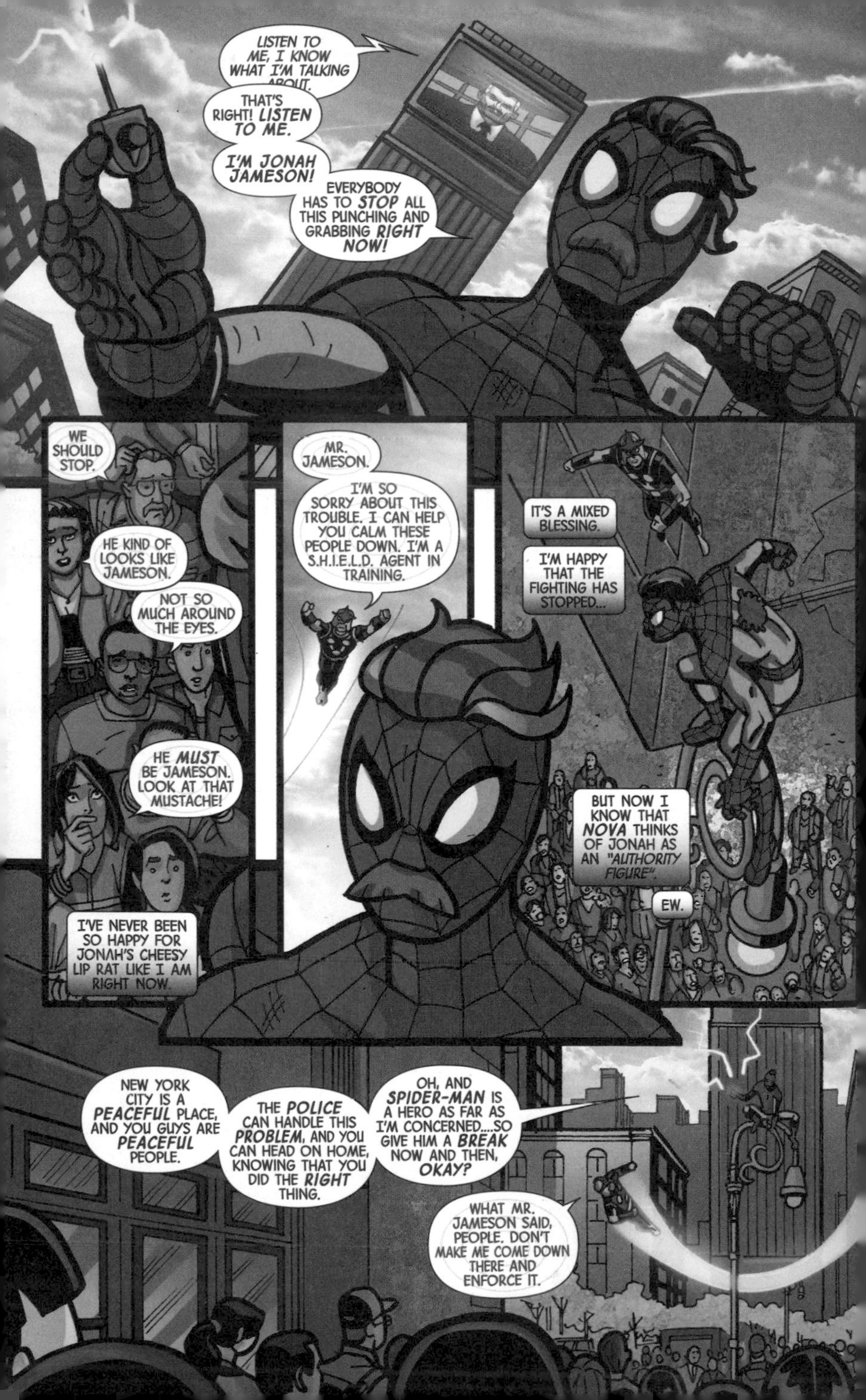
LISTEN TO ME, I KNOW WHAT I'M TALKING ABOUT.
THAT'S RIGHT! LISTEN TO ME.
I'M JONAH JAMESON!
EVERYBODY HAS TO STOP ALL THIS PUNCHING AND GRABBING RIGHT NOW!
WE SHOULD STOP.
HE KIND OF LOOKS LIKE JAMESON.
NOT SO MUCH AROUND THE EYES.
HE MUST BE JAMESON. LOOK AT THAT MUSTACHE!
I'VE NEVER BEEN SO HAPPY FOR JONAH'S CHEESY LIP RAT LIKE I AM RIGHT NOW.
MR. JAMESON.
I'M SO SORRY ABOUT THIS TROUBLE. I CAN HELP YOU CALM THESE PEOPLE DOWN. I'M A S.H.I.E.L.D. AGENT IN TRAINING.
IT'S A MIXED BLESSING.
I'M HAPPY THAT THE FIGHTING HAS STOPPED...
BUT NOW I KNOW THAT NOVA THINKS OF JONAH AS AN "AUTHORITY FIGURE".
EW.
NEW YORK CITY IS A PEACEFUL PLACE, AND YOU GUYS ARE PEACEFUL PEOPLE.
THE POLICE CAN HANDLE THIS PROBLEM, AND YOU CAN HEAD ON HOME, KNOWING THAT YOU DID THE RIGHT THING.
OH, AND SPIDER-MAN IS A HERO AS FAR AS I'M CONCERNED....SO GIVE HIM A BREAK NOW AND THEN, OKAY?
WHAT MR. JAMESON SAID, PEOPLE. DON'T MAKE ME COME DOWN THERE AND ENFORCE IT.

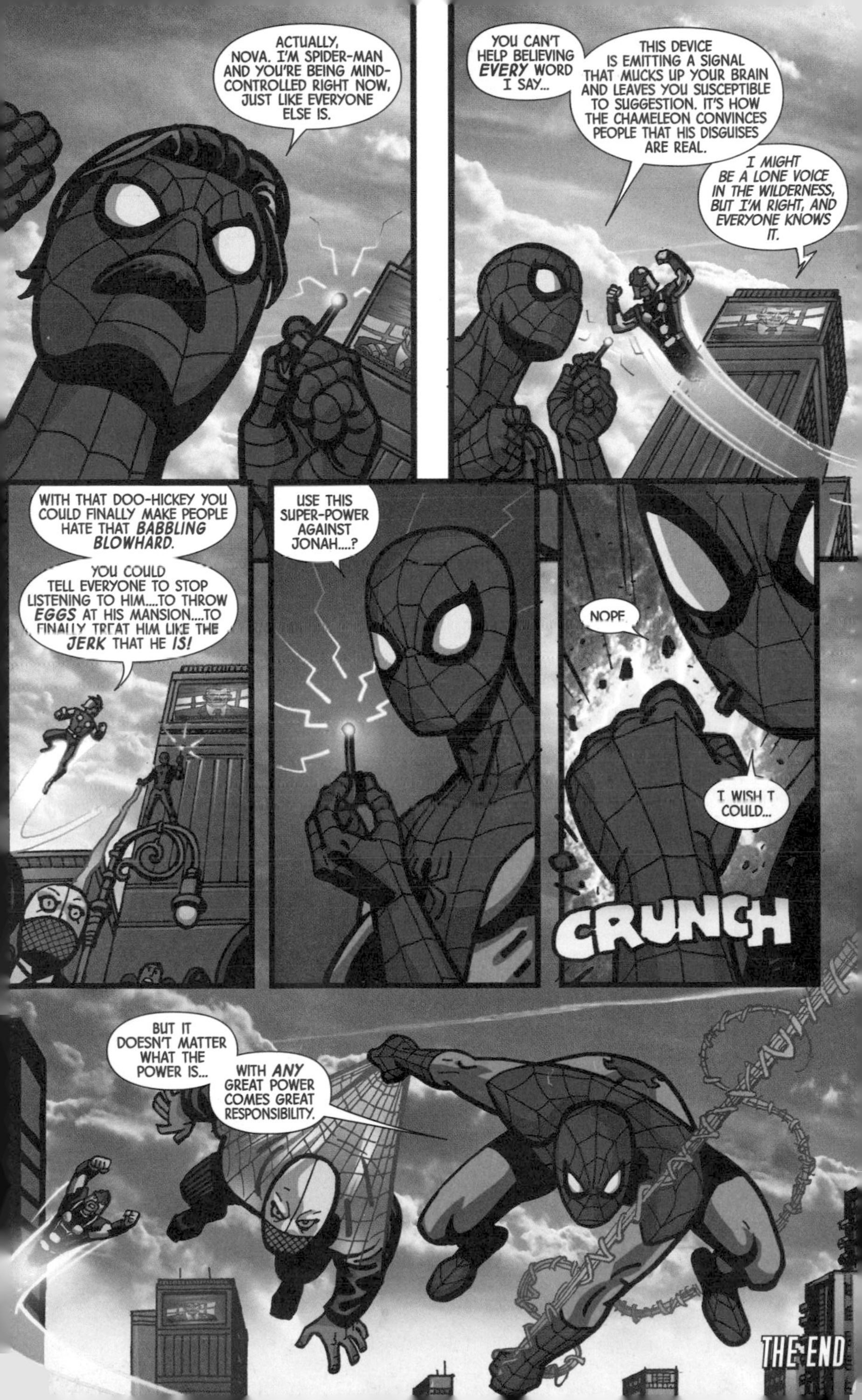
ACTUALLY, NOVA. I'M SPIDER-MAN AND YOU'RE BEING MIND-CONTROLLED RIGHT NOW, JUST LIKE EVERYONE ELSE IS.
YOU CAN'T HELP BELIEVING *EVERY* WORD I SAY...
THIS DEVICE IS EMITTING A SIGNAL THAT MUCKS UP YOUR BRAIN AND LEAVES YOU SUSCEPTIBLE TO SUGGESTION. IT'S HOW THE CHAMELEON CONVINCES PEOPLE THAT HIS DISGUISES ARE REAL.
I MIGHT BE A LONE VOICE IN THE WILDERNESS, BUT I'M RIGHT, AND EVERYONE KNOWS IT.
WITH THAT DOO-HICKEY YOU COULD FINALLY MAKE PEOPLE HATE THAT *BABBLING BLOWHARD*.
YOU COULD TELL EVERYONE TO STOP LISTENING TO HIM....TO THROW *EGGS* AT HIS MANSION....TO FINALLY TREAT HIM LIKE THE *JERK* THAT HE *IS!*
USE THIS SUPER-POWER AGAINST JONAH....?
NOPE.
I WISH I COULD...
CRUNCH
BUT IT DOESN'T MATTER WHAT THE POWER IS...
WITH *ANY* GREAT POWER COMES GREAT RESPONSIBILITY.
THE END

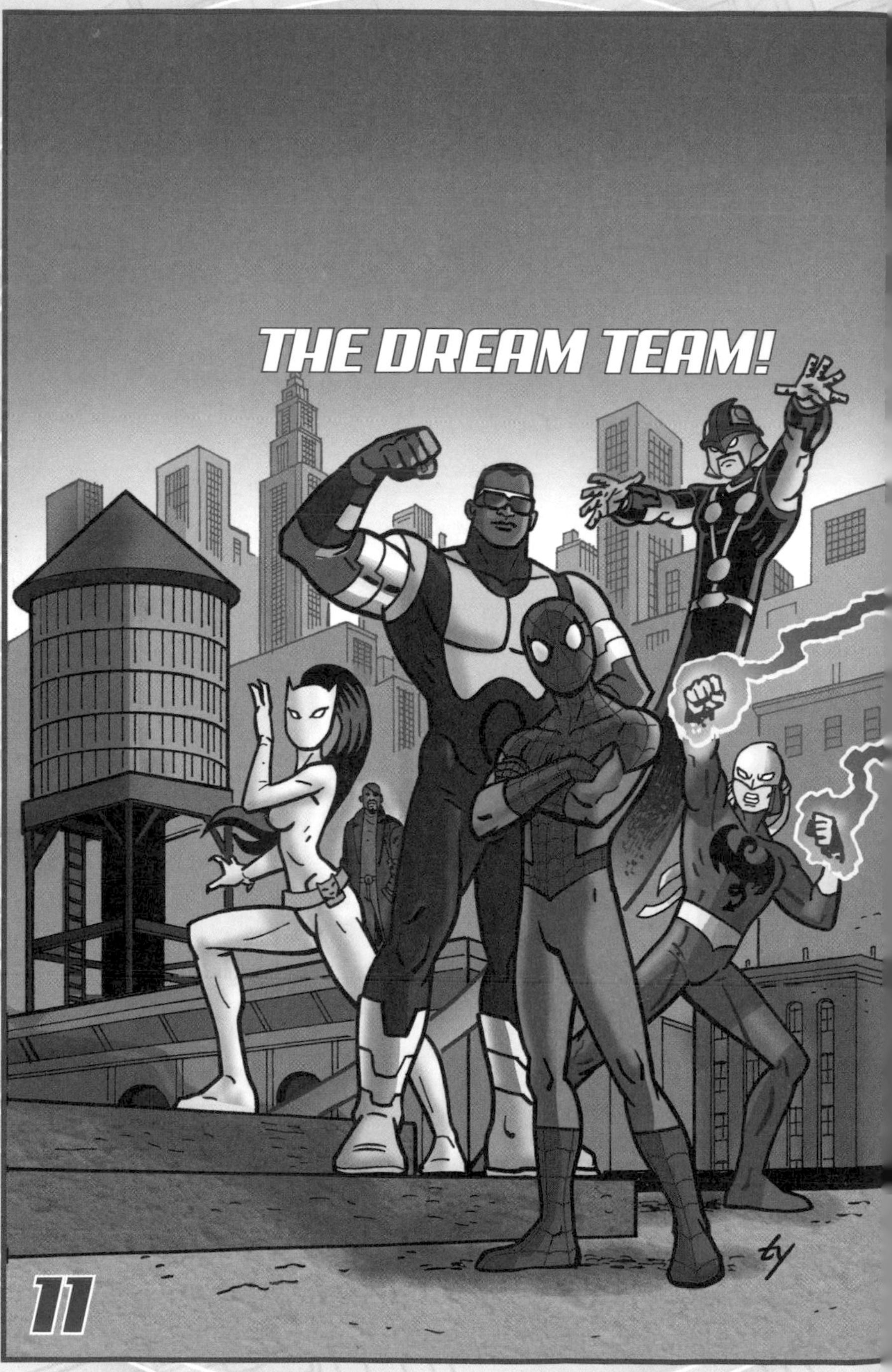
THE DREAM TEAM!
11

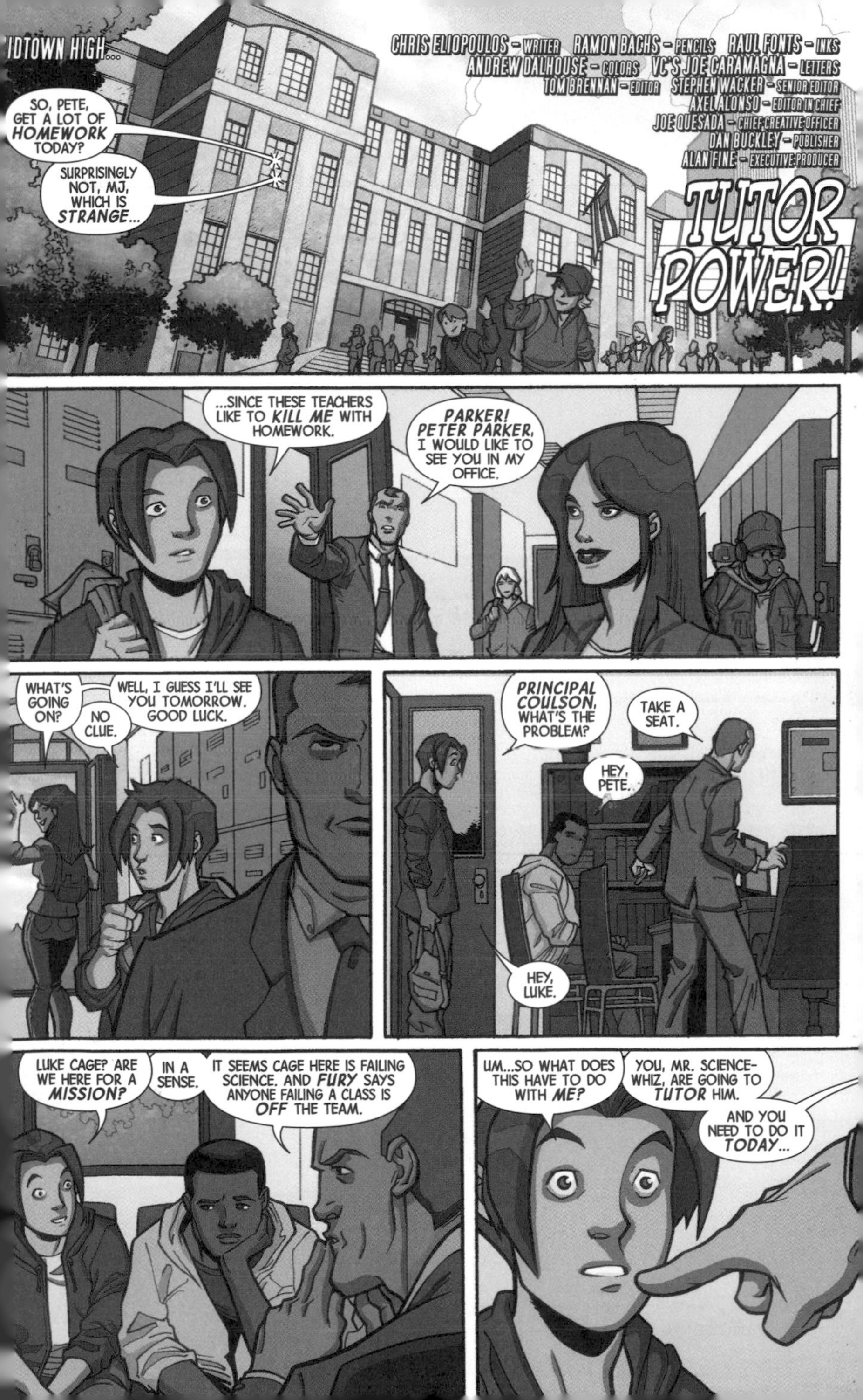
IDTOWN HIGH...
CHRIS ELIOPOULOS - WRITER RAMON BACHS - PENCILS RAUL FONTS - INKS
ANDREW DALHOUSE - COLORS VC'S JOE CARAMAGNA - LETTERS
TOM BRENNAN - EDITOR STEPHEN WACKER - SENIOR EDITOR
AXEL ALONSO - EDITOR IN CHIEF
JOE QUESADA - CHIEF CREATIVE OFFICER
DAN BUCKLEY - PUBLISHER
ALAN FINE - EXECUTIVE PRODUCER
SO, PETE, GET A LOT OF HOMEWORK TODAY?
SURPRISINGLY NOT, MJ, WHICH IS STRANGE...
TUTOR POWER!
...SINCE THESE TEACHERS LIKE TO KILL ME WITH HOMEWORK.
PARKER! PETER PARKER, I WOULD LIKE TO SEE YOU IN MY OFFICE.
WHAT'S GOING ON?
NO CLUE.
WELL, I GUESS I'LL SEE YOU TOMORROW. GOOD LUCK.
PRINCIPAL COULSON, WHAT'S THE PROBLEM?
TAKE A SEAT.
HEY, PETE.
HEY, LUKE.
LUKE CAGE? ARE WE HERE FOR A MISSION?
IN A SENSE.
IT SEEMS CAGE HERE IS FAILING SCIENCE. AND FURY SAYS ANYONE FAILING A CLASS IS OFF THE TEAM.
UM...SO WHAT DOES THIS HAVE TO DO WITH ME?
YOU, MR. SCIENCE-WHIZ, ARE GOING TO TUTOR HIM.
AND YOU NEED TO DO IT TODAY...

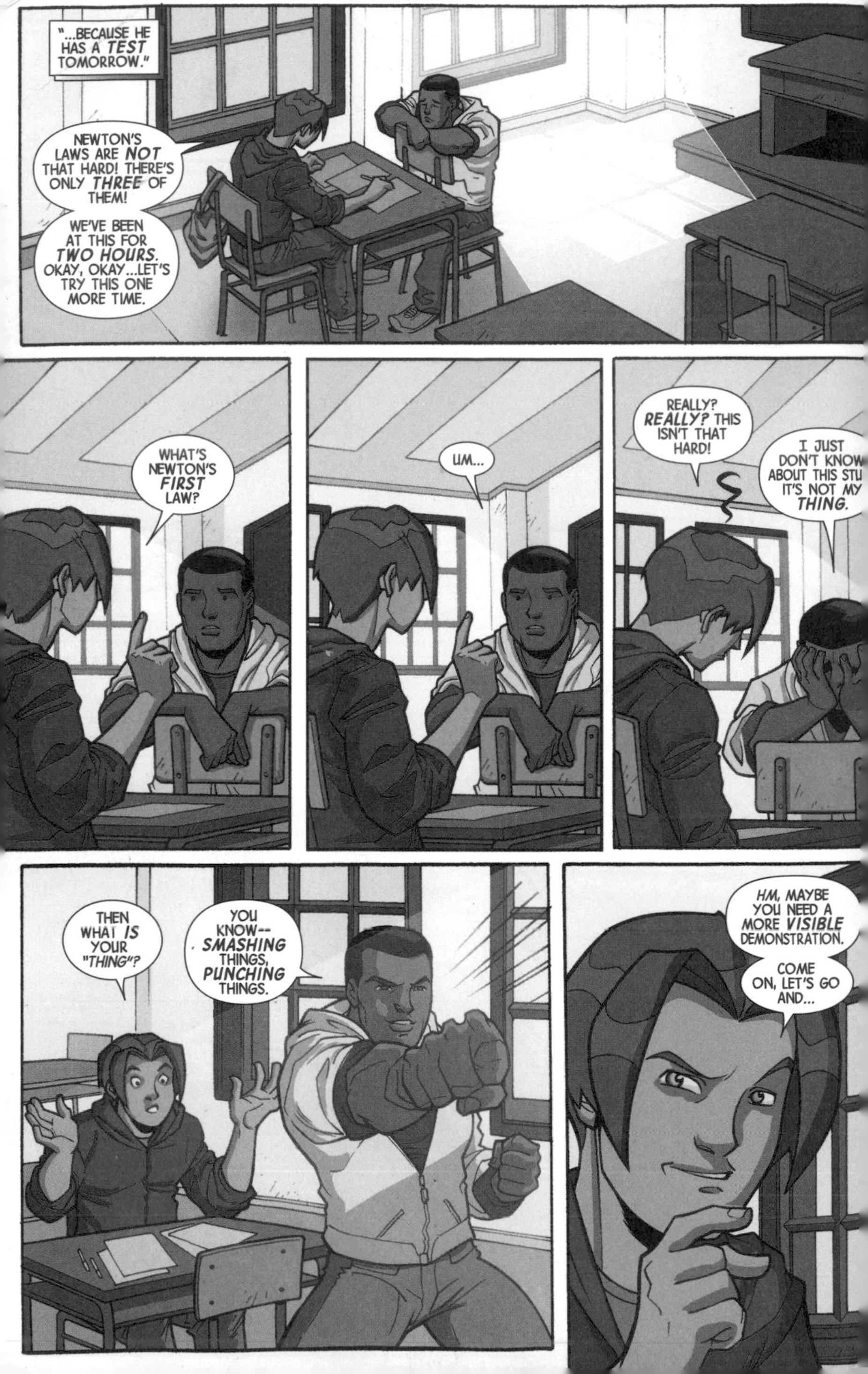
"...BECAUSE HE HAS A TEST TOMORROW."
NEWTON'S LAWS ARE NOT THAT HARD! THERE'S ONLY THREE OF THEM!
WE'VE BEEN AT THIS FOR TWO HOURS. OKAY, OKAY...LET'S TRY THIS ONE MORE TIME.
WHAT'S NEWTON'S FIRST LAW?
UM...
REALLY? REALLY? THIS ISN'T THAT HARD!
I JUST DON'T KNOW ABOUT THIS STU... IT'S NOT MY THING.
THEN WHAT IS YOUR "THING"?
YOU KNOW-- SMASHING THINGS, PUNCHING THINGS.
HM, MAYBE YOU NEED A MORE VISIBLE DEMONSTRATION.
COME ON, LET'S GO AND...

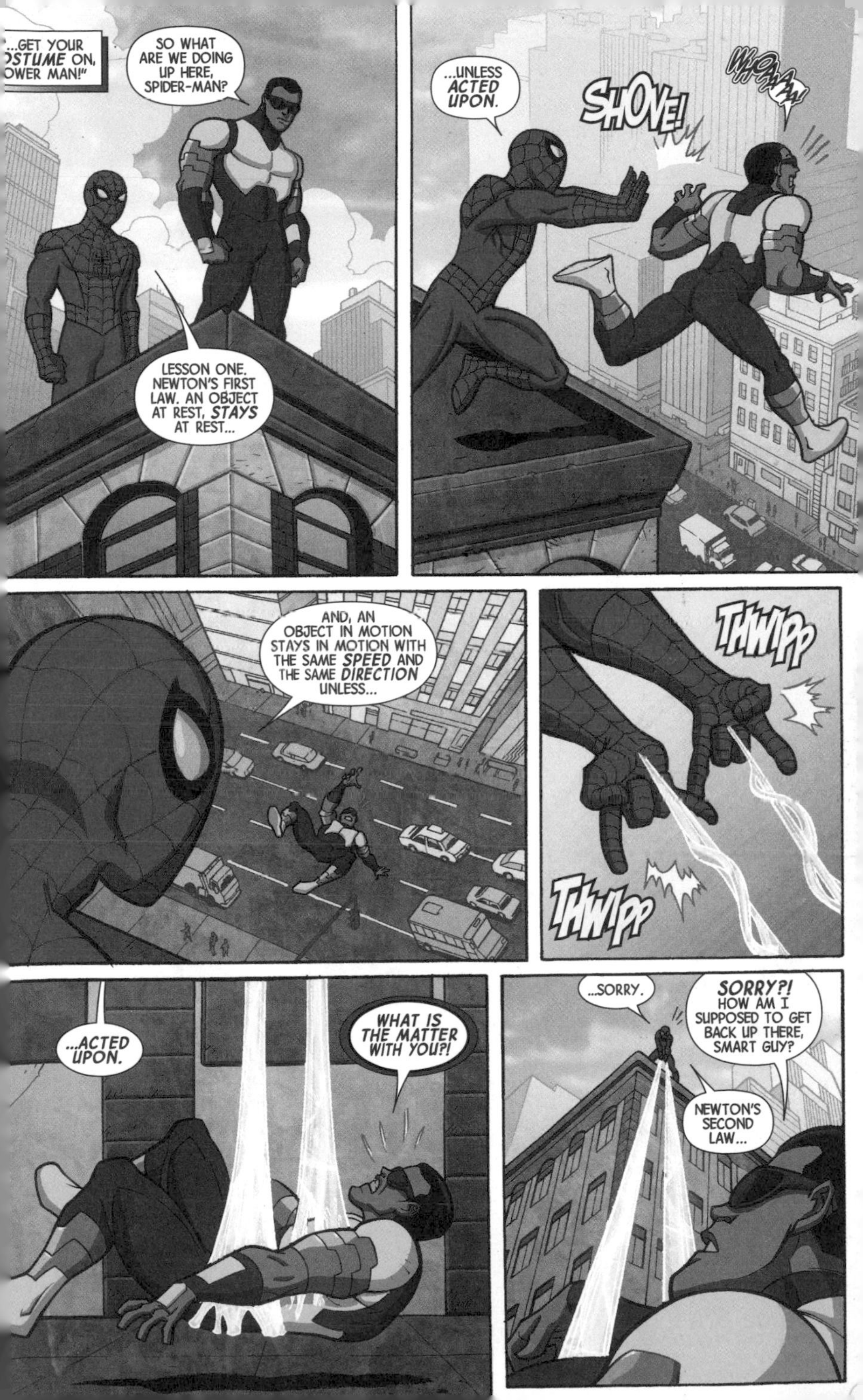
"...GET YOUR OSTUME ON, OWER MAN!"
SO WHAT ARE WE DOING UP HERE, SPIDER-MAN?
LESSON ONE. NEWTON'S FIRST LAW. AN OBJECT AT REST, STAYS AT REST...
...UNLESS ACTED UPON.
SHOVE!
AND, AN OBJECT IN MOTION STAYS IN MOTION WITH THE SAME SPEED AND THE SAME DIRECTION UNLESS...
THWIPP
THWIPP
...ACTED UPON.
WHAT IS THE MATTER WITH YOU?!
...SORRY.
SORRY?! HOW AM I SUPPOSED TO GET BACK UP THERE, SMART GUY?
NEWTON'S SECOND LAW...

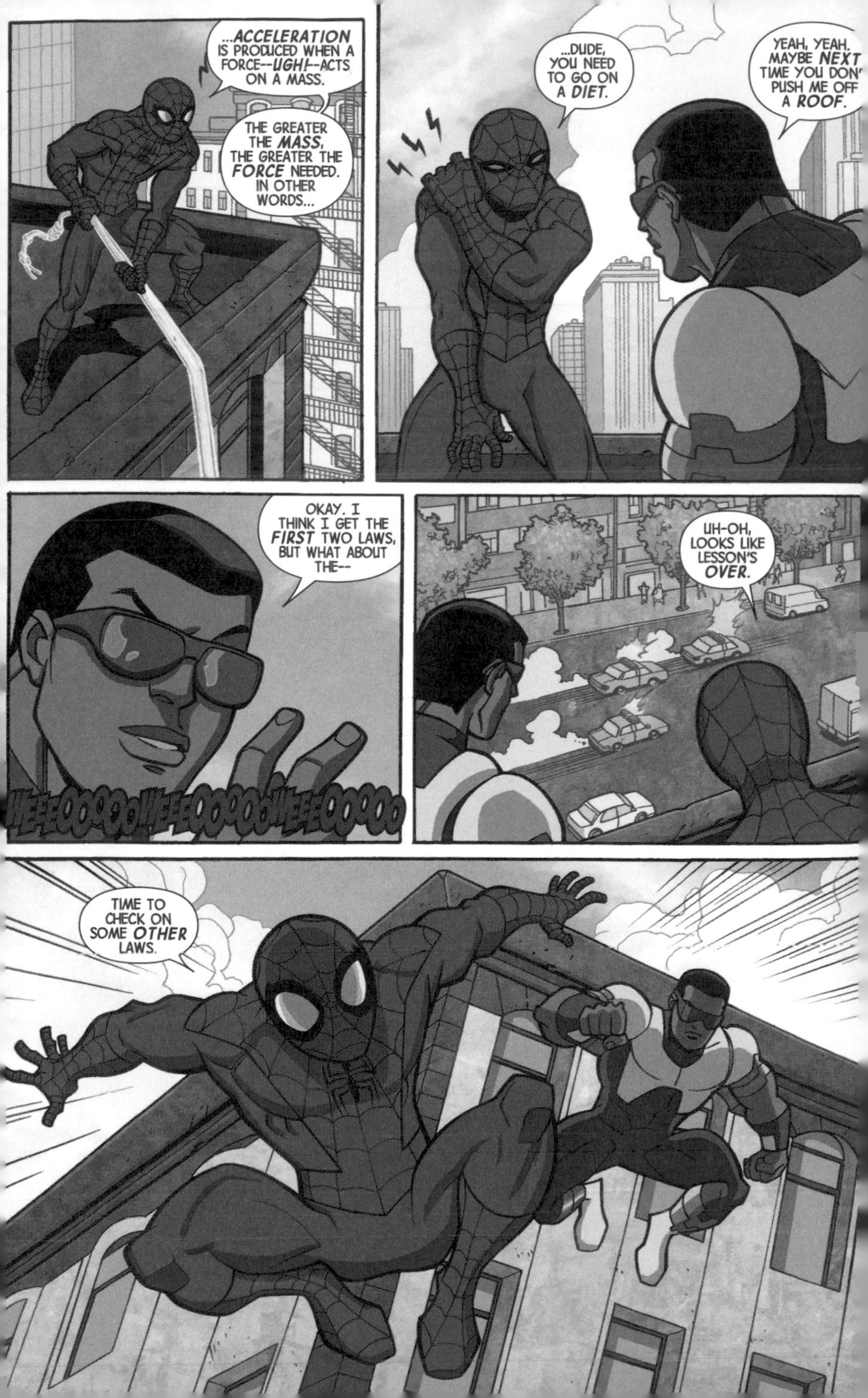

...ACCELERATION IS PRODUCED WHEN A FORCE--UGH!--ACTS ON A MASS.
THE GREATER THE MASS, THE GREATER THE FORCE NEEDED. IN OTHER WORDS...
...DUDE, YOU NEED TO GO ON A DIET.
YEAH, YEAH. MAYBE NEXT TIME YOU DON'T PUSH ME OFF A ROOF.
OKAY. I THINK I GET THE FIRST TWO LAWS, BUT WHAT ABOUT THE--
WEEEOOOOOWEEEOOOOOWEEEOOOOO
UH-OH, LOOKS LIKE LESSON'S OVER.
TIME TO CHECK ON SOME OTHER LAWS.

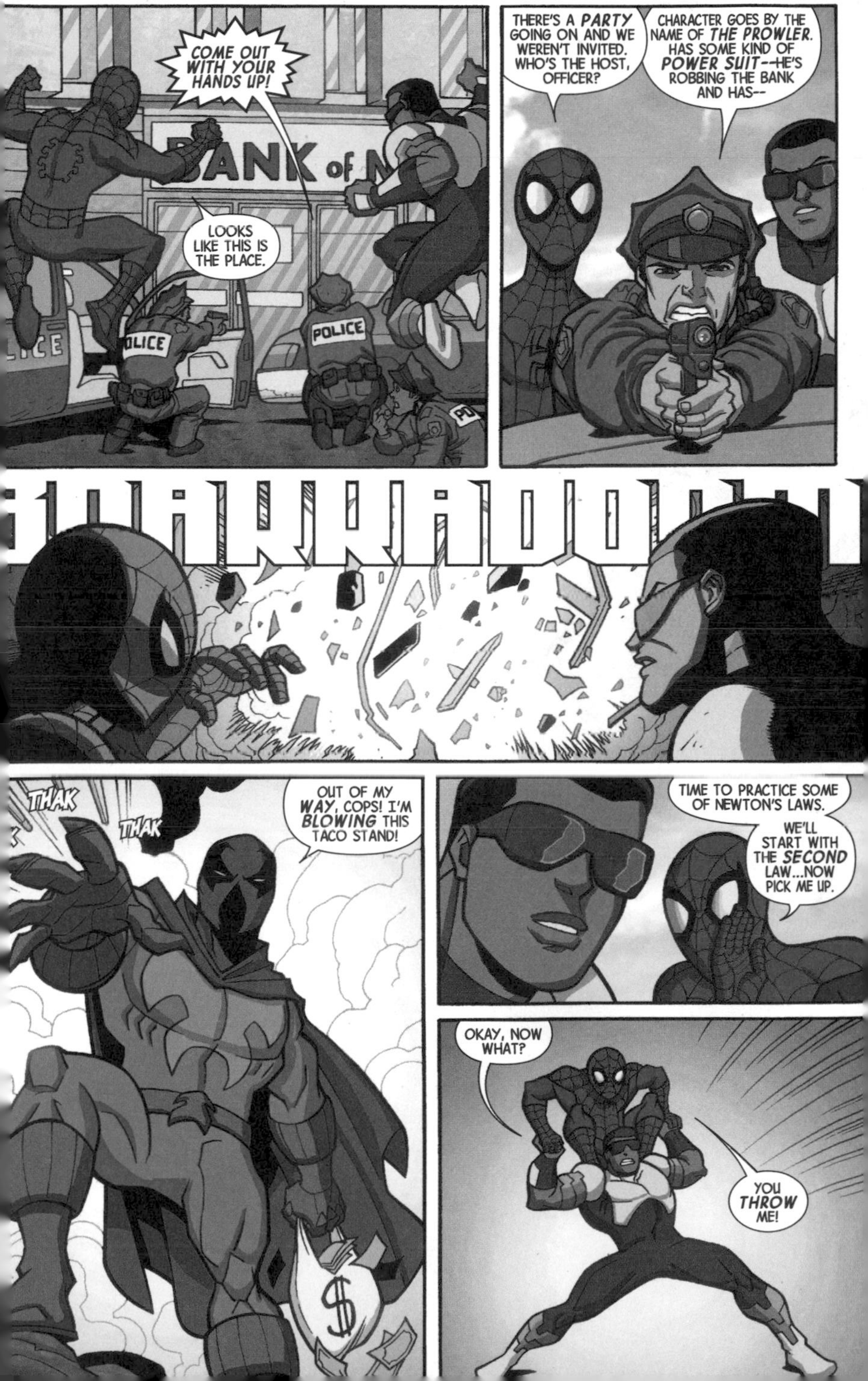
COME OUT WITH YOUR HANDS UP!
LOOKS LIKE THIS IS THE PLACE.
BANK of M
POLICE
POLICE
LICE
PD
THERE'S A PARTY GOING ON AND WE WEREN'T INVITED. WHO'S THE HOST, OFFICER?
CHARACTER GOES BY THE NAME OF THE PROWLER. HAS SOME KIND OF POWER SUIT--HE'S ROBBING THE BANK AND HAS--
THAK
THAK
OUT OF MY WAY, COPS! I'M BLOWING THIS TACO STAND!
TIME TO PRACTICE SOME OF NEWTON'S LAWS.
WE'LL START WITH THE SECOND LAW...NOW PICK ME UP.
OKAY, NOW WHAT?
YOU THROW ME!

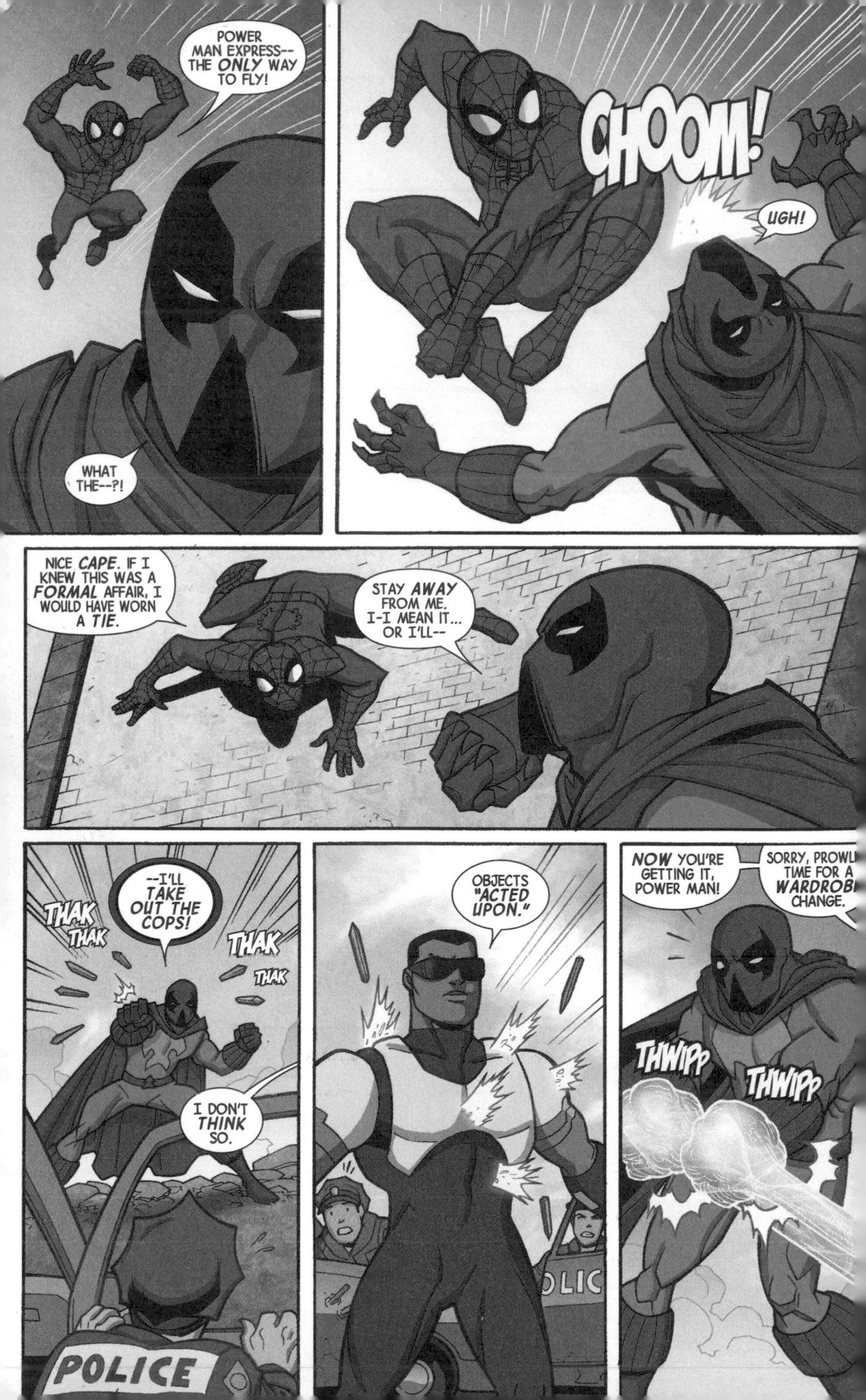
POWER MAN EXPRESS-- THE ONLY WAY TO FLY!
WHAT THE--?!
CHOOM!
UGH!
NICE CAPE. IF I KNEW THIS WAS A FORMAL AFFAIR, I WOULD HAVE WORN A TIE.
STAY AWAY FROM ME. I-I MEAN IT... OR I'LL--
--I'LL TAKE OUT THE COPS!
THAK THAK
THAK
THAK
I DON'T THINK SO.
OBJECTS "ACTED UPON."
POLICE
NOW YOU'RE GETTING IT, POWER MAN!
SORRY, PROWL
TIME FOR A
WARDROB
CHANGE.
THWIPP
THWIPP

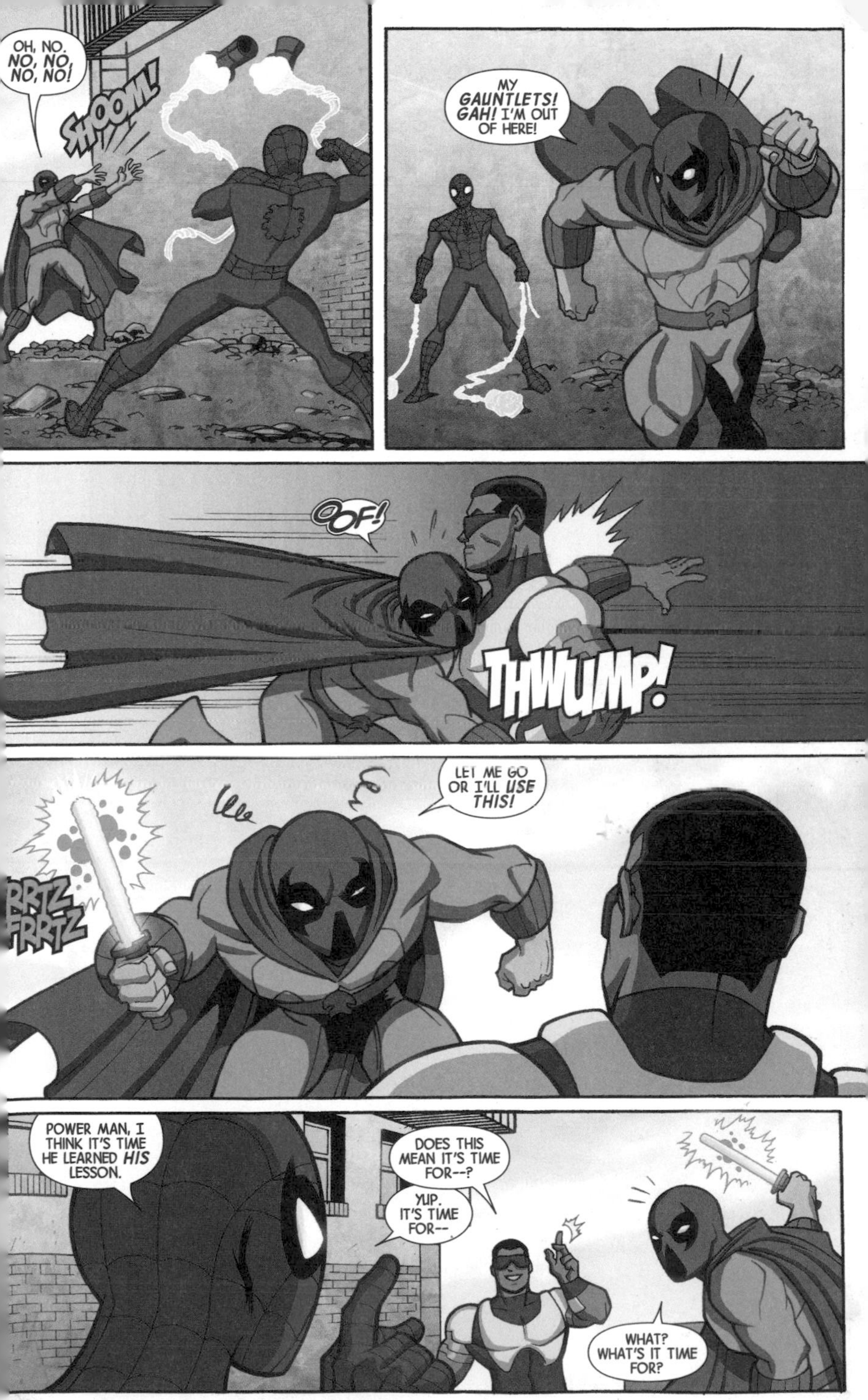
OH, NO. NO, NO, NO, NO!
SHOOM!
MY GAUNTLETS! GAH! I'M OUT OF HERE!
OOF!
THWUMP!
LET ME GO OR I'LL USE THIS!
RRTZ FRRTZ
POWER MAN, I THINK IT'S TIME HE LEARNED HIS LESSON.
DOES THIS MEAN IT'S TIME FOR--?
YUP. IT'S TIME FOR--
WHAT? WHAT'S IT TIME FOR?

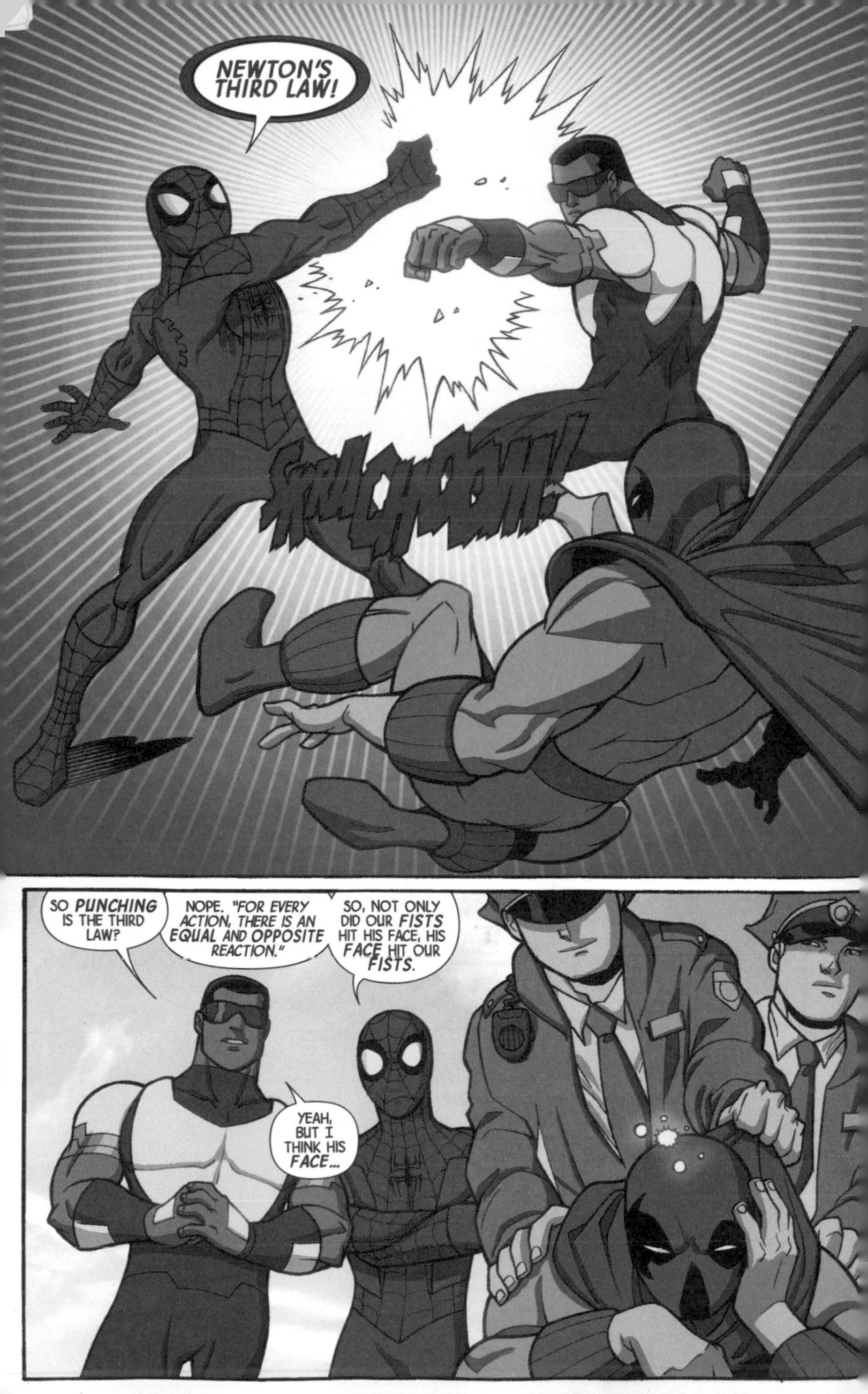
NEWTON'S THIRD LAW!
SO PUNCHING IS THE THIRD LAW?
NOPE. "FOR EVERY ACTION, THERE IS AN EQUAL AND OPPOSITE REACTION."
SO, NOT ONLY DID OUR FISTS HIT HIS FACE, HIS FACE HIT OUR FISTS.
YEAH, BUT I THINK HIS FACE...

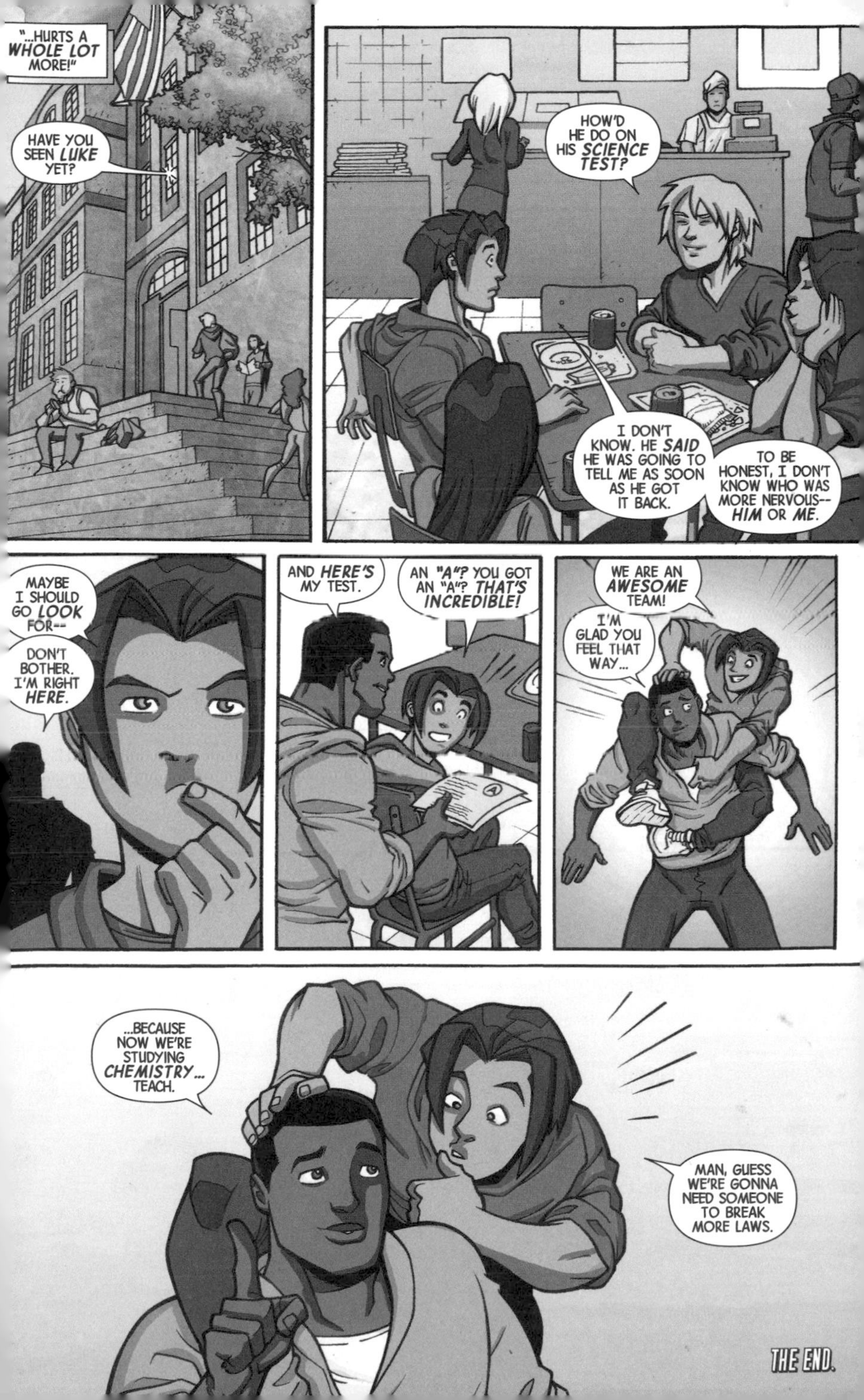
"...HURTS A WHOLE LOT MORE!"
HAVE YOU SEEN LUKE YET?
HOW'D HE DO ON HIS SCIENCE TEST?
I DON'T KNOW. HE SAID HE WAS GOING TO TELL ME AS SOON AS HE GOT IT BACK.
TO BE HONEST, I DON'T KNOW WHO WAS MORE NERVOUS-- HIM OR ME.
MAYBE I SHOULD GO LOOK FOR--
DON'T BOTHER. I'M RIGHT HERE.
AND HERE'S MY TEST.
AN "A"? YOU GOT AN "A"? THAT'S INCREDIBLE!
WE ARE AN AWESOME TEAM!
I'M GLAD YOU FEEL THAT WAY...
...BECAUSE NOW WE'RE STUDYING CHEMISTRY... TEACH.
MAN, GUESS WE'RE GONNA NEED SOMEONE TO BREAK MORE LAWS.
THE END.

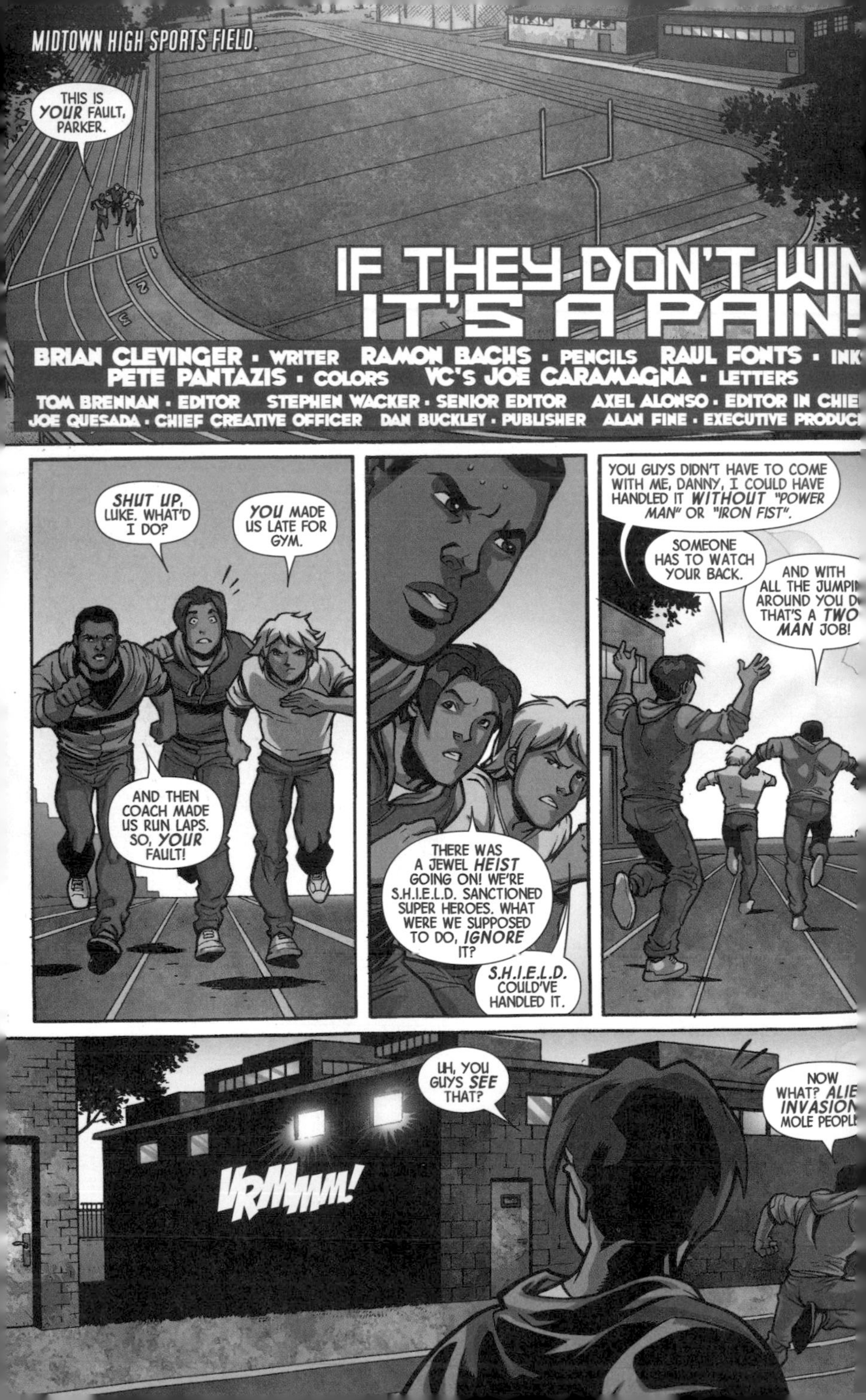
MIDTOWN HIGH SPORTS FIELD.
THIS IS YOUR FAULT, PARKER.
IF THEY DON'T WIN IT'S A PAIN!
BRIAN CLEVINGER · WRITER RAMON BACHS · PENCILS RAUL FONTS · INKS
PETE PANTAZIS · COLORS VC's JOE CARAMAGNA · LETTERS
TOM BRENNAN · EDITOR STEPHEN WACKER · SENIOR EDITOR AXEL ALONSO · EDITOR IN CHIEF
JOE QUESADA · CHIEF CREATIVE OFFICER DAN BUCKLEY · PUBLISHER ALAN FINE · EXECUTIVE PRODUCER
SHUT UP, LUKE. WHAT'D I DO?
YOU MADE US LATE FOR GYM.
AND THEN COACH MADE US RUN LAPS. SO, YOUR FAULT!
THERE WAS A JEWEL HEIST GOING ON! WE'RE S.H.I.E.L.D. SANCTIONED SUPER HEROES. WHAT WERE WE SUPPOSED TO DO, IGNORE IT?
S.H.I.E.L.D. COULD'VE HANDLED IT.
YOU GUYS DIDN'T HAVE TO COME WITH ME, DANNY, I COULD HAVE HANDLED IT WITHOUT "POWER MAN" OR "IRON FIST".
SOMEONE HAS TO WATCH YOUR BACK.
AND WITH ALL THE JUMPING AROUND YOU DO THAT'S A TWO MAN JOB!
UH, YOU GUYS SEE THAT?
NOW WHAT? ALIEN INVASION? MOLE PEOPLE?
VRMMMM!

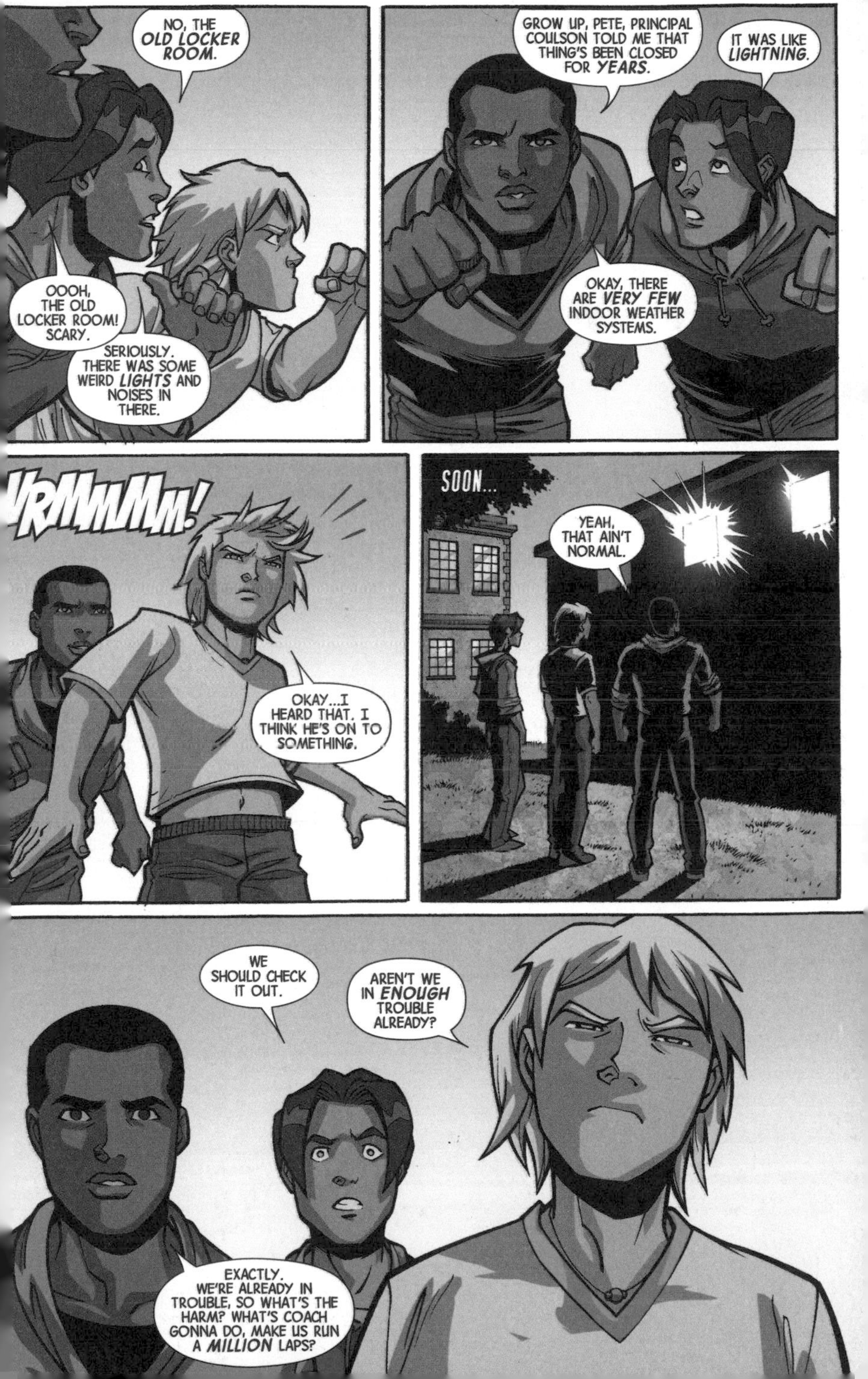
NO, THE OLD LOCKER ROOM.
OOOH, THE OLD LOCKER ROOM! SCARY.
SERIOUSLY. THERE WAS SOME WEIRD LIGHTS AND NOISES IN THERE.
GROW UP, PETE, PRINCIPAL COULSON TOLD ME THAT THING'S BEEN CLOSED FOR YEARS.
IT WAS LIKE LIGHTNING.
OKAY, THERE ARE VERY FEW INDOOR WEATHER SYSTEMS.
VRMMMM!
OKAY...I HEARD THAT. I THINK HE'S ON TO SOMETHING.
SOON...
YEAH, THAT AIN'T NORMAL.
WE SHOULD CHECK IT OUT.
AREN'T WE IN ENOUGH TROUBLE ALREADY?
EXACTLY. WE'RE ALREADY IN TROUBLE, SO WHAT'S THE HARM? WHAT'S COACH GONNA DO, MAKE US RUN A MILLION LAPS?

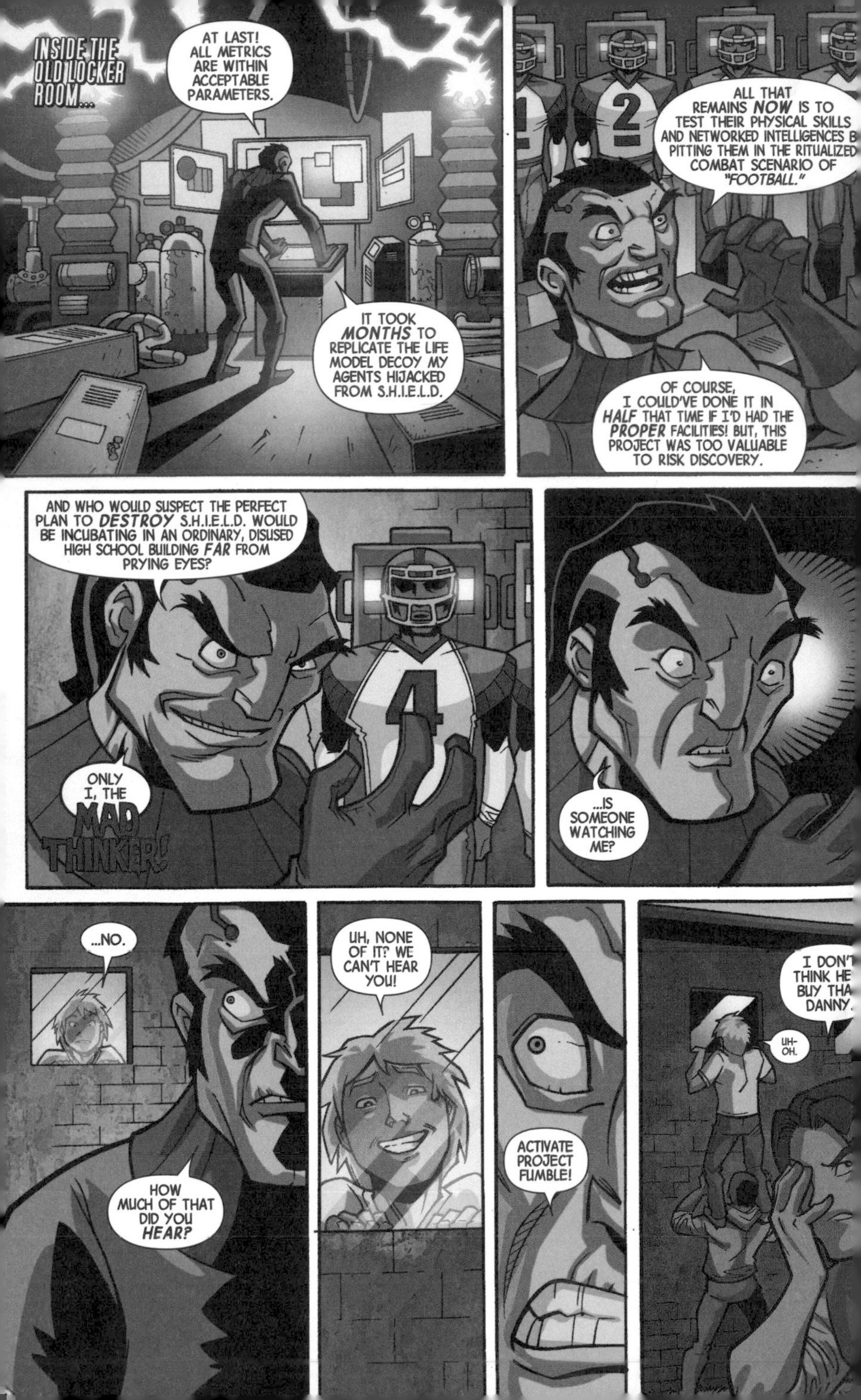
INSIDE THE OLD LOCKER ROOM...
AT LAST! ALL METRICS ARE WITHIN ACCEPTABLE PARAMETERS.
IT TOOK MONTHS TO REPLICATE THE LIFE MODEL DECOY MY AGENTS HIJACKED FROM S.H.I.E.L.D.
ALL THAT REMAINS NOW IS TO TEST THEIR PHYSICAL SKILLS AND NETWORKED INTELLIGENCES B PITTING THEM IN THE RITUALIZED COMBAT SCENARIO OF "FOOTBALL."
OF COURSE, I COULD'VE DONE IT IN HALF THAT TIME IF I'D HAD THE PROPER FACILITIES! BUT, THIS PROJECT WAS TOO VALUABLE TO RISK DISCOVERY.
AND WHO WOULD SUSPECT THE PERFECT PLAN TO DESTROY S.H.I.E.L.D. WOULD BE INCUBATING IN AN ORDINARY, DISUSED HIGH SCHOOL BUILDING FAR FROM PRYING EYES?
ONLY I, THE MAD THINKER!
...IS SOMEONE WATCHING ME?
...NO.
HOW MUCH OF THAT DID YOU HEAR?
UH, NONE OF IT? WE CAN'T HEAR YOU!
ACTIVATE PROJECT FUMBLE!
I DON'T THINK HE BUY THA DANNY.
UH-OH.

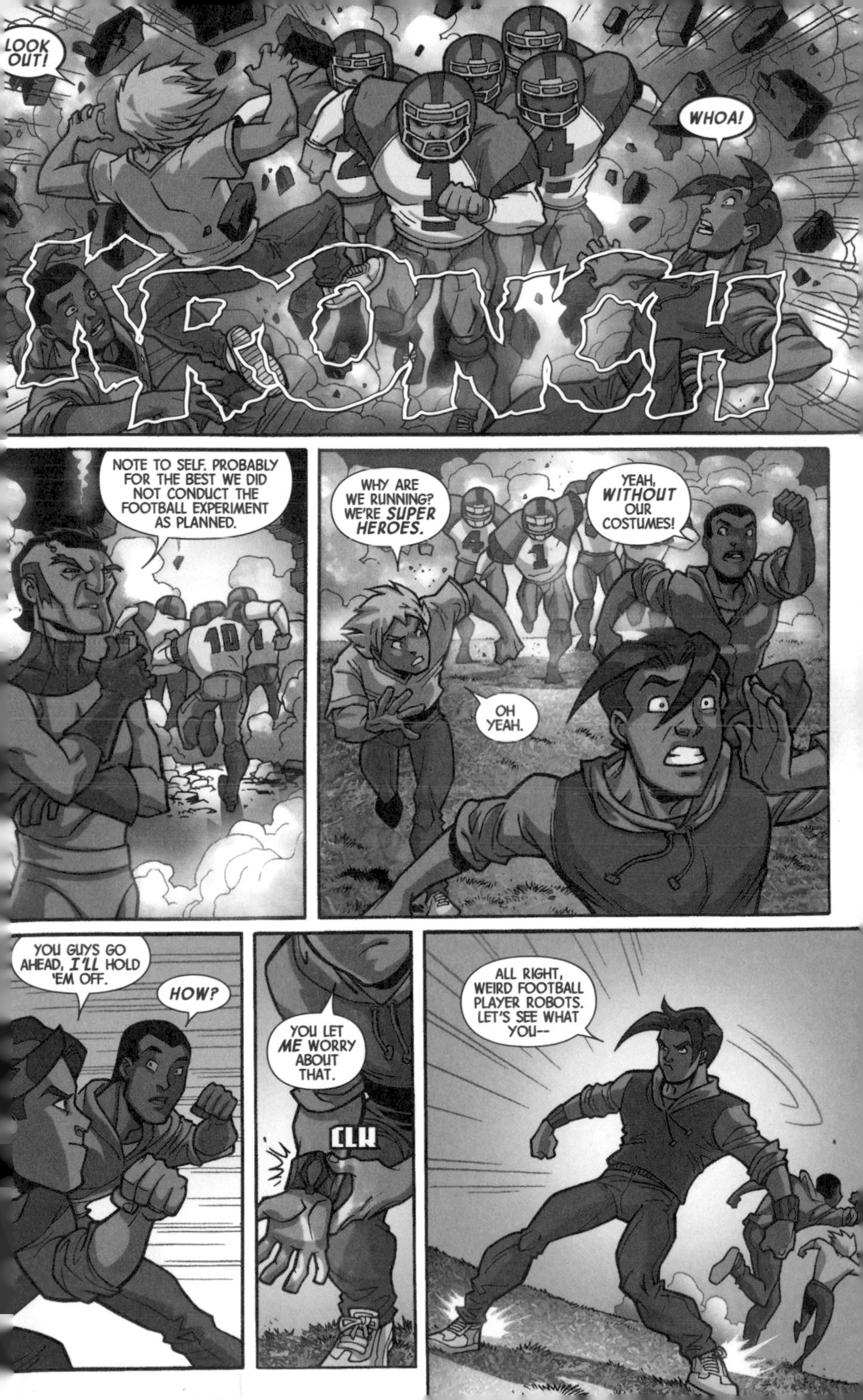
LOOK OUT!
WHOA!
KRUNCH
NOTE TO SELF. PROBABLY FOR THE BEST WE DID NOT CONDUCT THE FOOTBALL EXPERIMENT AS PLANNED.
WHY ARE WE RUNNING? WE'RE SUPER HEROES.
YEAH, WITHOUT OUR COSTUMES!
OH YEAH.
YOU GUYS GO AHEAD, I'LL HOLD 'EM OFF.
HOW?
YOU LET ME WORRY ABOUT THAT.
CLK
ALL RIGHT, WEIRD FOOTBALL PLAYER ROBOTS. LET'S SEE WHAT YOU--

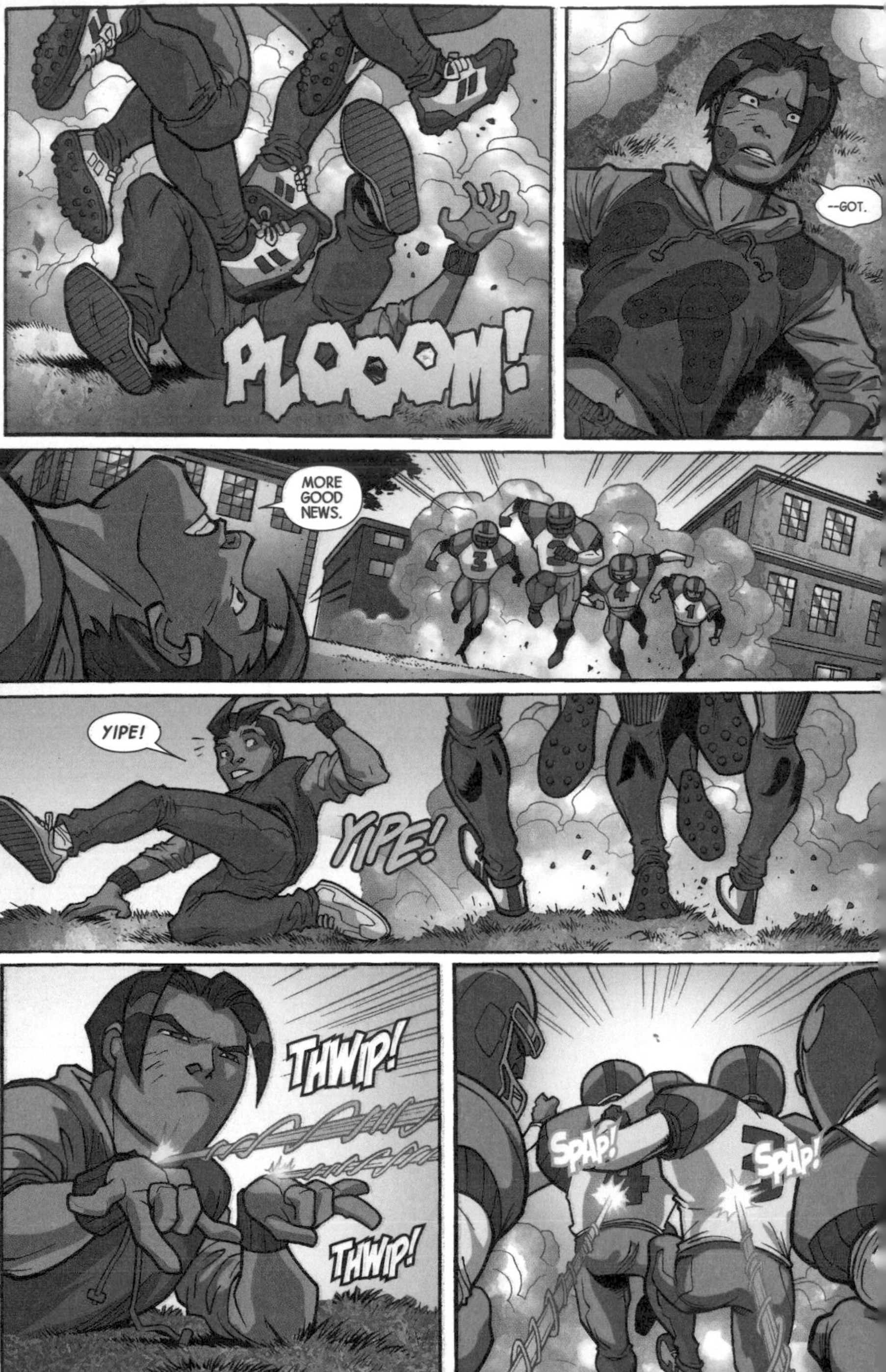
PLOOOM!
--GOT.
MORE GOOD NEWS.
YIPE!
YIPE!
THWIP!
THWIP!
SPAP!
SPAP!

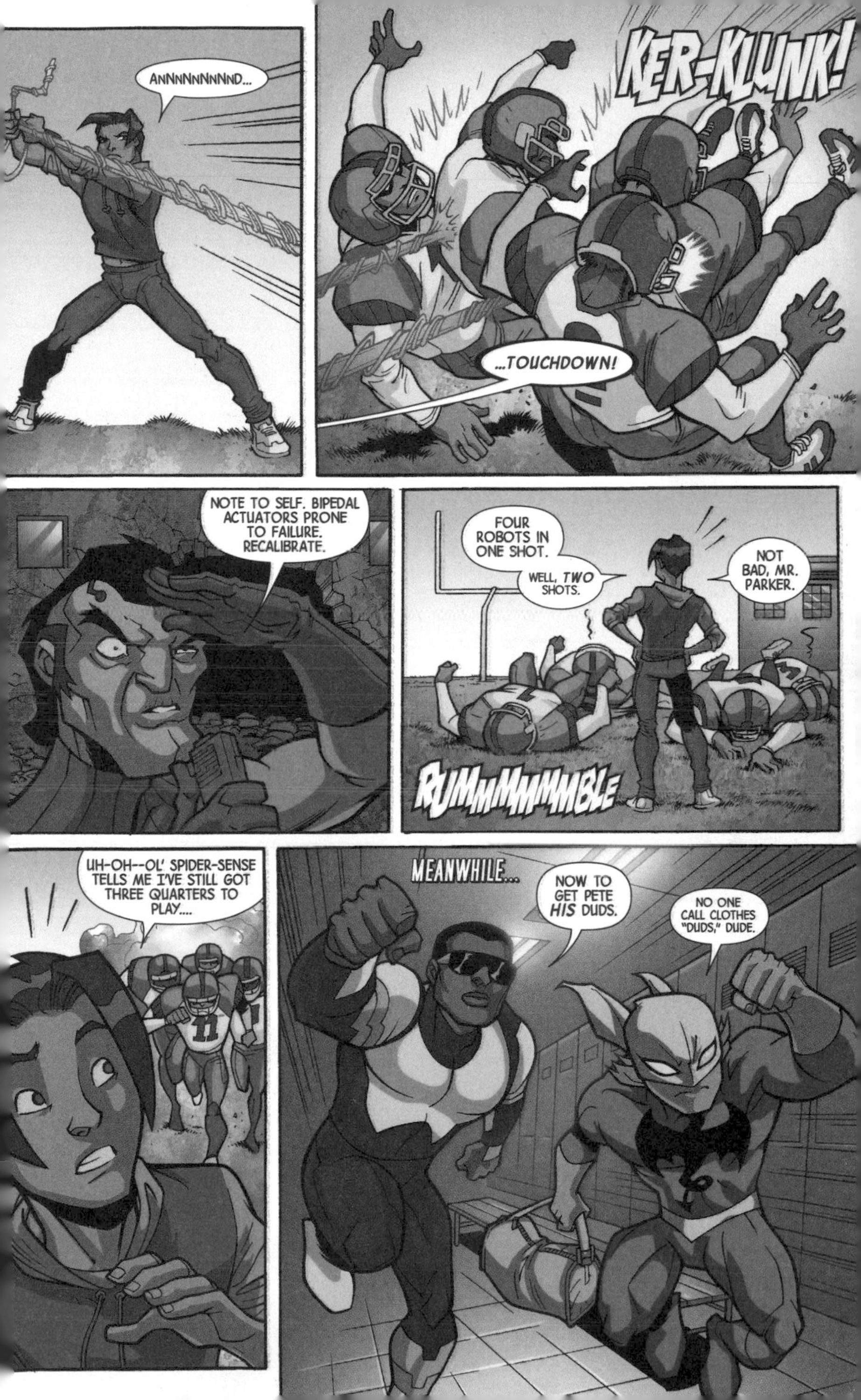
ANNNNNNNND...
KER-KLUNK!
...TOUCHDOWN!
NOTE TO SELF. BIPEDAL ACTUATORS PRONE TO FAILURE. RECALIBRATE.
FOUR ROBOTS IN ONE SHOT.
WELL, TWO SHOTS.
NOT BAD, MR. PARKER.
RUMMMMMMMBLE
UH-OH--OL' SPIDER-SENSE TELLS ME I'VE STILL GOT THREE QUARTERS TO PLAY....
MEANWHILE...
NOW TO GET PETE HIS DUDS.
NO ONE CALL CLOTHES "DUDS," DUDE.

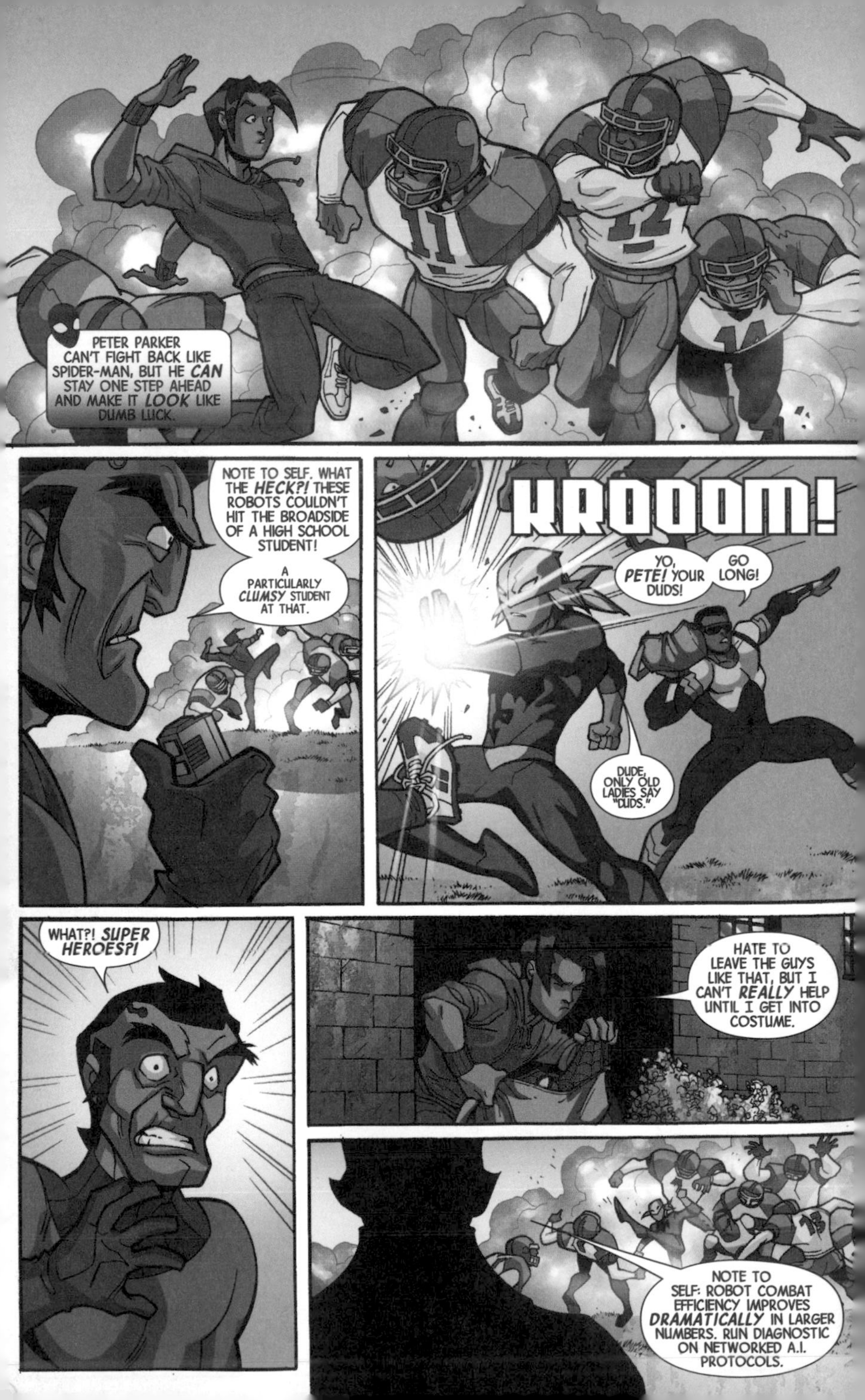
PETER PARKER CAN'T FIGHT BACK LIKE SPIDER-MAN, BUT HE CAN STAY ONE STEP AHEAD AND MAKE IT LOOK LIKE DUMB LUCK.
NOTE TO SELF. WHAT THE HECK?! THESE ROBOTS COULDN'T HIT THE BROADSIDE OF A HIGH SCHOOL STUDENT!
A PARTICULARLY CLUMSY STUDENT AT THAT.
KROOOM!
YO, PETE! YOUR DUDS!
GO LONG!
DUDE, ONLY OLD LADIES SAY "DUDS."
WHAT?! SUPER HEROES?!
HATE TO LEAVE THE GUYS LIKE THAT, BUT I CAN'T REALLY HELP UNTIL I GET INTO COSTUME.
NOTE TO SELF: ROBOT COMBAT EFFICIENCY IMPROVES DRAMATICALLY IN LARGER NUMBERS. RUN DIAGNOSTIC ON NETWORKED A.I. PROTOCOLS.

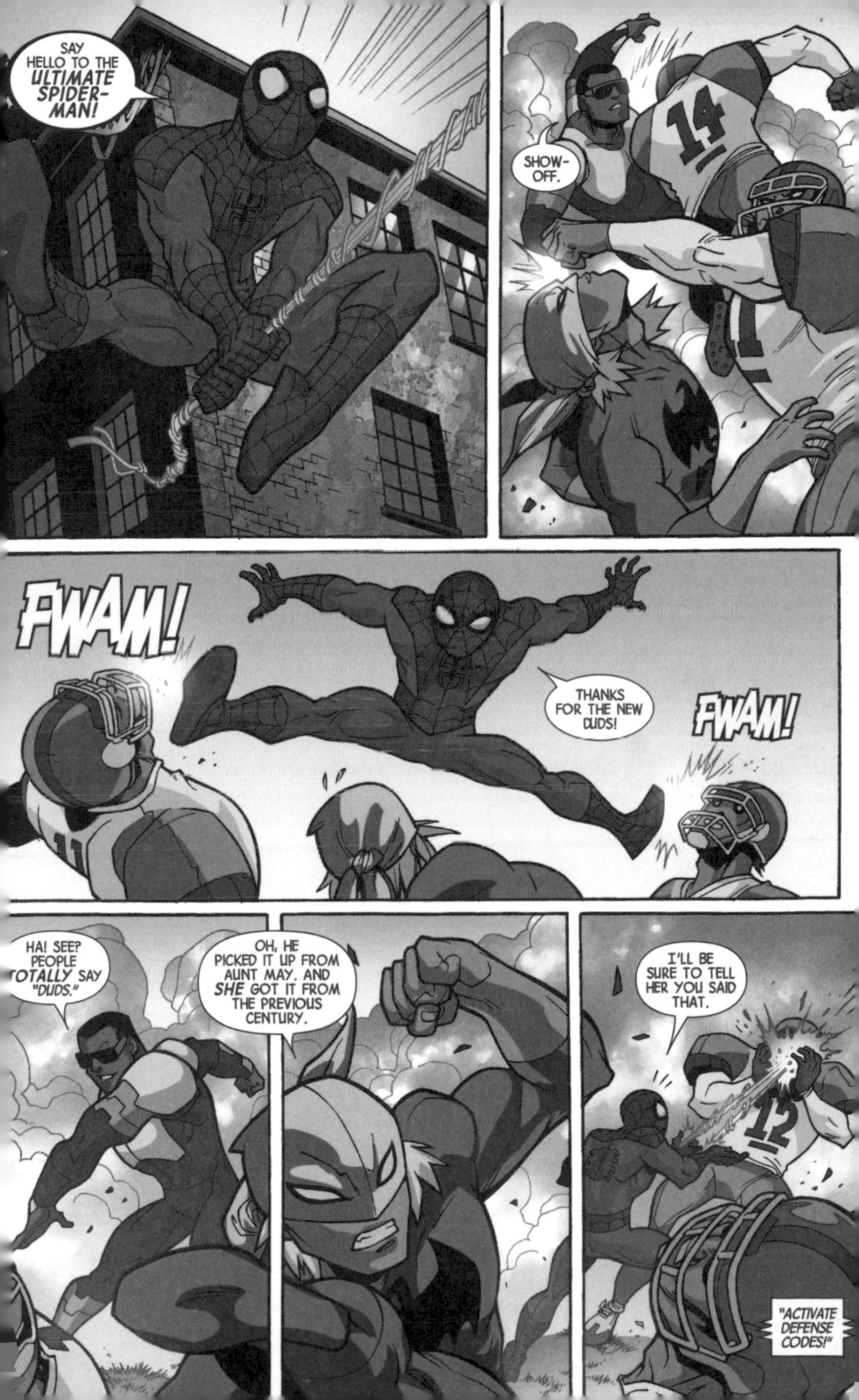
SAY HELLO TO THE *ULTIMATE SPIDER-MAN!*
SHOW-OFF.
FWAM!
THANKS FOR THE NEW DUDS!
FWAM!
HA! SEE? PEOPLE *TOTALLY* SAY *"DUDS."*
OH, HE PICKED IT UP FROM AUNT MAY. AND *SHE* GOT IT FROM THE PREVIOUS CENTURY.
I'LL BE SURE TO TELL HER YOU SAID THAT.
"ACTIVATE DEFENSE CODES!"

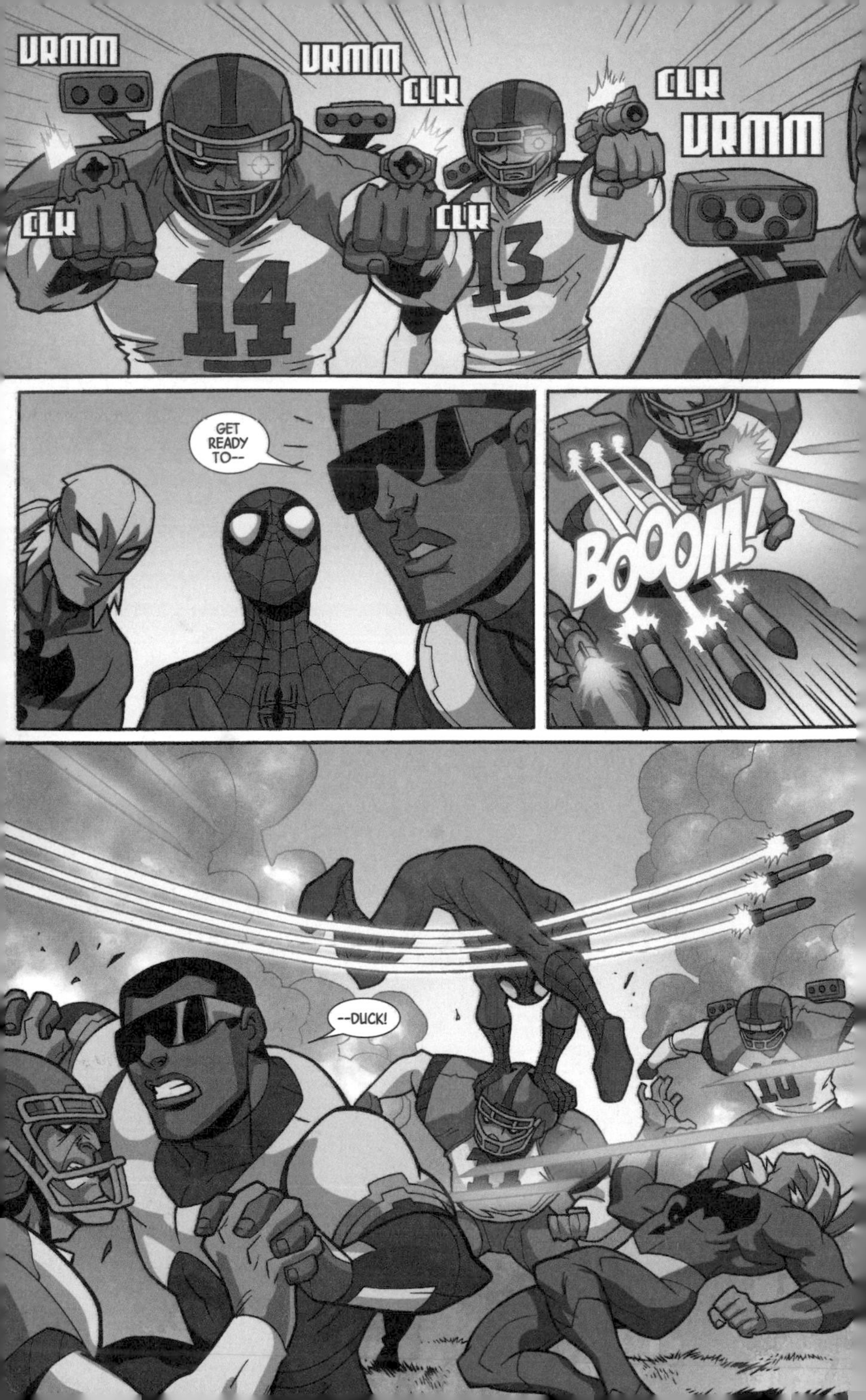
VRMM
VRMM
CLK
CLK
VRMM
CLK
CLK
GET READY TO--
BOOOM!
--DUCK!

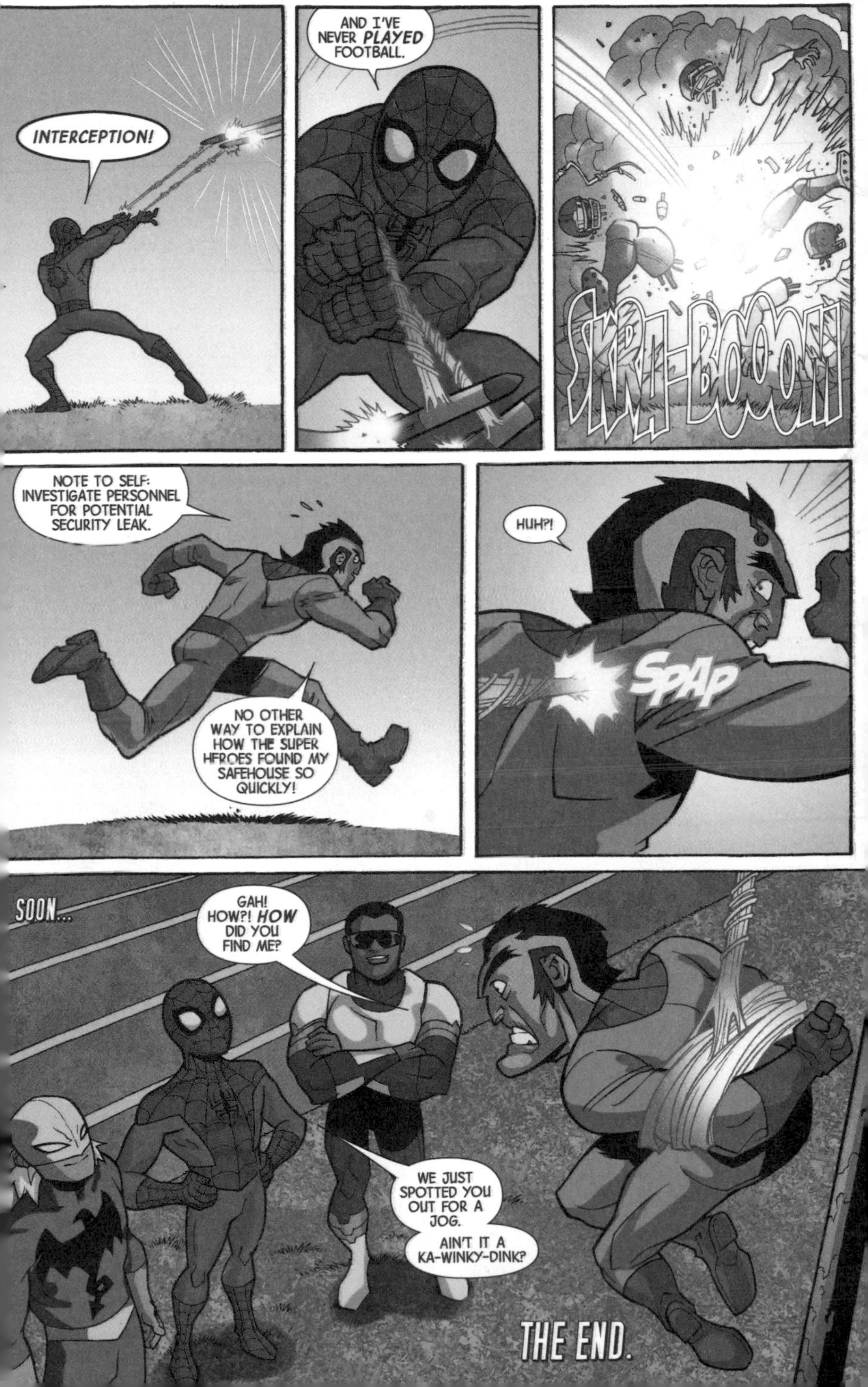
INTERCEPTION!
AND I'VE NEVER PLAYED FOOTBALL.
SKRA-BOOOM
NOTE TO SELF: INVESTIGATE PERSONNEL FOR POTENTIAL SECURITY LEAK.
NO OTHER WAY TO EXPLAIN HOW THE SUPER HEROES FOUND MY SAFEHOUSE SO QUICKLY!
HUH?!
SPAP
SOON...
GAH! HOW?! HOW DID YOU FIND ME?
WE JUST SPOTTED YOU OUT FOR A JOG.
AIN'T IT A KA-WINKY-DINK?
THE END.

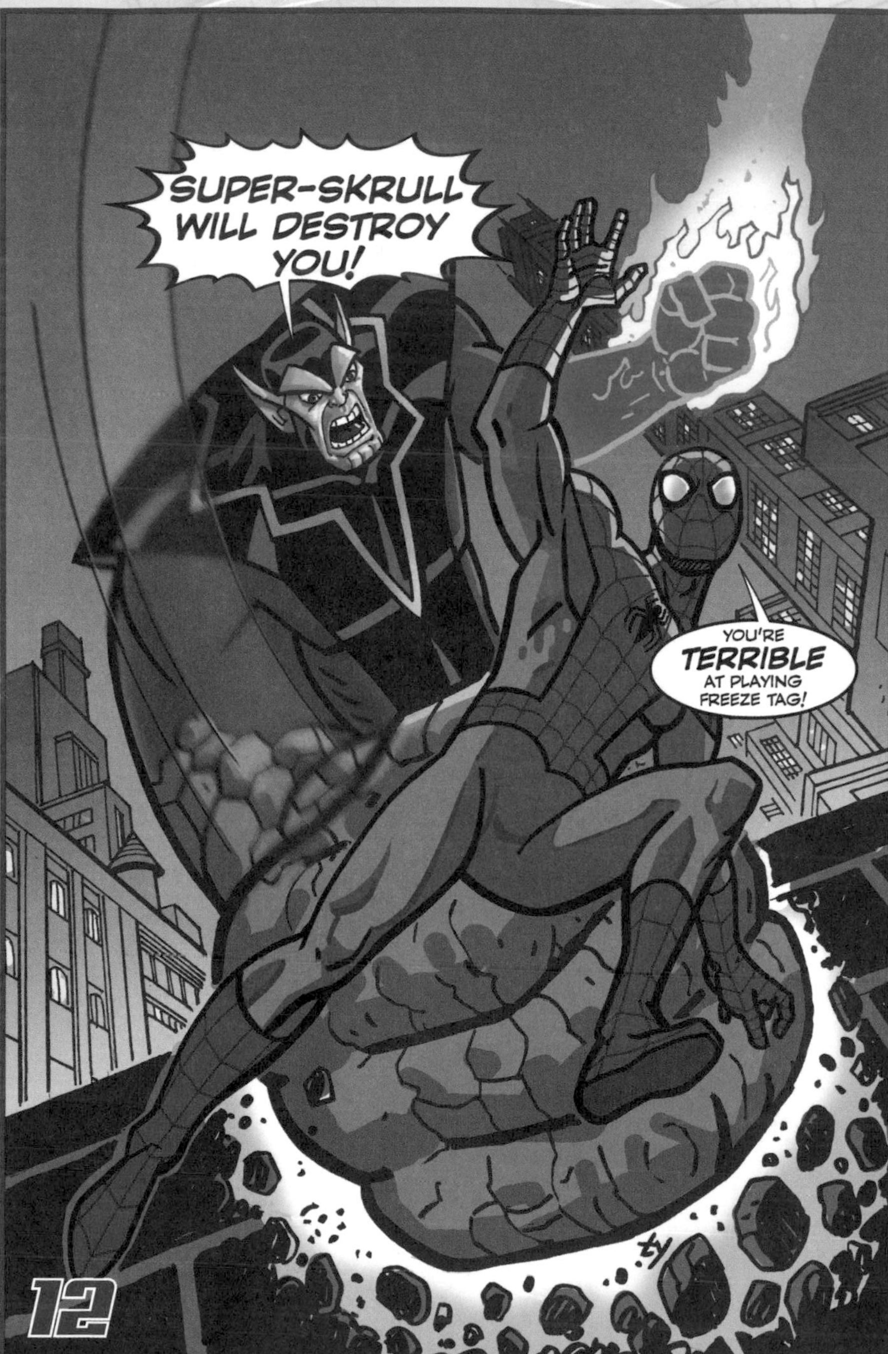
SUPER-SKRULL WILL DESTROY YOU!
YOU'RE TERRIBLE AT PLAYING FREEZE TAG!

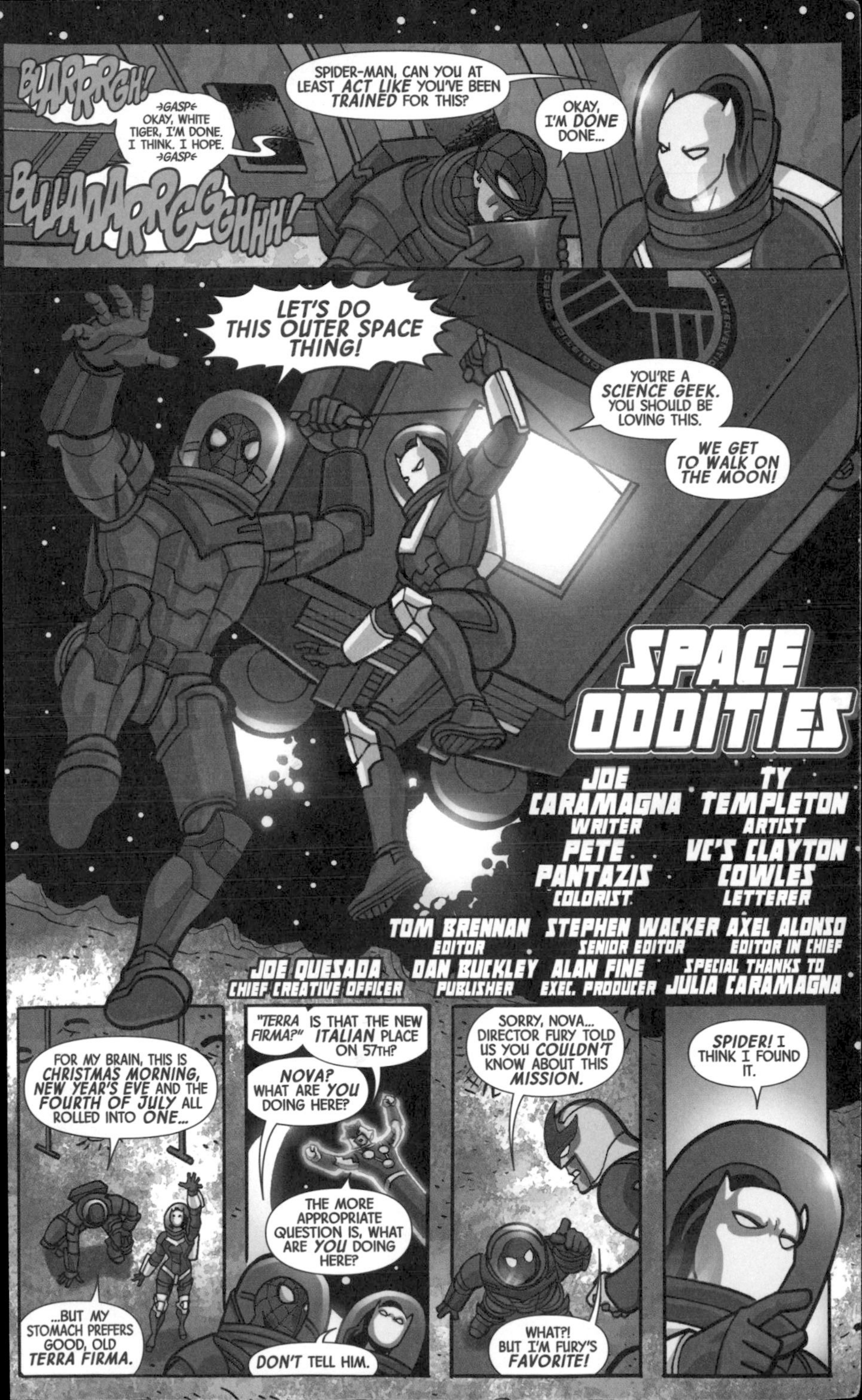
BLARRRGH!
>GASP< OKAY, WHITE TIGER, I'M DONE. I THINK. I HOPE. >GASP<
BLLLAAARRRGGGHHH!
SPIDER-MAN, CAN YOU AT LEAST ACT LIKE YOU'VE BEEN TRAINED FOR THIS?
OKAY, I'M DONE DONE...
LET'S DO THIS OUTER SPACE THING!
YOU'RE A SCIENCE GEEK. YOU SHOULD BE LOVING THIS.
WE GET TO WALK ON THE MOON!
SPACE ODDITIES
JOE CARAMAGNA WRITER
TY TEMPLETON ARTIST
PETE PANTAZIS COLORIST
VC'S CLAYTON COWLES LETTERER
TOM BRENNAN EDITOR
STEPHEN WACKER SENIOR EDITOR
AXEL ALONSO EDITOR IN CHIEF
JOE QUESADA CHIEF CREATIVE OFFICER
DAN BUCKLEY PUBLISHER
ALAN FINE EXEC. PRODUCER
SPECIAL THANKS TO JULIA CARAMAGNA
FOR MY BRAIN, THIS IS CHRISTMAS MORNING, NEW YEAR'S EVE AND THE FOURTH OF JULY ALL ROLLED INTO ONE...
...BUT MY STOMACH PREFERS GOOD, OLD TERRA FIRMA.
"TERRA FIRMA?"
IS THAT THE NEW ITALIAN PLACE ON 57TH?
NOVA? WHAT ARE YOU DOING HERE?
THE MORE APPROPRIATE QUESTION IS, WHAT ARE YOU DOING HERE?
DON'T TELL HIM.
SORRY, NOVA... DIRECTOR FURY TOLD US YOU COULDN'T KNOW ABOUT THIS MISSION.
WHAT?! BUT I'M FURY'S FAVORITE!
SPIDER! I THINK I FOUND IT.

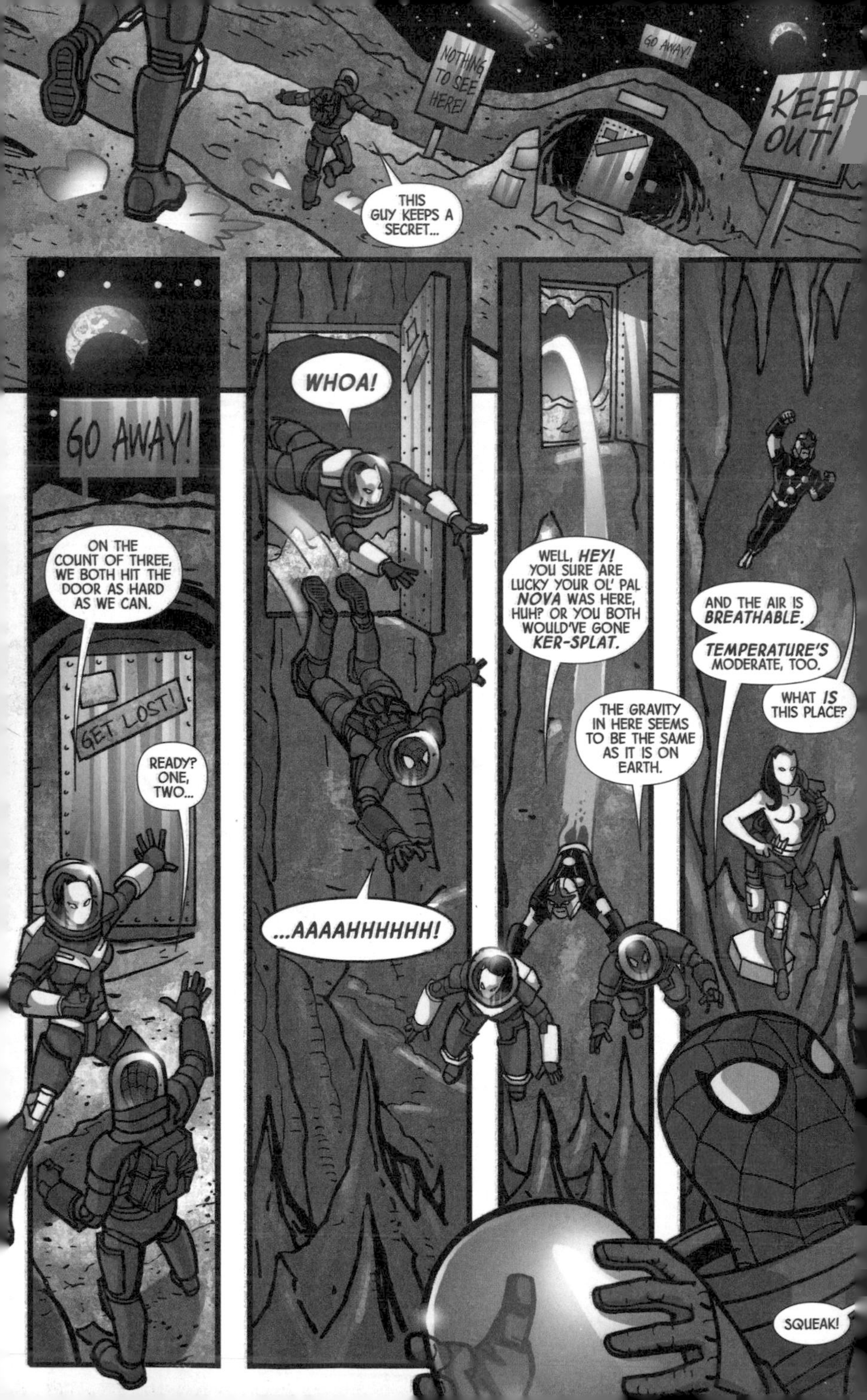
NOTHING TO SEE HERE!
GO AWAY!
KEEP OUT!
THIS GUY KEEPS A SECRET...
GO AWAY!
ON THE COUNT OF THREE, WE BOTH HIT THE DOOR AS HARD AS WE CAN.
GET LOST!
READY? ONE, TWO...
WHOA!
...AAAAHHHHHH!
WELL, HEY! YOU SURE ARE LUCKY YOUR OL' PAL NOVA WAS HERE, HUH? OR YOU BOTH WOULD'VE GONE KER-SPLAT.
THE GRAVITY IN HERE SEEMS TO BE THE SAME AS IT IS ON EARTH.
AND THE AIR IS BREATHABLE.
TEMPERATURE'S MODERATE, TOO.
WHAT IS THIS PLACE?
SQUEAK!

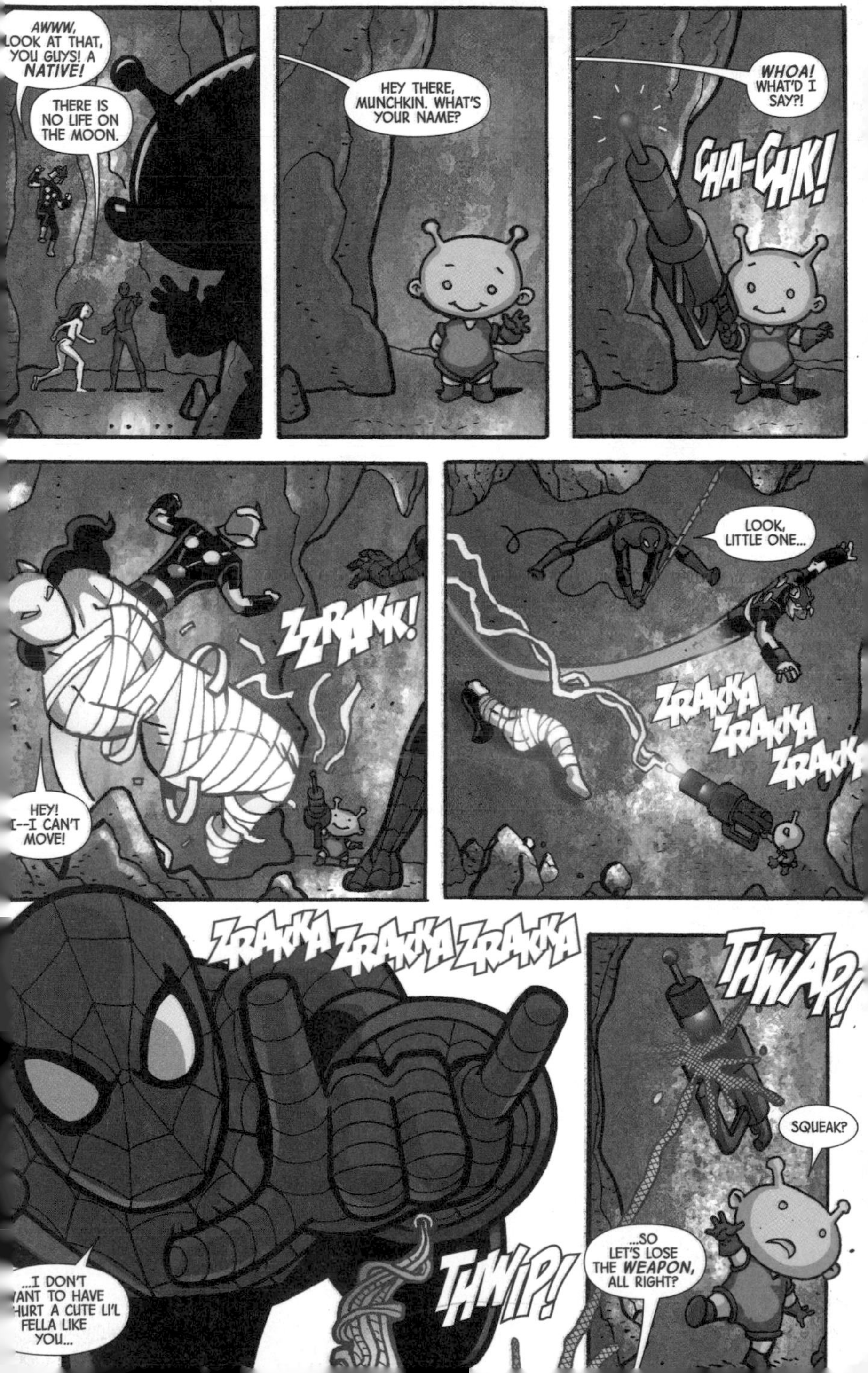
AWWW, LOOK AT THAT, YOU GUYS! A NATIVE!
THERE IS NO LIFE ON THE MOON.
HEY THERE, MUNCHKIN. WHAT'S YOUR NAME?
WHOA! WHAT'D I SAY?!
CHA-CHK!
ZZRAKK!
HEY! I--I CAN'T MOVE!
LOOK, LITTLE ONE...
ZRAKKA ZRAKKA ZRAKKA
ZRAKKA ZRAKKA ZRAKKA
...I DON'T WANT TO HAVE HURT A CUTE LI'L FELLA LIKE YOU...
THWIP!
THWAP!
SQUEAK?
...SO LET'S LOSE THE WEAPON, ALL RIGHT?

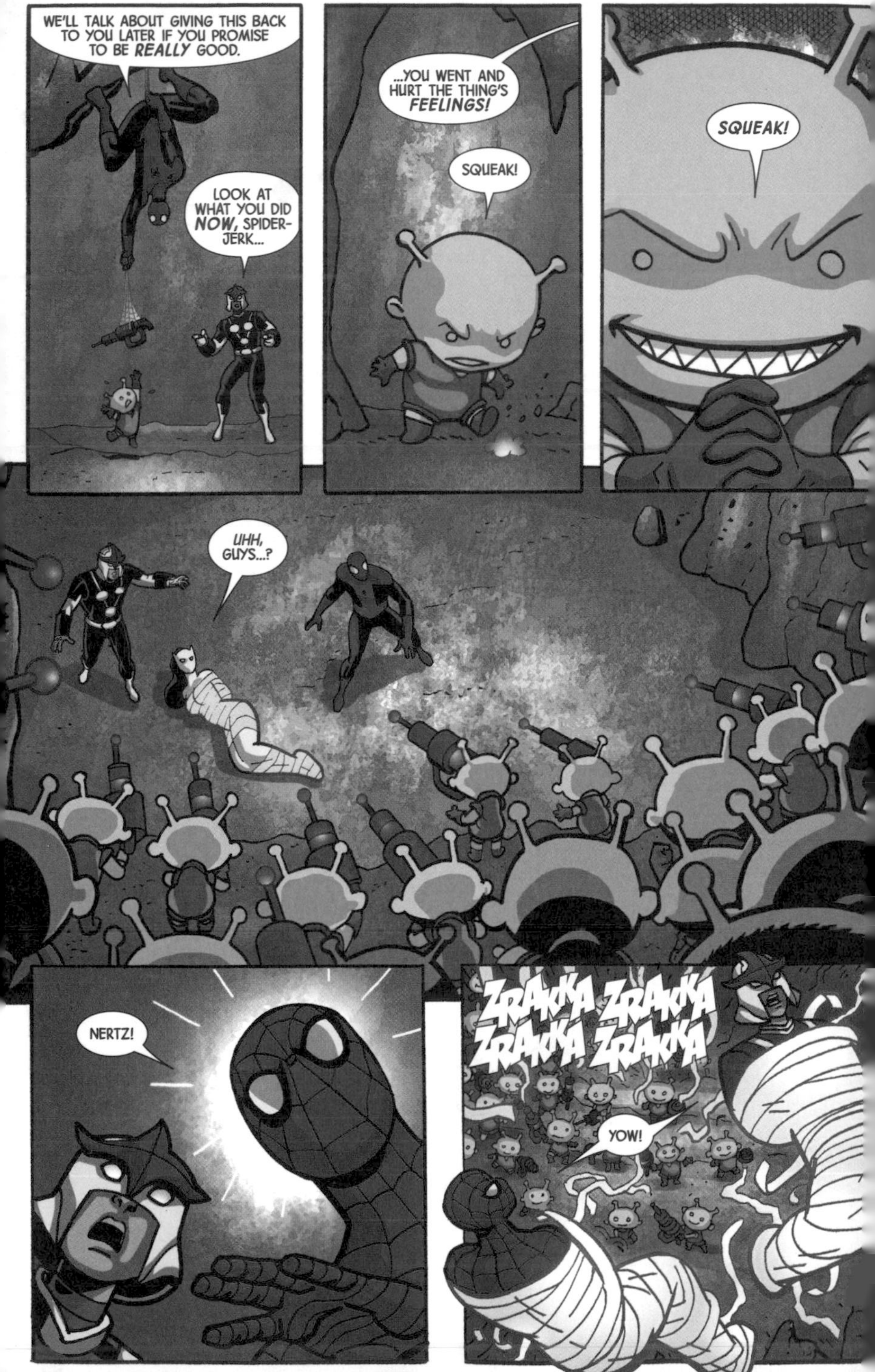
WE'LL TALK ABOUT GIVING THIS BACK TO YOU LATER IF YOU PROMISE TO BE REALLY GOOD.
LOOK AT WHAT YOU DID NOW, SPIDER-JERK...
...YOU WENT AND HURT THE THING'S FEELINGS!
SQUEAK!
SQUEAK!
UHH, GUYS...?
NERTZ!
ZRAKKA ZRAKKA ZRAKKA ZRAKKA
YOW!

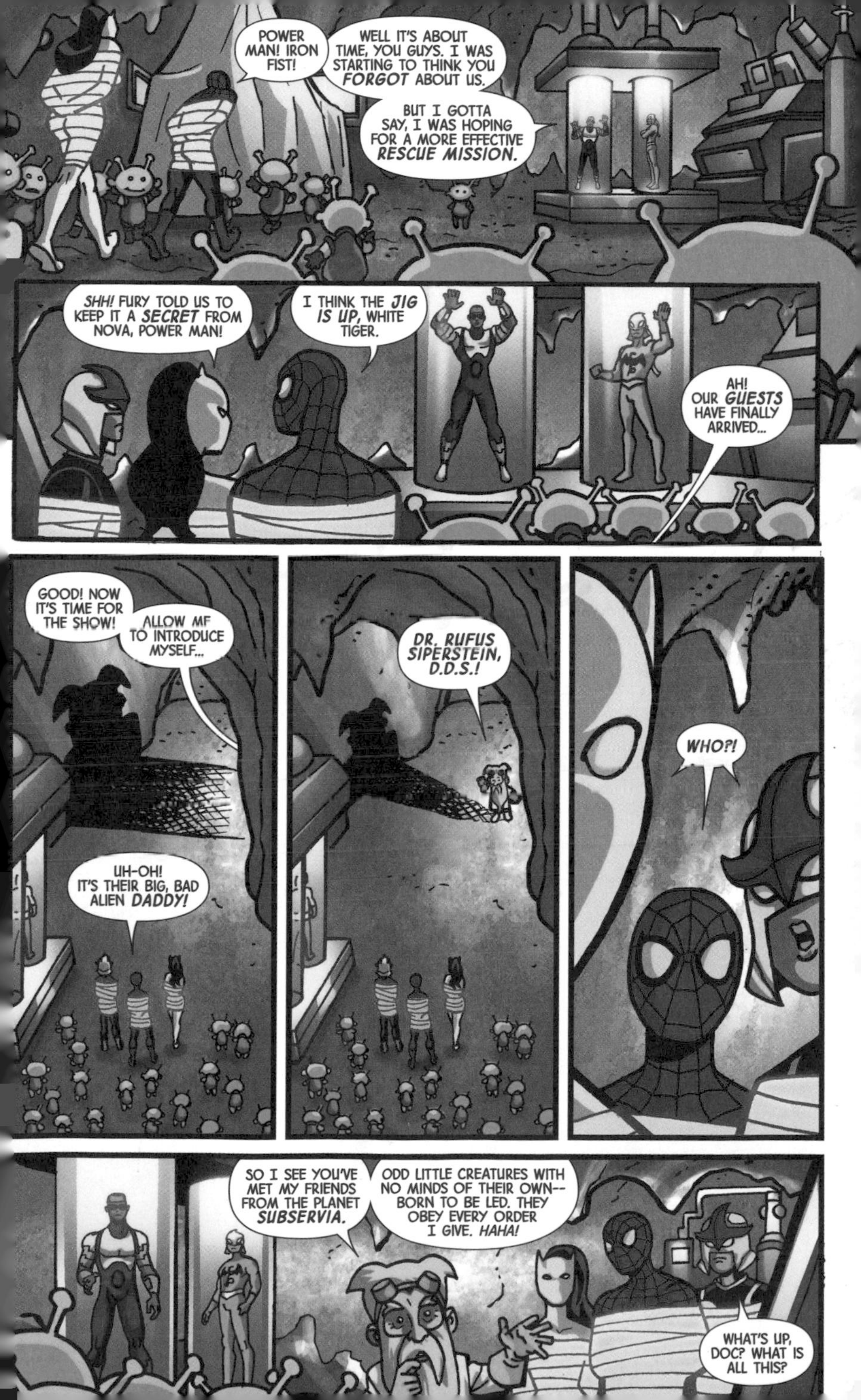
POWER MAN! IRON FIST!
WELL IT'S ABOUT TIME, YOU GUYS. I WAS STARTING TO THINK YOU FORGOT ABOUT US.
BUT I GOTTA SAY, I WAS HOPING FOR A MORE EFFECTIVE RESCUE MISSION.
SHH! FURY TOLD US TO KEEP IT A SECRET FROM NOVA, POWER MAN!
I THINK THE JIG IS UP, WHITE TIGER.
AH! OUR GUESTS HAVE FINALLY ARRIVED...
GOOD! NOW IT'S TIME FOR THE SHOW!
ALLOW ME TO INTRODUCE MYSELF...
UH-OH! IT'S THEIR BIG, BAD ALIEN DADDY!
DR. RUFUS SIPERSTEIN, D.D.S.!
WHO?!
SO I SEE YOU'VE MET MY FRIENDS FROM THE PLANET SUBSERVIA.
ODD LITTLE CREATURES WITH NO MINDS OF THEIR OWN-- BORN TO BE LED. THEY OBEY EVERY ORDER I GIVE. HAHA!
WHAT'S UP, DOC? WHAT IS ALL THIS?

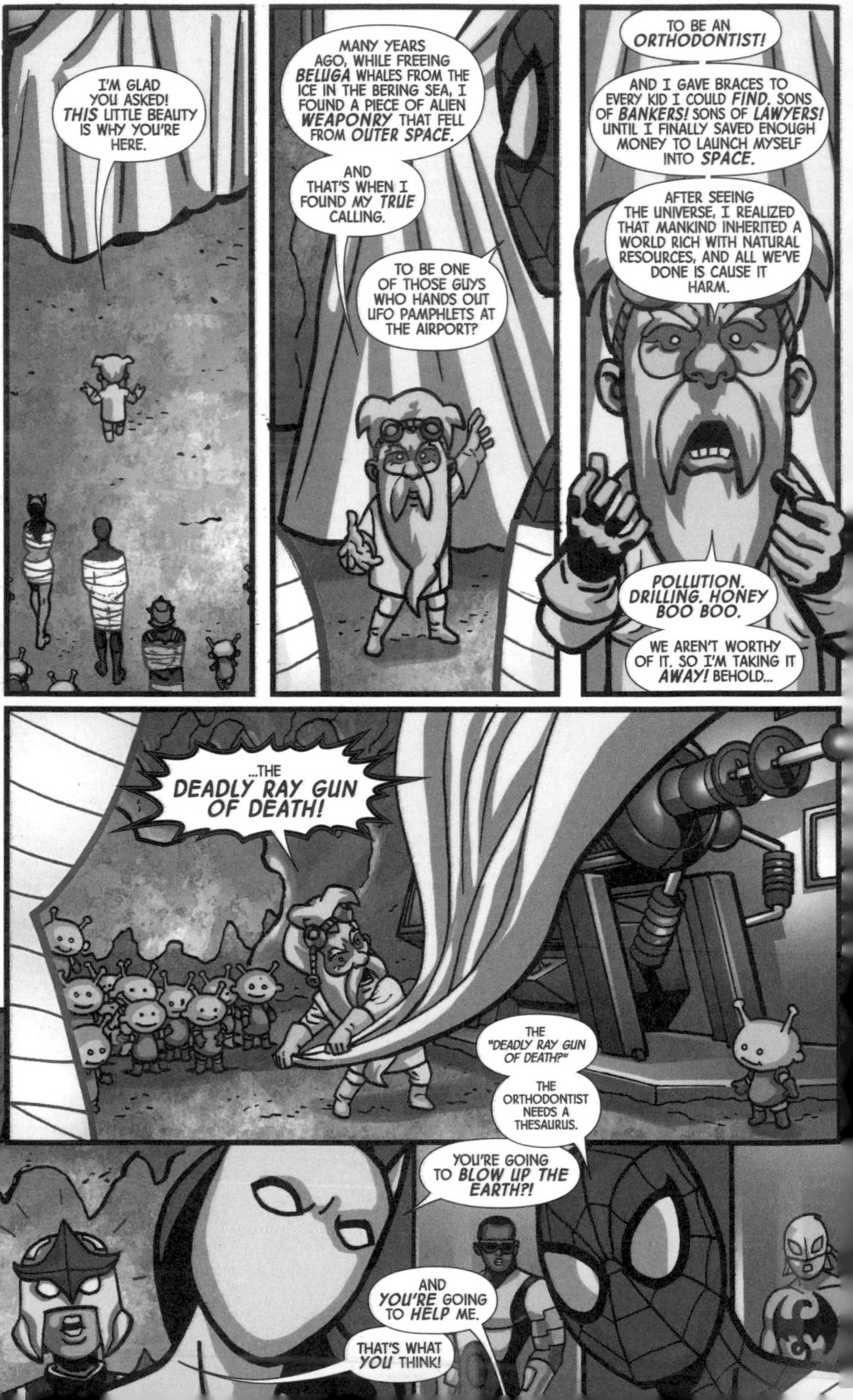
I'M GLAD YOU ASKED! THIS LITTLE BEAUTY IS WHY YOU'RE HERE.
MANY YEARS AGO, WHILE FREEING BELUGA WHALES FROM THE ICE IN THE BERING SEA, I FOUND A PIECE OF ALIEN WEAPONRY THAT FELL FROM OUTER SPACE.
AND THAT'S WHEN I FOUND MY TRUE CALLING.
TO BE ONE OF THOSE GUYS WHO HANDS OUT UFO PAMPHLETS AT THE AIRPORT?
TO BE AN ORTHODONTIST!
AND I GAVE BRACES TO EVERY KID I COULD FIND. SONS OF BANKERS! SONS OF LAWYERS! UNTIL I FINALLY SAVED ENOUGH MONEY TO LAUNCH MYSELF INTO SPACE.
AFTER SEEING THE UNIVERSE, I REALIZED THAT MANKIND INHERITED A WORLD RICH WITH NATURAL RESOURCES, AND ALL WE'VE DONE IS CAUSE IT HARM.
POLLUTION. DRILLING. HONEY BOO BOO.
WE AREN'T WORTHY OF IT. SO I'M TAKING IT AWAY! BEHOLD...
...THE DEADLY RAY GUN OF DEATH!
THE "DEADLY RAY GUN OF DEATH?"
THE ORTHODONTIST NEEDS A THESAURUS.
YOU'RE GOING TO BLOW UP THE EARTH?!
AND YOU'RE GOING TO HELP ME.
THAT'S WHAT YOU THINK!

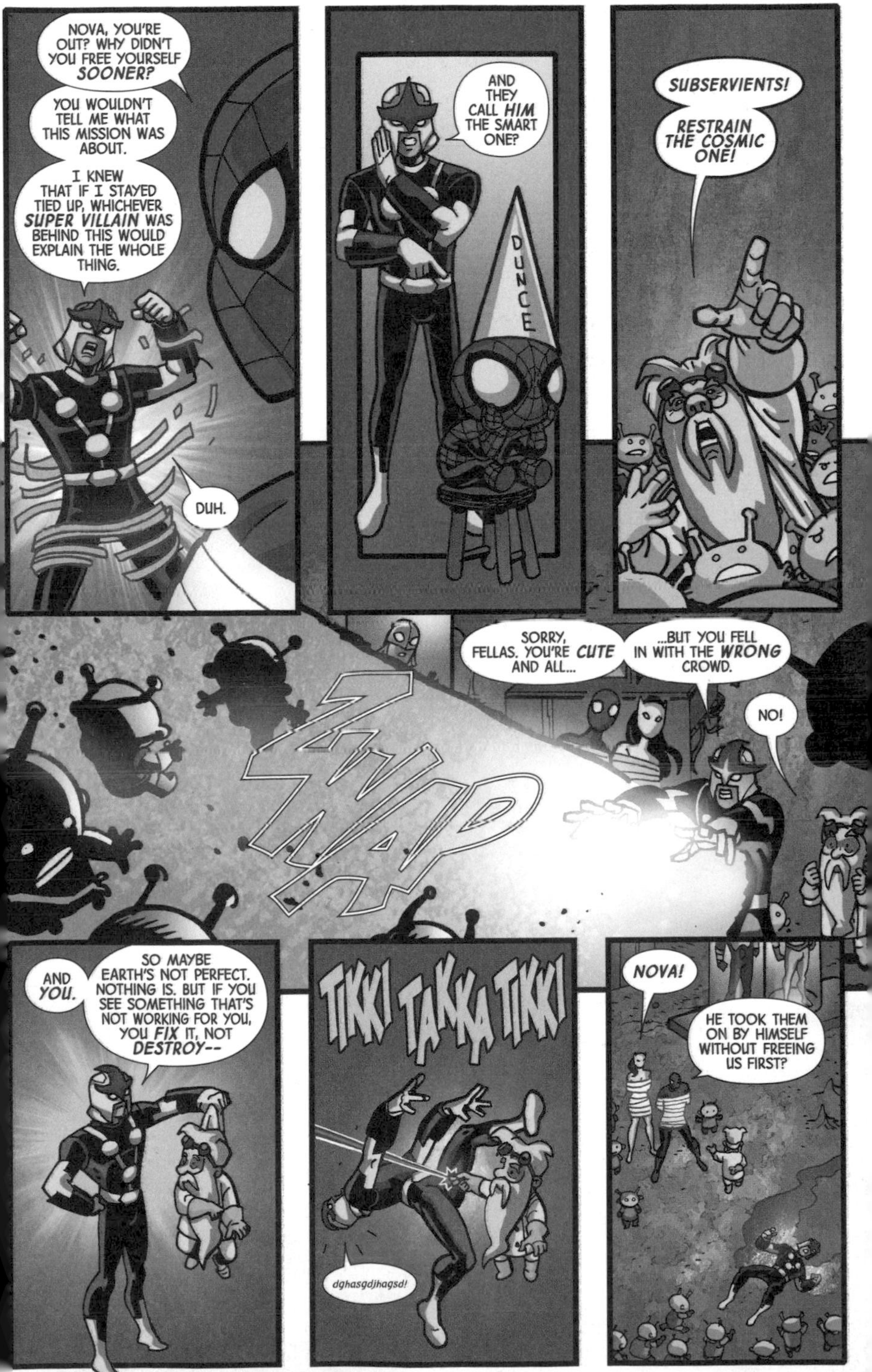
NOVA, YOU'RE OUT? WHY DIDN'T YOU FREE YOURSELF SOONER?
YOU WOULDN'T TELL ME WHAT THIS MISSION WAS ABOUT.
I KNEW THAT IF I STAYED TIED UP, WHICHEVER SUPER VILLAIN WAS BEHIND THIS WOULD EXPLAIN THE WHOLE THING.
DUH.
AND THEY CALL HIM THE SMART ONE?
DUNCE
SUBSERVIENTS!
RESTRAIN THE COSMIC ONE!
ZWAP
SORRY, FELLAS. YOU'RE CUTE AND ALL...
...BUT YOU FELL IN WITH THE WRONG CROWD.
NO!
AND YOU.
SO MAYBE EARTH'S NOT PERFECT. NOTHING IS. BUT IF YOU SEE SOMETHING THAT'S NOT WORKING FOR YOU, YOU FIX IT, NOT DESTROY--
TIKKI TAKKA TIKKI
dghasgdjhagsd!
NOVA!
HE TOOK THEM ON BY HIMSELF WITHOUT FREEING US FIRST?

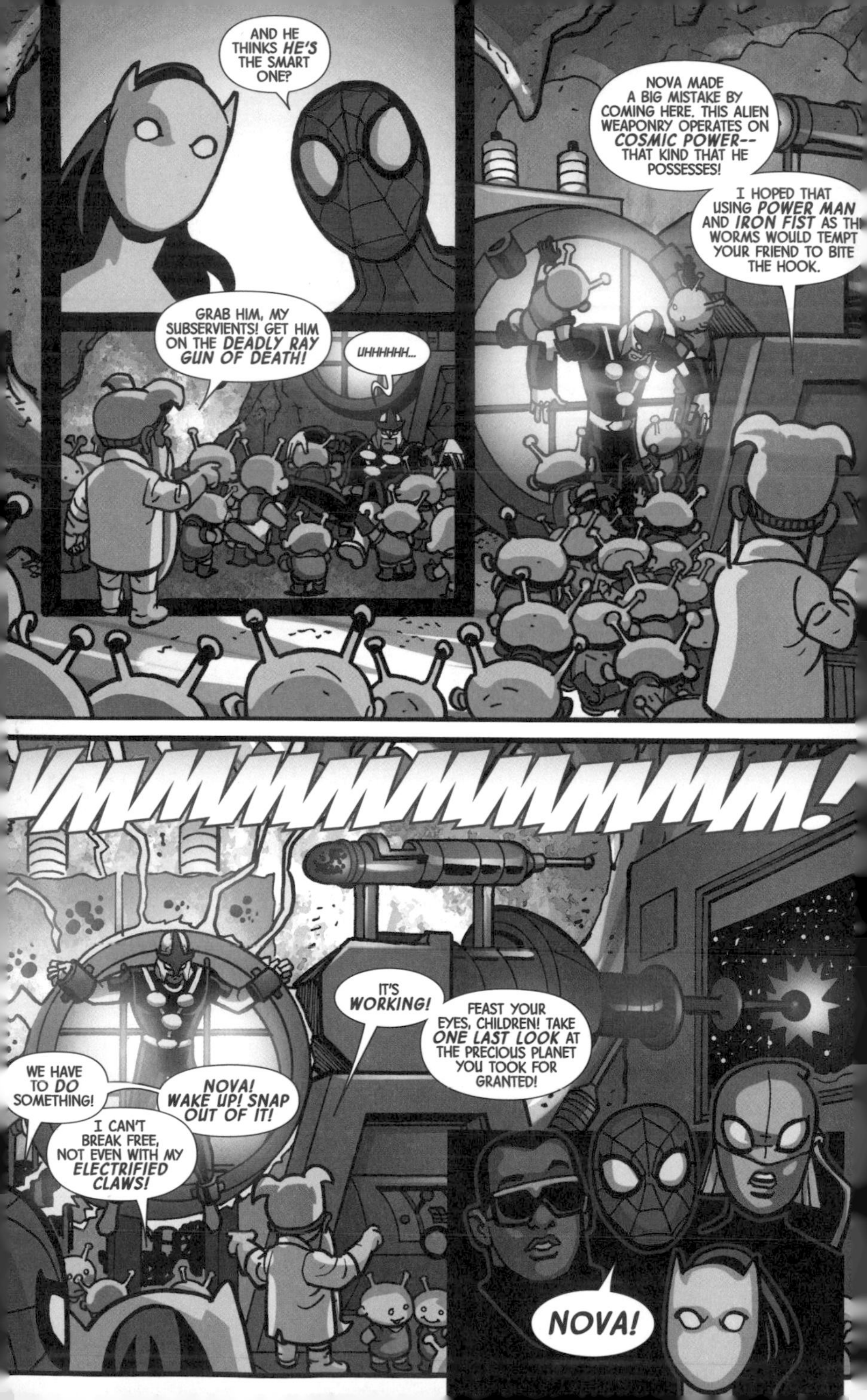
AND HE THINKS HE'S THE SMART ONE?
NOVA MADE A BIG MISTAKE BY COMING HERE. THIS ALIEN WEAPONRY OPERATES ON COSMIC POWER-- THAT KIND THAT HE POSSESSES!
I HOPED THAT USING POWER MAN AND IRON FIST AS TH WORMS WOULD TEMPT YOUR FRIEND TO BITE THE HOOK.
GRAB HIM, MY SUBSERVIENTS! GET HIM ON THE DEADLY RAY GUN OF DEATH!
UHHHHHH...
VMMMMMMMMMMMM!
IT'S WORKING!
FEAST YOUR EYES, CHILDREN! TAKE ONE LAST LOOK AT THE PRECIOUS PLANET YOU TOOK FOR GRANTED!
WE HAVE TO DO SOMETHING!
NOVA! WAKE UP! SNAP OUT OF IT!
I CAN'T BREAK FREE, NOT EVEN WITH MY ELECTRIFIED CLAWS!
NOVA!

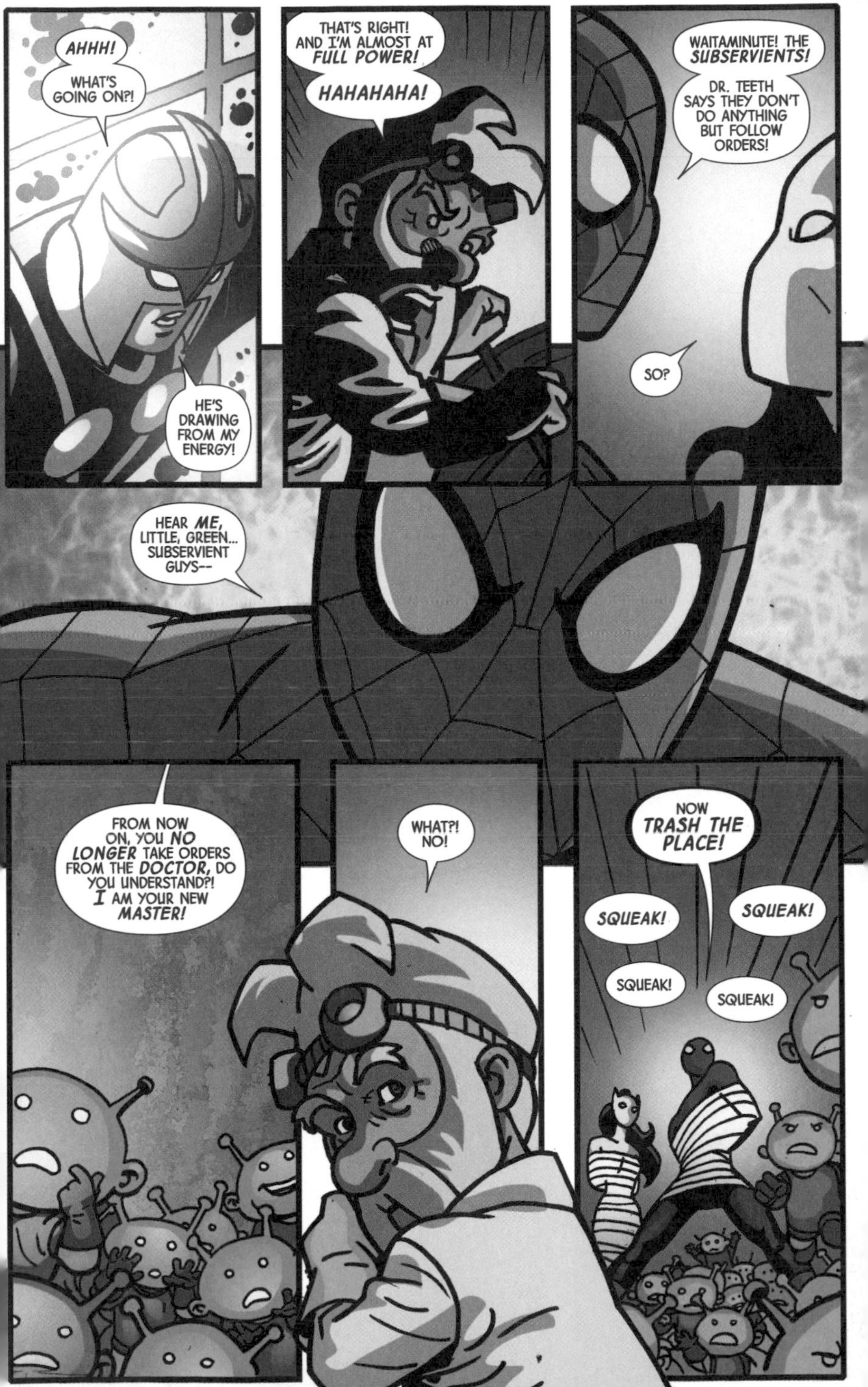
AHHH!
WHAT'S GOING ON?!
HE'S DRAWING FROM MY ENERGY!
THAT'S RIGHT! AND I'M ALMOST AT FULL POWER!
HAHAHAHA!
WAITAMINUTE! THE SUBSERVIENTS!
DR. TEETH SAYS THEY DON'T DO ANYTHING BUT FOLLOW ORDERS!
SO?
HEAR ME, LITTLE, GREEN... SUBSERVIENT GUYS--
FROM NOW ON, YOU NO LONGER TAKE ORDERS FROM THE DOCTOR, DO YOU UNDERSTAND?! I AM YOUR NEW MASTER!
WHAT?! NO!
NOW TRASH THE PLACE!
SQUEAK!
SQUEAK!
SQUEAK!
SQUEAK!

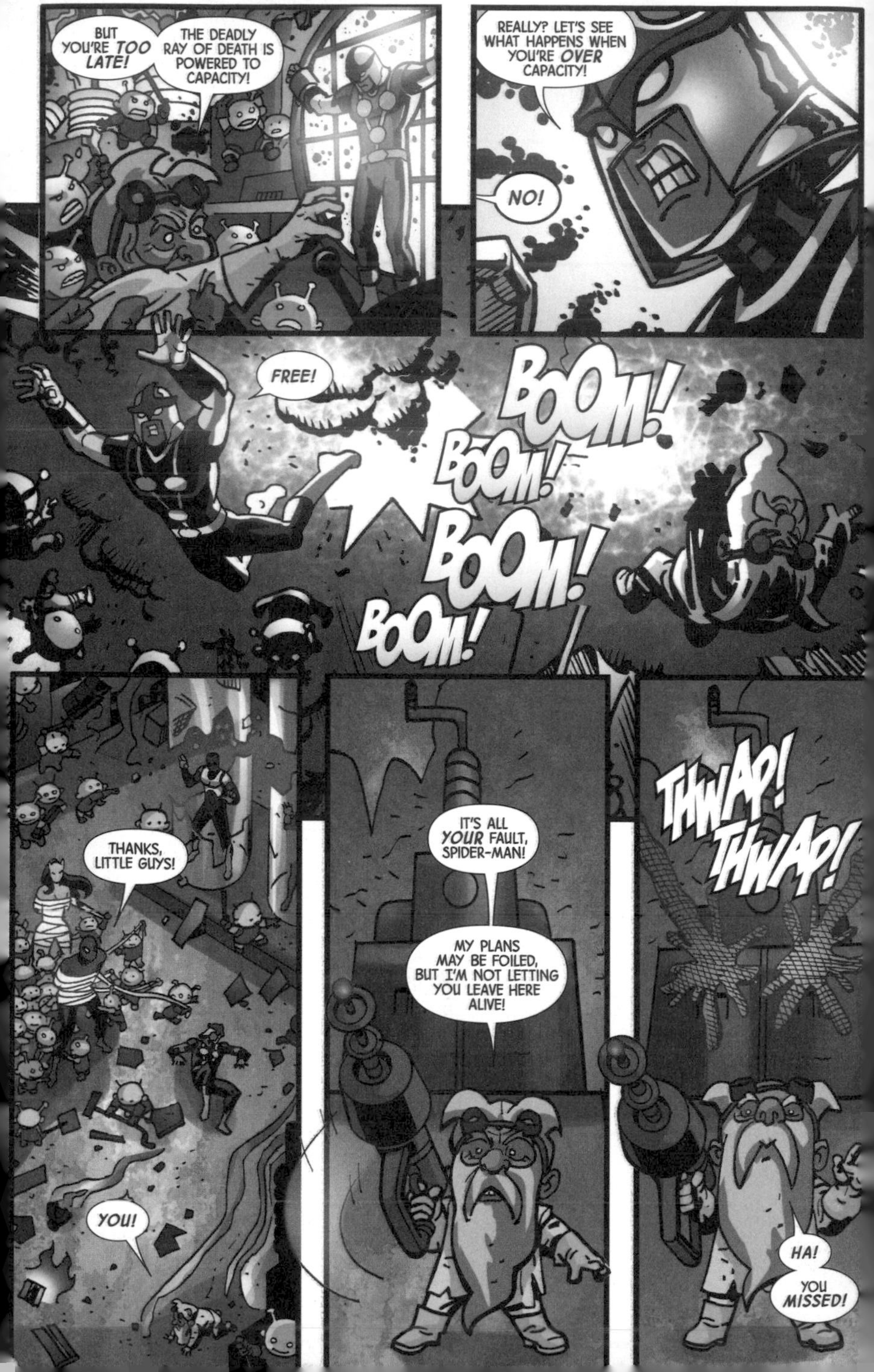

BUT YOU'RE TOO LATE!
THE DEADLY RAY OF DEATH IS POWERED TO CAPACITY!
REALLY? LET'S SEE WHAT HAPPENS WHEN YOU'RE OVER CAPACITY!
NO!
FREE!
BOOM!
BOOM!
BOOM!
BOOM!
THANKS, LITTLE GUYS!
YOU!
IT'S ALL YOUR FAULT, SPIDER-MAN!
MY PLANS MAY BE FOILED, BUT I'M NOT LETTING YOU LEAVE HERE ALIVE!
THWAP!
THWAP!
HA!
YOU MISSED!

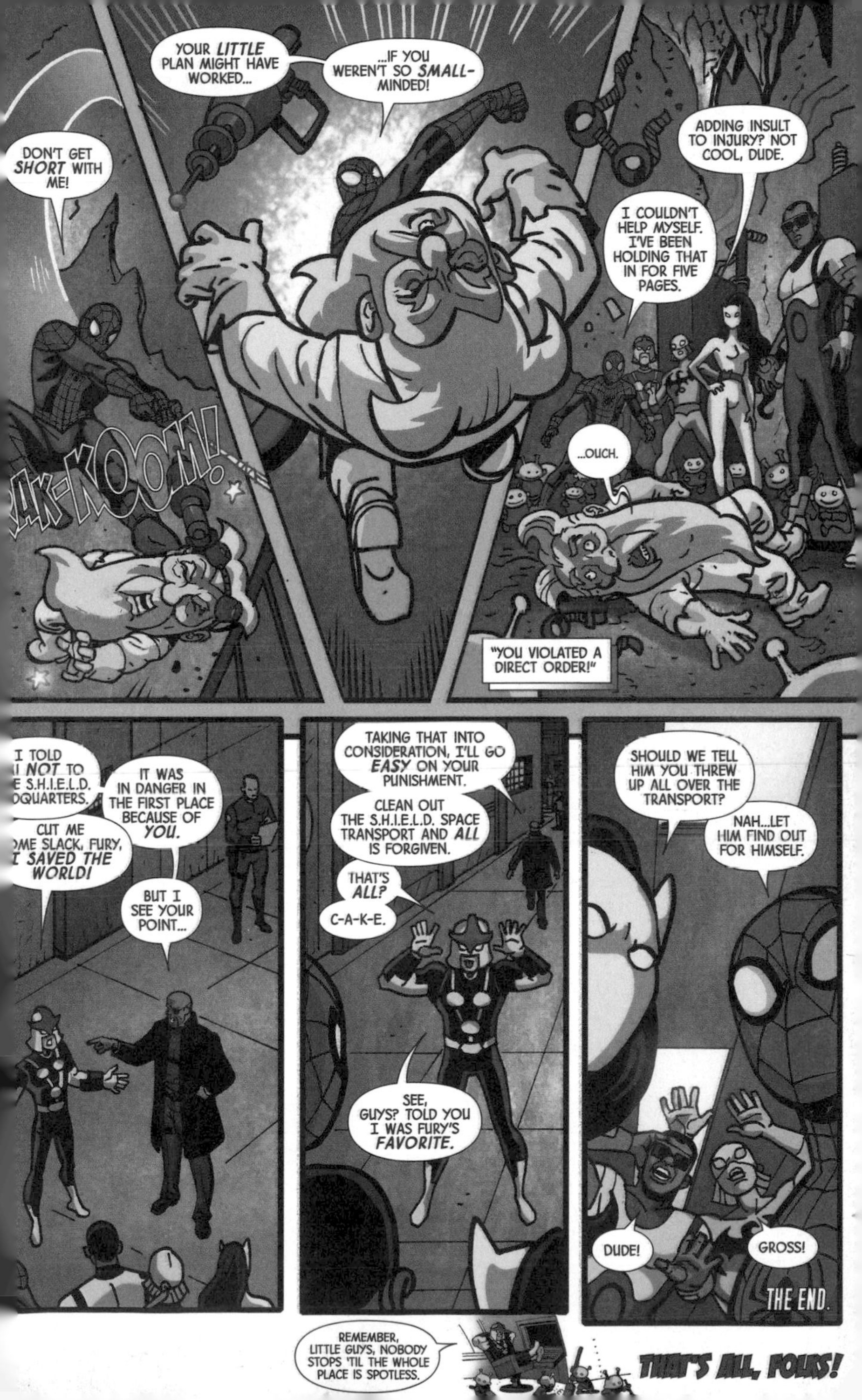

YOUR LITTLE PLAN MIGHT HAVE WORKED...
...IF YOU WEREN'T SO SMALL-MINDED!
DON'T GET SHORT WITH ME!
RAK-KOOM!
ADDING INSULT TO INJURY? NOT COOL, DUDE.
I COULDN'T HELP MYSELF. I'VE BEEN HOLDING THAT IN FOR FIVE PAGES.
...OUCH.
"YOU VIOLATED A DIRECT ORDER!"
I TOLD I NOT TO E S.H.I.E.L.D. DQUARTERS.
IT WAS IN DANGER IN THE FIRST PLACE BECAUSE OF YOU.
CUT ME ME SLACK, FURY, I SAVED THE WORLD!
BUT I SEE YOUR POINT...
TAKING THAT INTO CONSIDERATION, I'LL GO EASY ON YOUR PUNISHMENT.
CLEAN OUT THE S.H.I.E.L.D. SPACE TRANSPORT AND ALL IS FORGIVEN.
THAT'S ALL?
C-A-K-E.
SEE, GUYS? TOLD YOU I WAS FURY'S FAVORITE.
SHOULD WE TELL HIM YOU THREW UP ALL OVER THE TRANSPORT?
NAH...LET HIM FIND OUT FOR HIMSELF.
DUDE!
GROSS!
THE END.
REMEMBER, LITTLE GUYS, NOBODY STOPS 'TIL THE WHOLE PLACE IS SPOTLESS.
THAT'S ALL, FOLKS!

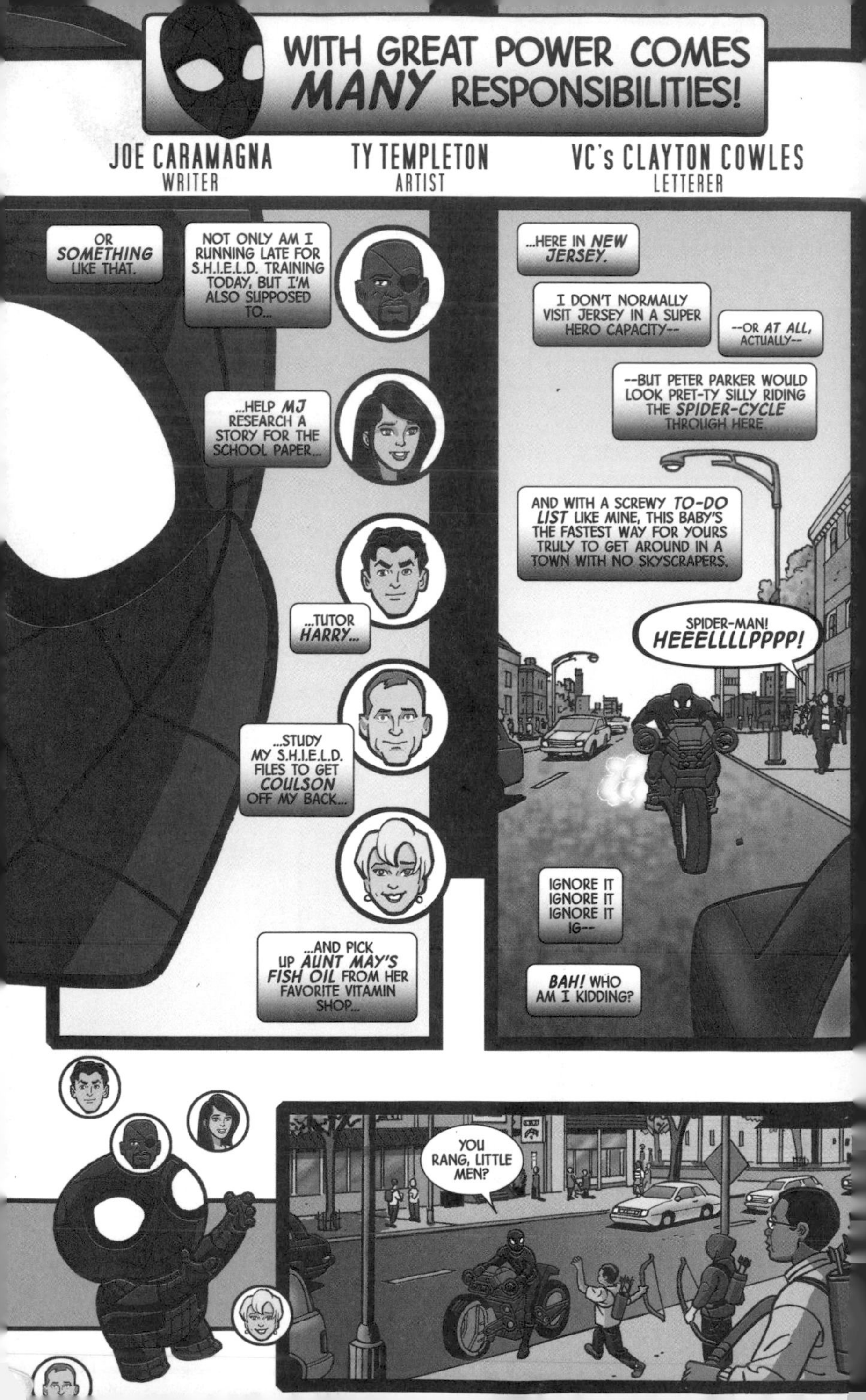
WITH GREAT POWER COMES MANY RESPONSIBILITIES!
JOE CARAMAGNA WRITER
TY TEMPLETON ARTIST
VC's CLAYTON COWLES LETTERER
OR SOMETHING LIKE THAT.
NOT ONLY AM I RUNNING LATE FOR S.H.I.E.L.D. TRAINING TODAY, BUT I'M ALSO SUPPOSED TO...
...HELP MJ RESEARCH A STORY FOR THE SCHOOL PAPER...
...TUTOR HARRY...
...STUDY MY S.H.I.E.L.D. FILES TO GET COULSON OFF MY BACK...
...AND PICK UP AUNT MAY'S FISH OIL FROM HER FAVORITE VITAMIN SHOP...
...HERE IN NEW JERSEY.
I DON'T NORMALLY VISIT JERSEY IN A SUPER HERO CAPACITY--
--OR AT ALL, ACTUALLY--
--BUT PETER PARKER WOULD LOOK PRET-TY SILLY RIDING THE SPIDER-CYCLE THROUGH HERE.
AND WITH A SCREWY TO-DO LIST LIKE MINE, THIS BABY'S THE FASTEST WAY FOR YOURS TRULY TO GET AROUND IN A TOWN WITH NO SKYSCRAPERS.
SPIDER-MAN! HEEELLLLPPPP!
IGNORE IT IGNORE IT IGNORE IT IG--
BAH! WHO AM I KIDDING?
YOU RANG, LITTLE MEN?

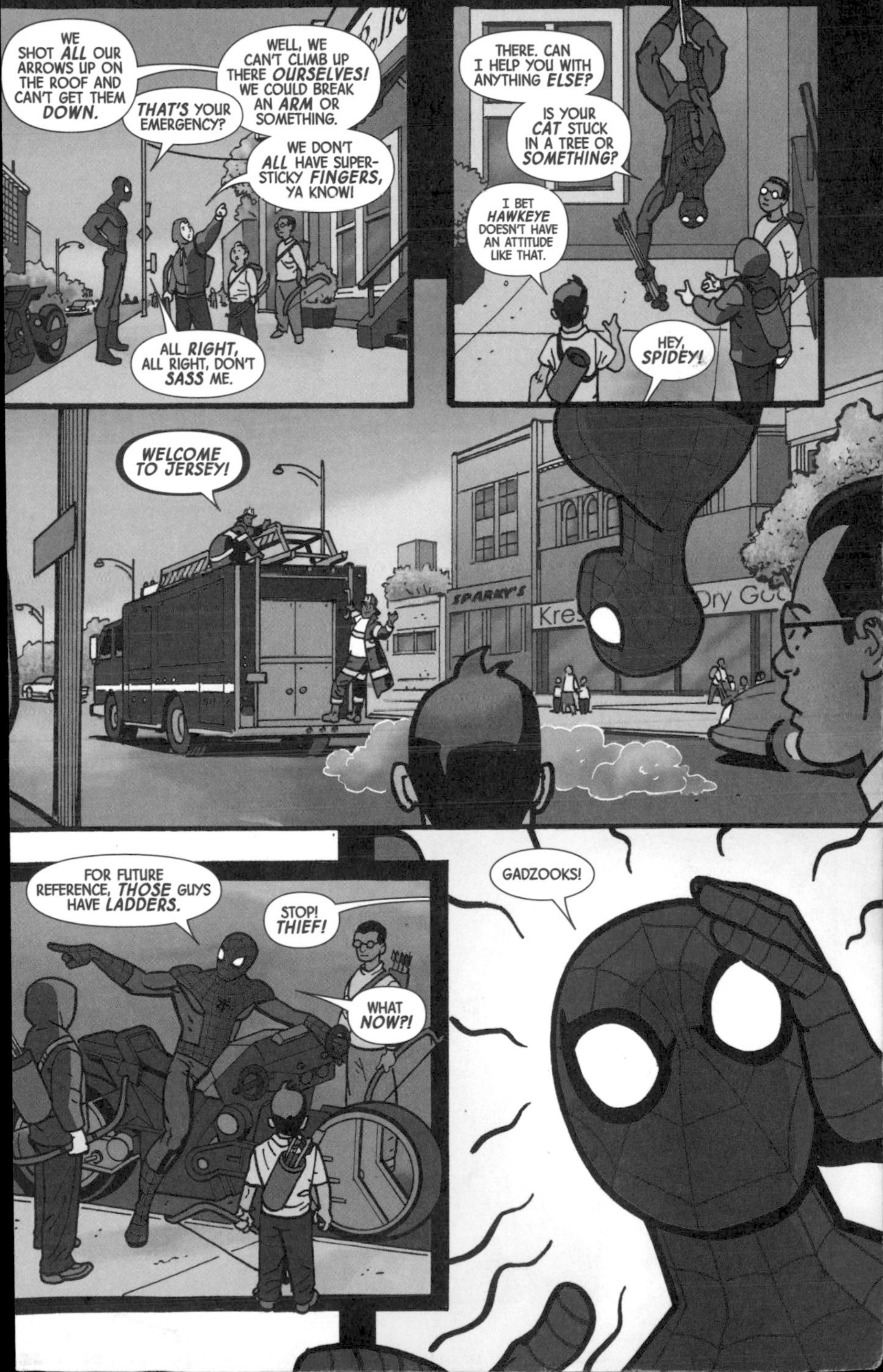
WE SHOT ALL OUR ARROWS UP ON THE ROOF AND CAN'T GET THEM DOWN.
THAT'S YOUR EMERGENCY?
WELL, WE CAN'T CLIMB UP THERE OURSELVES! WE COULD BREAK AN ARM OR SOMETHING.
WE DON'T ALL HAVE SUPER-STICKY FINGERS, YA KNOW!
ALL RIGHT, ALL RIGHT, DON'T SASS ME.
THERE. CAN I HELP YOU WITH ANYTHING ELSE?
IS YOUR CAT STUCK IN A TREE OR SOMETHING?
I BET HAWKEYE DOESN'T HAVE AN ATTITUDE LIKE THAT.
HEY, SPIDEY!
WELCOME TO JERSEY!
SPARKY'S
Kres
Dry Goo
FOR FUTURE REFERENCE, THOSE GUYS HAVE LADDERS.
STOP! THIEF!
WHAT NOW?!
GADZOOKS!

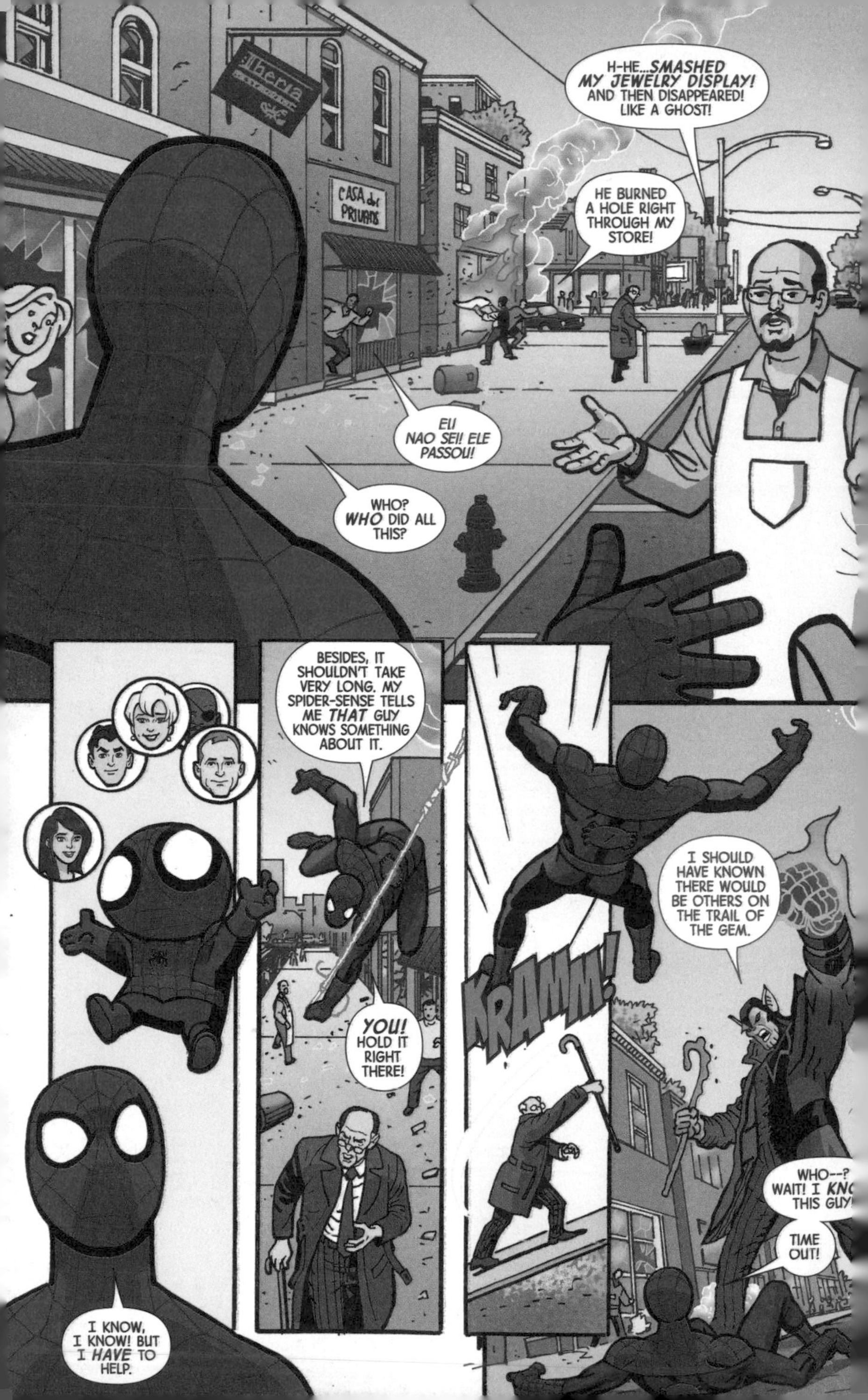
H-HE...SMASHED MY JEWELRY DISPLAY! AND THEN DISAPPEARED! LIKE A GHOST!
HE BURNED A HOLE RIGHT THROUGH MY STORE!
EU NAO SEI! ELE PASSOU!
WHO? WHO DID ALL THIS?
CASA do PRIURDS
I KNOW, I KNOW! BUT I HAVE TO HELP.
BESIDES, IT SHOULDN'T TAKE VERY LONG. MY SPIDER-SENSE TELLS ME THAT GUY KNOWS SOMETHING ABOUT IT.
YOU! HOLD IT RIGHT THERE!
KRAMM!
I SHOULD HAVE KNOWN THERE WOULD BE OTHERS ON THE TRAIL OF THE GEM.
WHO--? WAIT! I KN THIS GUY!
TIME OUT!

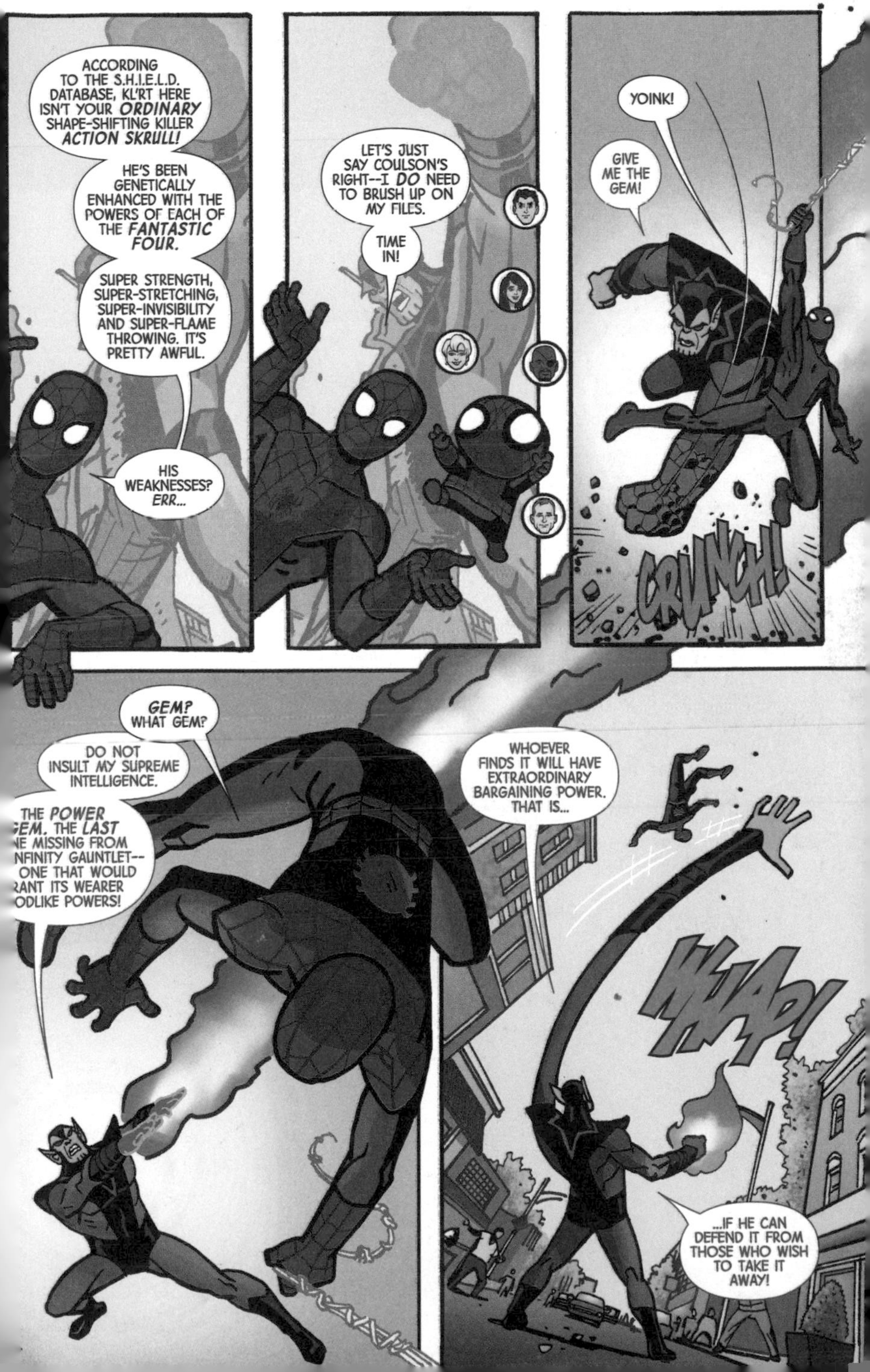

ACCORDING TO THE S.H.I.E.L.D. DATABASE, KL'RT HERE ISN'T YOUR ORDINARY SHAPE-SHIFTING KILLER ACTION SKRULL!
HE'S BEEN GENETICALLY ENHANCED WITH THE POWERS OF EACH OF THE FANTASTIC FOUR.
SUPER STRENGTH, SUPER-STRETCHING, SUPER-INVISIBILITY AND SUPER-FLAME THROWING. IT'S PRETTY AWFUL.
HIS WEAKNESSES? ERR...
LET'S JUST SAY COULSON'S RIGHT--I DO NEED TO BRUSH UP ON MY FILES.
TIME IN!
YOINK!
GIVE ME THE GEM!
CRUNCH!
GEM? WHAT GEM?
DO NOT INSULT MY SUPREME INTELLIGENCE.
THE POWER GEM. THE LAST ONE MISSING FROM INFINITY GAUNTLET--ONE THAT WOULD GRANT ITS WEARER GODLIKE POWERS!
WHOEVER FINDS IT WILL HAVE EXTRAORDINARY BARGAINING POWER. THAT IS...
WHAP!
...IF HE CAN DEFEND IT FROM THOSE WHO WISH TO TAKE IT AWAY!

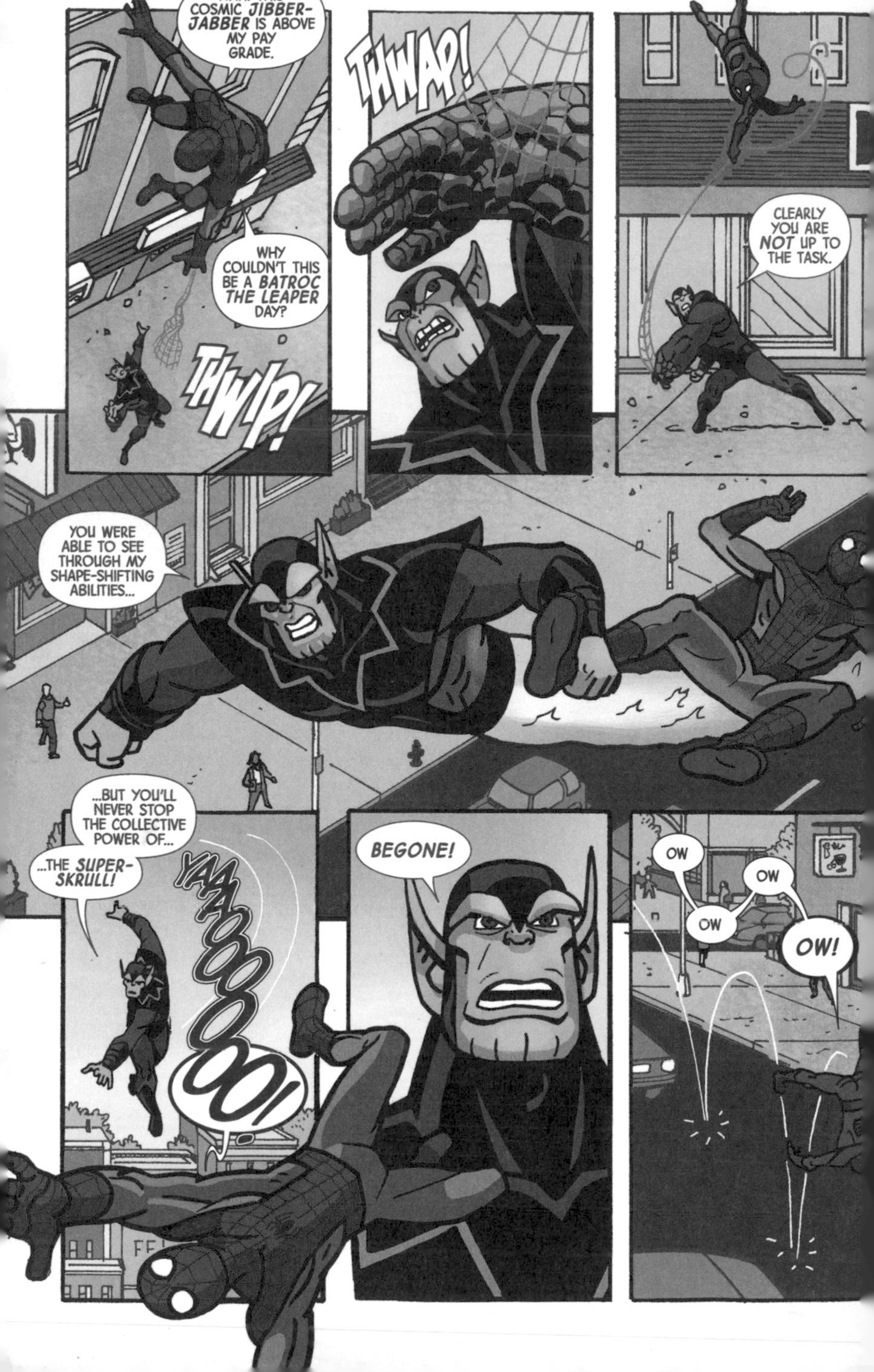
NNH! THIS COSMIC JIBBER-JABBER IS ABOVE MY PAY GRADE.
WHY COULDN'T THIS BE A BATROC THE LEAPER DAY?
THWIP!
THWAP!
CLEARLY YOU ARE NOT UP TO THE TASK.
YOU WERE ABLE TO SEE THROUGH MY SHAPE-SHIFTING ABILITIES...
...BUT YOU'LL NEVER STOP THE COLLECTIVE POWER OF...
...THE SUPER-SKRULL!
YAAAOOOOOO!
BEGONE!
OW
OW
OW
OW!

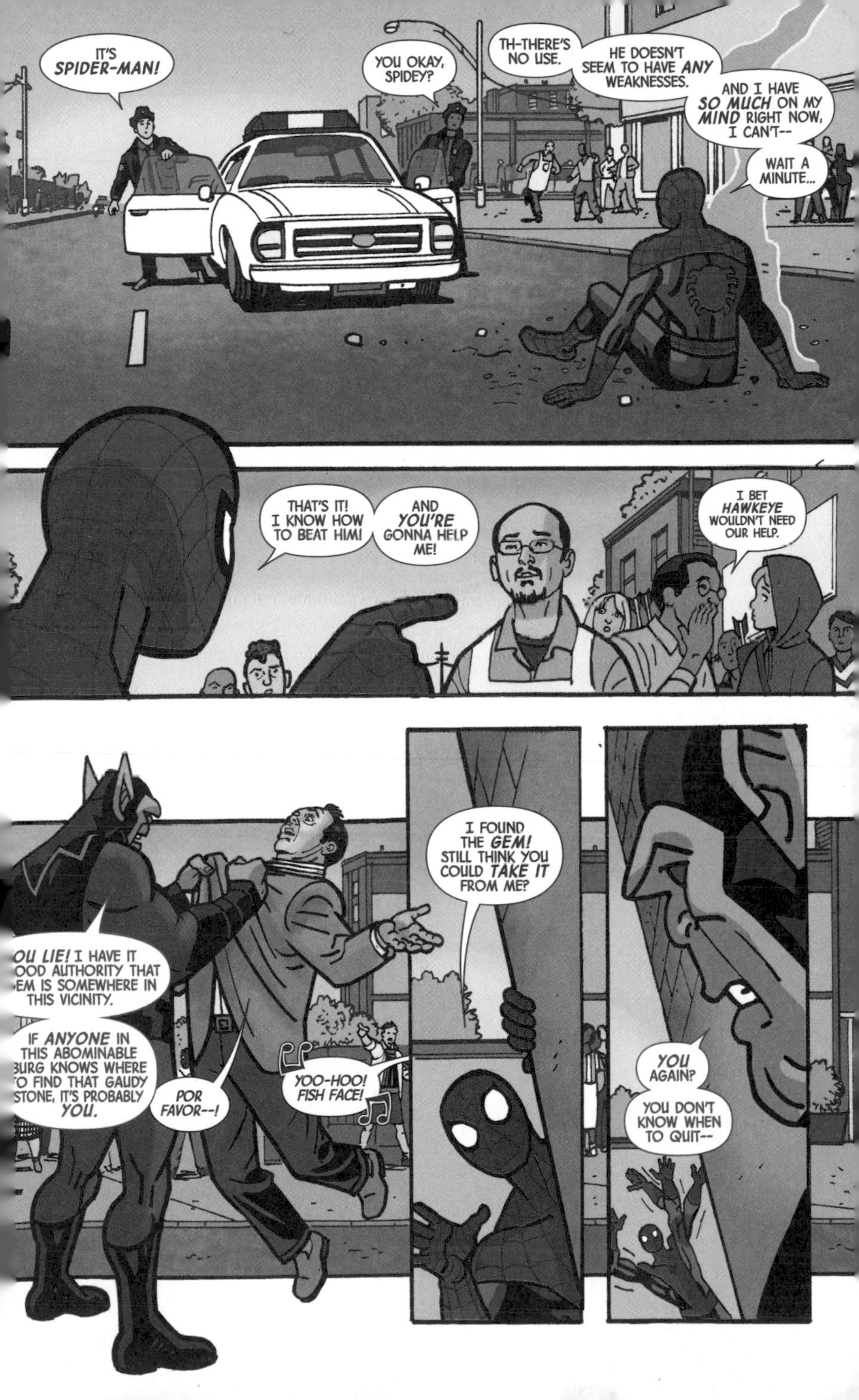
IT'S SPIDER-MAN!
YOU OKAY, SPIDEY?
TH-THERE'S NO USE.
HE DOESN'T SEEM TO HAVE ANY WEAKNESSES.
AND I HAVE SO MUCH ON MY MIND RIGHT NOW, I CAN'T--
WAIT A MINUTE...
THAT'S IT! I KNOW HOW TO BEAT HIM!
AND YOU'RE GONNA HELP ME!
I BET HAWKEYE WOULDN'T NEED OUR HELP.
OU LIE! I HAVE IT OOD AUTHORITY THAT EM IS SOMEWHERE IN THIS VICINITY.
IF ANYONE IN THIS ABOMINABLE BURG KNOWS WHERE O FIND THAT GAUDY STONE, IT'S PROBABLY YOU.
POR FAVOR--!
YOO-HOO! FISH FACE!
I FOUND THE GEM! STILL THINK YOU COULD TAKE IT FROM ME?
YOU AGAIN?
YOU DON'T KNOW WHEN TO QUIT--

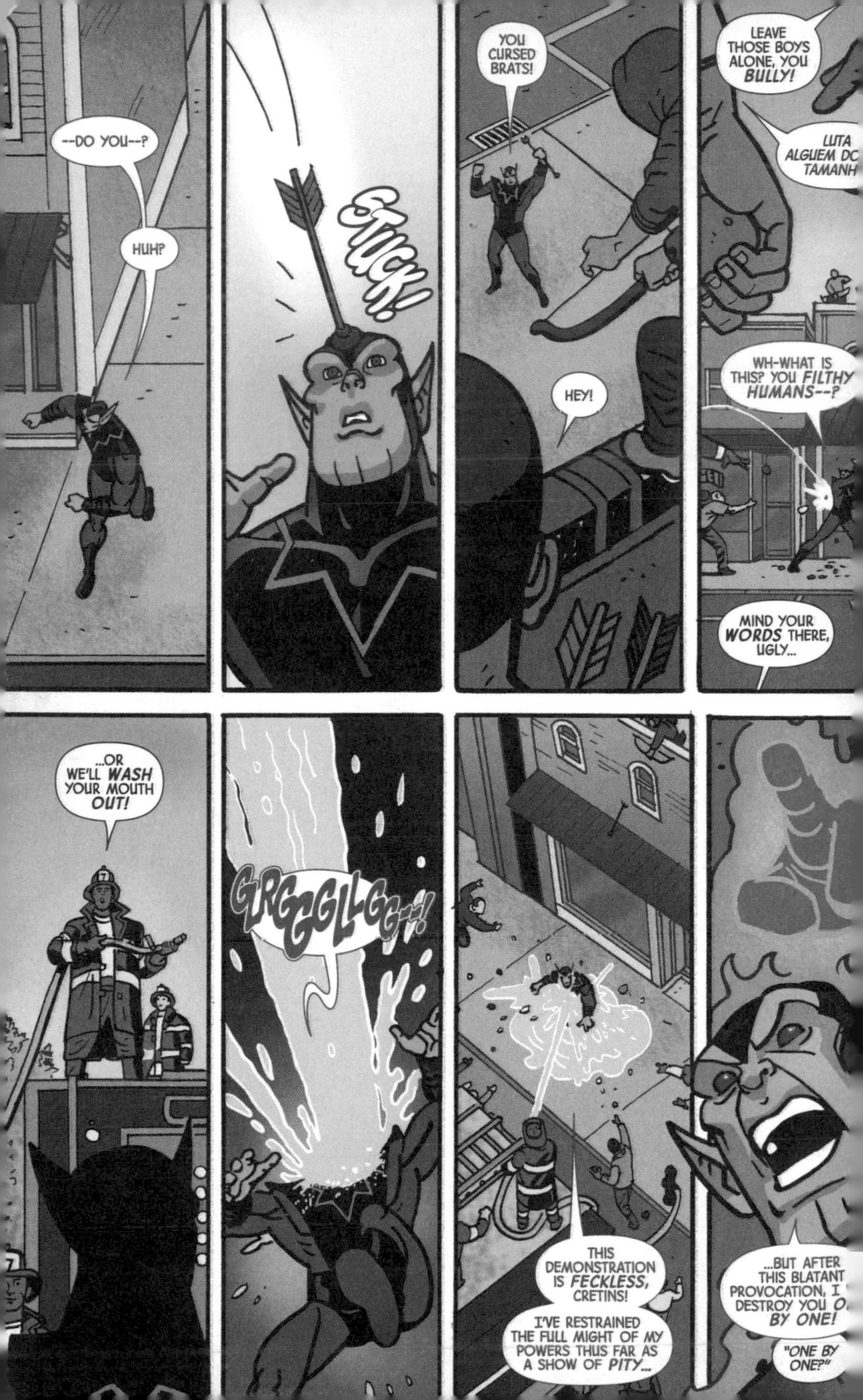
--DO YOU--?
HUH?
STUCK!
YOU CURSED BRATS!
HEY!
LEAVE THOSE BOYS ALONE, YOU BULLY!
LUTA ALGUEM DO TAMANH
WH-WHAT IS THIS? YOU FILTHY HUMANS--?
MIND YOUR WORDS THERE, UGLY...
...OR WE'LL WASH YOUR MOUTH OUT!
GLRGGGLLGG!
THIS DEMONSTRATION IS FECKLESS, CRETINS!
I'VE RESTRAINED THE FULL MIGHT OF MY POWERS THUS FAR AS A SHOW OF PITY...
...BUT AFTER THIS BLATANT PROVOCATION, I DESTROY YOU O BY ONE!
"ONE BY ONE?"

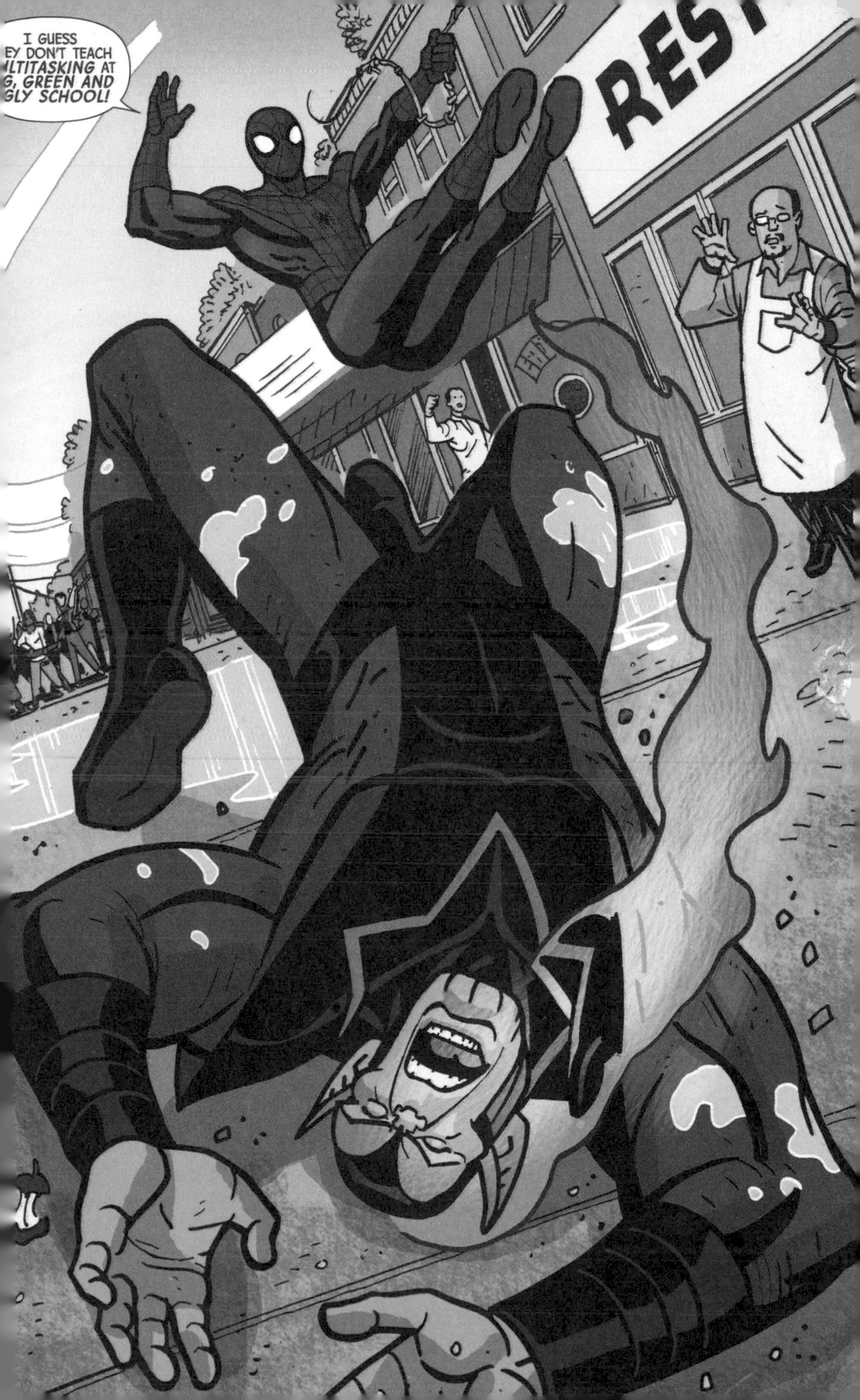
I GUESS
EY DON'T TEACH
ILTITASKING AT
G, GREEN AND
GLY SCHOOL!
REST

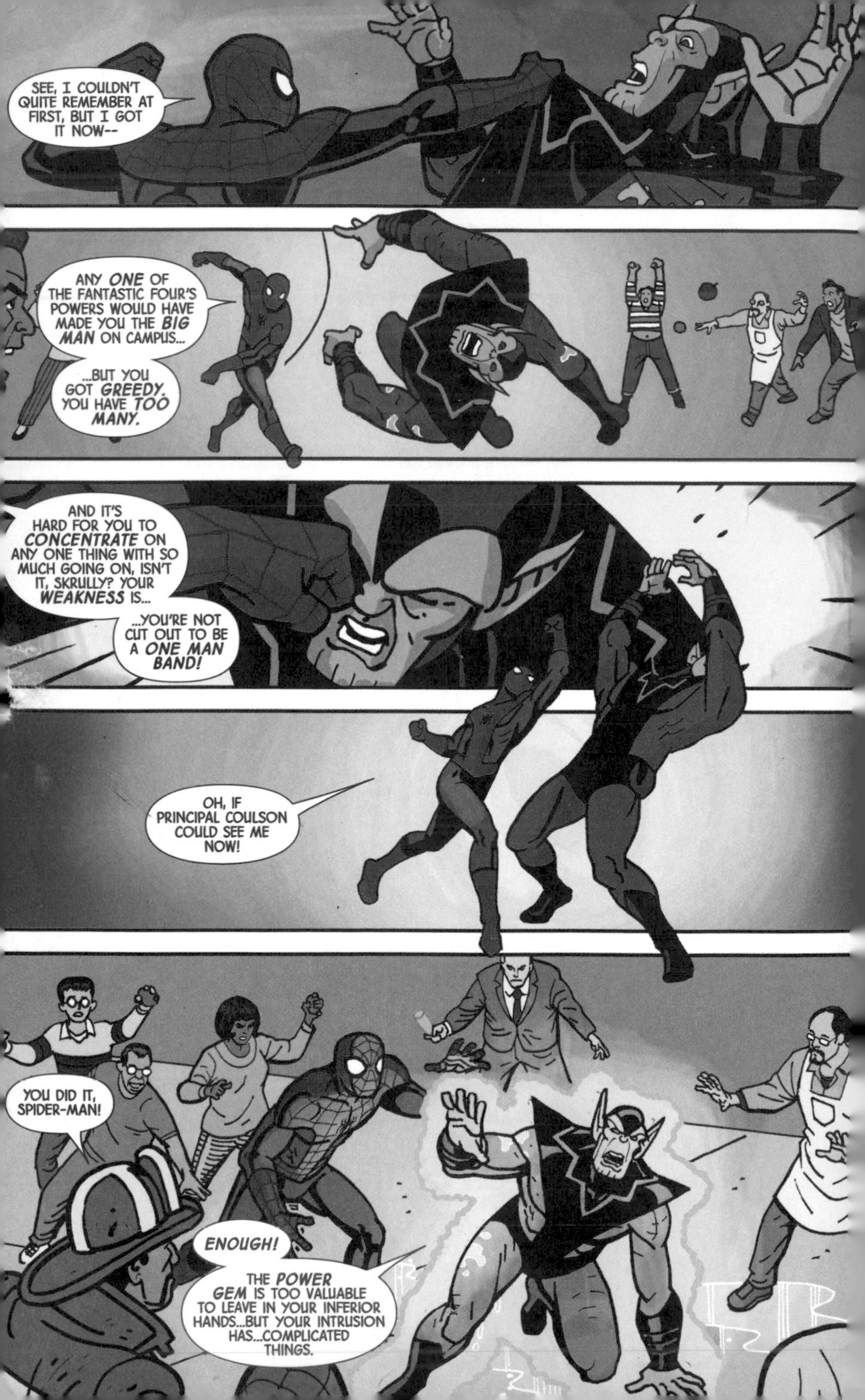
SEE, I COULDN'T QUITE REMEMBER AT FIRST, BUT I GOT IT NOW--
ANY ONE OF THE FANTASTIC FOUR'S POWERS WOULD HAVE MADE YOU THE BIG MAN ON CAMPUS...
...BUT YOU GOT GREEDY. YOU HAVE TOO MANY.
AND IT'S HARD FOR YOU TO CONCENTRATE ON ANY ONE THING WITH SO MUCH GOING ON, ISN'T IT, SKRULLY? YOUR WEAKNESS IS...
...YOU'RE NOT CUT OUT TO BE A ONE MAN BAND!
OH, IF PRINCIPAL COULSON COULD SEE ME NOW!
YOU DID IT, SPIDER-MAN!
ENOUGH!
THE POWER GEM IS TOO VALUABLE TO LEAVE IN YOUR INFERIOR HANDS...BUT YOUR INTRUSION HAS...COMPLICATED THINGS.

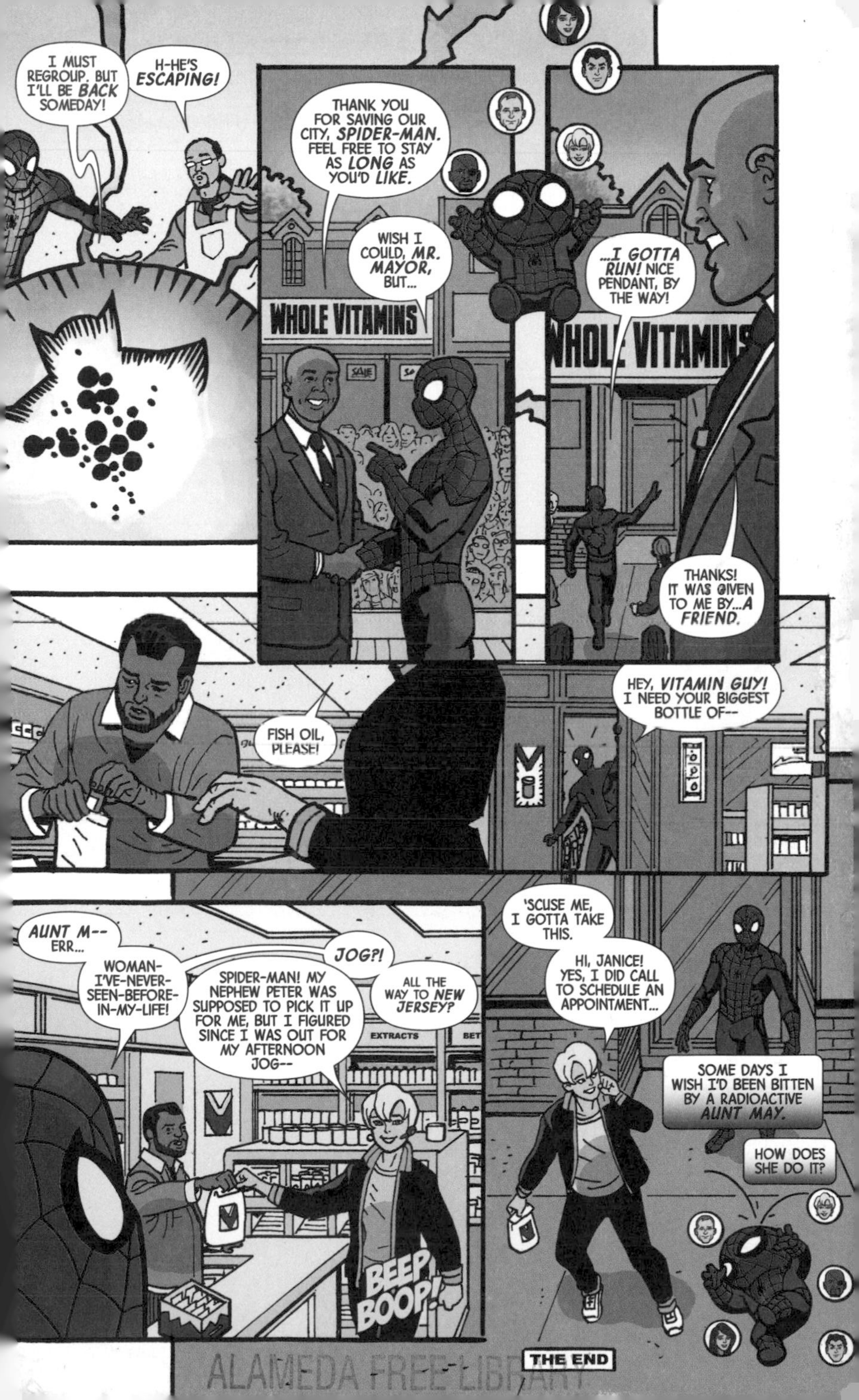

I MUST REGROUP. BUT I'LL BE BACK SOMEDAY!
H-HE'S ESCAPING!
THANK YOU FOR SAVING OUR CITY, SPIDER-MAN. FEEL FREE TO STAY AS LONG AS YOU'D LIKE.
WISH I COULD, MR. MAYOR, BUT...
WHOLE VITAMINS
...I GOTTA RUN! NICE PENDANT, BY THE WAY!
WHOLE VITAMINS
THANKS! IT WAS GIVEN TO ME BY...A FRIEND.
FISH OIL, PLEASE!
HEY, VITAMIN GUY! I NEED YOUR BIGGEST BOTTLE OF--
AUNT M-- ERR...
WOMAN-I'VE-NEVER-SEEN-BEFORE-IN-MY-LIFE!
SPIDER-MAN! MY NEPHEW PETER WAS SUPPOSED TO PICK IT UP FOR ME, BUT I FIGURED SINCE I WAS OUT FOR MY AFTERNOON JOG--
JOG?!
ALL THE WAY TO NEW JERSEY?
EXTRACTS
BEEP BOOP!
'SCUSE ME, I GOTTA TAKE THIS.
HI, JANICE! YES, I DID CALL TO SCHEDULE AN APPOINTMENT...
SOME DAYS I WISH I'D BEEN BITTEN BY A RADIOACTIVE AUNT MAY.
HOW DOES SHE DO IT?
THE END

LIVE! ON PAPER! IT'S TIME AGAIN FOR... MARVEL MASH-UP

COMICS YOU LOVE...REWRITT BY THE PEOPLE YOU DON'T.

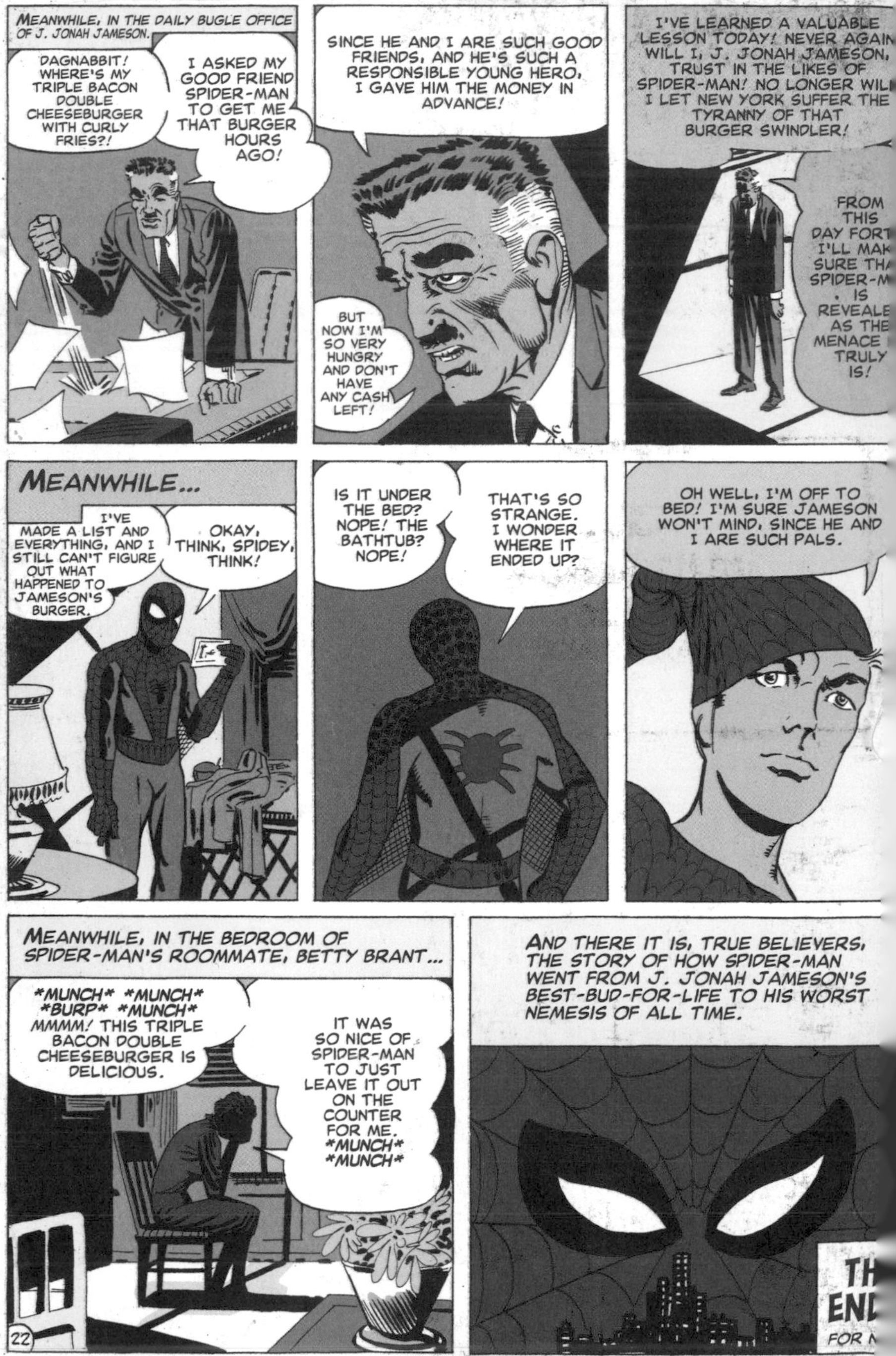

MEANWHILE, IN THE DAILY BUGLE OFFICE OF J. JONAH JAMESON.
DAGNABBIT! WHERE'S MY TRIPLE BACON DOUBLE CHEESEBURGER WITH CURLY FRIES?!
I ASKED MY GOOD FRIEND SPIDER-MAN TO GET ME THAT BURGER HOURS AGO!
SINCE HE AND I ARE SUCH GOOD FRIENDS, AND HE'S SUCH A RESPONSIBLE YOUNG HERO, I GAVE HIM THE MONEY IN ADVANCE!
BUT NOW I'M SO VERY HUNGRY AND DON'T HAVE ANY CASH LEFT!
I'VE LEARNED A VALUABLE LESSON TODAY! NEVER AGAIN WILL I, J. JONAH JAMESON, TRUST IN THE LIKES OF SPIDER-MAN! NO LONGER WILL I LET NEW YORK SUFFER THE TYRANNY OF THAT BURGER SWINDLER!
FROM THIS DAY FORT I'LL MAK SURE THA SPIDER-M . IS REVEALE AS THE MENACE TRULY IS!
MEANWHILE...
I'VE MADE A LIST AND EVERYTHING, AND I STILL CAN'T FIGURE OUT WHAT HAPPENED TO JAMESON'S BURGER.
OKAY, THINK, SPIDEY, THINK!
IS IT UNDER THE BED? NOPE! THE BATHTUB? NOPE!
THAT'S SO STRANGE. I WONDER WHERE IT ENDED UP?
OH WELL, I'M OFF TO BED! I'M SURE JAMESON WON'T MIND, SINCE HE AND I ARE SUCH PALS.
MEANWHILE, IN THE BEDROOM OF SPIDER-MAN'S ROOMMATE, BETTY BRANT...
MUNCH *MUNCH* *BURP* *MUNCH* MMMM! THIS TRIPLE BACON DOUBLE CHEESEBURGER IS DELICIOUS.
IT WAS SO NICE OF SPIDER-MAN TO JUST LEAVE IT OUT ON THE COUNTER FOR ME. *MUNCH* *MUNCH*
AND THERE IT IS, TRUE BELIEVERS, THE STORY OF HOW SPIDER-MAN WENT FROM J. JONAH JAMESON'S BEST-BUD-FOR-LIFE TO HIS WORST NEMESIS OF ALL TIME.
TH END FOR
22

ORIGINAL BY STAN LEE & STEVE DITKO

NEW DIALOGUE BY HARRISON WILCOX

LETTERED BY VC'S CLAYTON COWLES